# VOCAL TECHNIQUE

# VOCAL TECHNIQUE

## A Guide for Conductors, Teachers, and Singers

Julia Davids, D.M.

Stephen LaTour, Ph.D.

Long Grove, Illinois

For information about this book, contact:
Waveland Press, Inc.
4180 IL Route 83, Suite 101
Long Grove, Illinois 60047-9580
(847) 634-0081
info@waveland.com
www.waveland.com

Illustrations and cover design by Evelyn LaTour



10-digit ISBN 1-57766-782-4
13-digit ISBN 978-1-57766-782-7



Printed in the United States of America

7 6 5 4 3 2

# Table of Contents

## Acknowledgements

We want to extend special thanks to:

- Sarah Ponder, mezzo-soprano extraordinaire, for serving as our photography model and for comments on early drafts of chapters.
- Evelyn LaTour for her beautiful cover design and wonderful illustrations that make complex anatomy understandable.
- Professor Karen Brunssen and Dr. Darryl Edwards for particularly detailed comments on and suggestions about the complete manuscript.
- Professor Sarah Beatty for her encouragement and use of an early version of our book in her course on vocal technique for music educators.
- Dr. Jerry Blackstone for helpful comments on an early draft.
- Dr. Antonia Syson for observations and guidance throughout the process.

We are grateful to the following individuals who read and commented on a number of initial chapters: Dr. Karen Bauer, Sammi Block, Tom Board, Christopher Bowman, Barry Davids, John Darrow, Anne Harkonen, Dr. Anne Heider, Professor Freda Herseth, Chris Hoffmeyer, Nancy Johnston, Dr. Nicole Jordan, Dr. Victoria Meredith, Sarah Jean Morrison, Christina Murray, Linda Olson, Ryan O'Mealey, Dr. David Perry, Dr. Ken Rasinski, Karen Anne Schuessler, Lauren Sklar, Joel Tranquilla, and Alison Vernon.

Carrie Ericksen provided helpful advice on numerous book design issues. Emily Rivera's comments on cover design helped us to choose among a number of excellent alternatives. Joseph Kellner, Jordanna Glueckauf, and Shane Holmes performed yeoman copyediting.

Tom Curtin is our superb editor at Waveland Press, consistently giving us excellent advice. Jeni Ogilvie at Waveland was our wonderfully meticulous copyeditor for the final manuscript. Any remaining errors are ours!

Thanks to the North Shore Choral Society, North Park University choirs, Trinity United Methodist Church Chancel Choir, the Canadian Chamber Choir, and Julia's studio students for encouraging us and putting many of the ideas contained in this book into practice.

Julia wants to thank: all those who have taught me how to sing—conductors, voice teachers, students, and choristers. I especially want to thank Lorna Haywood, my dear voice teacher at the University of Michigan, who inspired my interest in vocal technique and encouraged me to share it with choirs. Huge thanks to my parents, Linda and Ron Olson, my in-laws Carol and Cary Davids, my siblings Karen and Dan, and dear friends who support me and have been especially encouraging in this endeavor. To my amazing husband Marty and our children, Judith and Solomon—thank you for allowing time for this huge project, and for literally being there from beginning to end. No words can describe the inspiration you give me. And to Steve—this book wouldn't have happened without your encouragement, incredible work ethic, wisdom, patience, and kindness. You're a great partner—thank you for believing in this!

Steve wants to thank: my wife, Pauline, my partner in life and in research, who has been extraordinarily supportive of this project; my children, Paul and Evelyn, for their love and support—you consistently amaze me! Special thanks to Evelyn whose art and photography adorn our home, and whose elegant illustrations for *Vocal Technique* provide clarity about anatomy. My parents, Jean and Parvin, encouraged my love for music during my formative years. My early elementary school music teacher, Joyce Taylor, helped me to realize the joy of singing, and my junior high choral director, Gene Klein, made singing fun and enjoyable during those difficult years of voice change. Julia, you inspired me to see new possibilities in my own voice and are infinitely patient when I want to discuss every new vocal science journal article. You are the consummate professional; it has been a joy to work with you in creating this book!

# Introduction: Our Philosophy of Vocal Technique

## Good vocal technique is essential for great sound

The more conductors, teachers, and singers understand vocal technique and the science underlying it, the more readily they can apply these concepts in both individual and ensemble singing. There are excellent resources that concentrate on one of three areas: vocal science, vocal pedagogy, or choral rehearsal technique. This book integrates the three. As such it is intended as a guide to good technique in all settings.

Consistently addressing good vocal technique will vastly improve the sound of both soloists and choral groups. Conductors and teachers must work with their singers over time, during warm-ups and throughout rehearsals, to improve their singing skills.

### Importance of attention to vocal technique in the choral setting

We believe knowledge of good vocal technique applies to all singing and all singers deserve the opportunity to sing well. That said, choral singing, in particular, presents some unique vocal demands. Focus on vocal technique can assist singers in meeting these demands and help conductors to communicate more clearly how to achieve the results that they desire.

Even singers who regularly study with a voice teacher will likely spend more time singing with their choral conductor. For many amateur singers such as those in school and community choirs, conductors may be the only source of information about vocal technique. The choral conductor thus has a valuable opportunity and indeed, a responsibility to encourage great vocal technique and vocal health.

Attention to vocal technique is indispensable for untrained singers, but it is important as well for developing and trained singers, who will benefit from reminders to apply appropriate technique in a choral setting.

Addressing vocal technique during warm-up and rehearsal also allows singers to understand vocal goals. In the choral context, trained and untrained singers will speak the same language and singers can be active participants in improving choral singing. They can work on specific technical solutions for singing challenges and avoid some common pitfalls.

## Some benefits of good vocal technique

There are a number of ways that singing can be improved by utilizing excellent vocal technique. A few examples are listed below.

### Rich resonance

Most untrained singers have limited resonance in their voices. By gaining an understanding of vocal resonance and using a number of exercises over time, resonance can be enhanced. As a result, individual singers and ensembles will have a richer sound that will also carry better over instrumental ensembles. Moreover, there will be fewer blend problems in the choral setting due to marked difference in the resonance of individual singers.

### Better tone

One of the major benefits of good vocal technique is that it improves the quality of sound. Better resonance contributes to this, but so do consistent approaches to vowel formation, vowel modification for higher pitches, techniques for quick enunciation of consonants, approaches to easing register transitions, and methods for reducing unproductive tension.

### Improved and more consistent range

As singers learn more about register transitions and methods of negotiating them, they will find both more consistent tone quality and improved range. This avoids problems such as basses and altos having difficulty accessing upper pitches, tenors forcing sound in the higher portions of their range, and sopranos sounding breathy.

### Better intonation

Conductors, teachers, and singers are all concerned about good intonation. While no singer seeks to sing out of tune, deficiencies in technique (e.g., lack of proper breath support, lack of appropriate shaping of the vocal tract) often cause this to happen. With proper vocal technique there are fewer situations where singers sound flat/sharp or scoop to a pitch. Good vocal technique provides the "tool box" for in-tune singing.

### Expressive flexibility

Vocal technique is not an end unto itself; it is a means to expressive singing. This includes, for example, the ability to:

- Sing varying dynamic levels, particularly at the extremes of range

- Vary tone color to better match repertoire indications (e.g., musical theatre, barbershop, belt versus legit, general darker versus lighter tone depending upon desired emotional response)
- Vary the amount of vibrato
- Negotiate rapid passages
- Use proper articulation in a healthy manner (legato, staccato, accents, melismas)

## Singing with greater ease and efficiency

A major benefit of good vocal technique is the ability to sing with less effort. Efficient singing involves:

- Good posture
- Proper breathing technique
- Better resonance to help sing loud passages—rather than just increased singing effort
- Appropriate vowel modification to reduce strain in singing high pitches
- Elimination of extraneous tensions that tire singers and result in reduced sound quality

## Improved choral blend

Often, choral conductors must create an ensemble sound from a disparate group of singers, be they members of a junior high or high school chorus, voice majors at a university, or amateurs in a community chorus (or a combination). Good vocal technique, with particular focus on vowel formation, vowel modification for higher pitches, and efficient enunciation of consonants can go a long way toward creating a unified sound without sacrificing the individual singer.

## Better singing through life's changes

Understanding what is happening to the voice due to hormonal changes (related to adolescence, menopause, or general aging) can help conductors, teachers, and singers to cope more effectively with potentially disruptive events. Too many adolescents and older individuals stop singing due to changes in the voice that occur during these phases of human development. This can be prevented with knowledge about the physiology of the changes and practical techniques to assist singers during these life transitions.

## Good vocal technique preserves singers' voices

Proper technique is essential for vocal health. Most amateurs sing once or twice a week at the most, but desire to use their voices well into the later years of their lives. Professional singers are required to use their instruments for long periods of time most days and will appreciate attempts to preserve their vocal health. Knowledge of vocal technique enables conductors to help amateur adults to experience good occasional use as well as long-term vocal facility. Young singers will find that applied vocal technique facilitates healthy vocal development and assists in avoiding the bad habits that choral singing can allow to go unchecked.

## Intentional use of warm-ups is essential to vocal development

Most choral conductors, teachers, and singers agree that some sort of vocal warm-up is essential prior to the singing of repertoire. Some use warm-ups as a time to focus on the repertoire to be rehearsed, while others see it as a few minutes to literally warm up unused voices. We contend, however, that warm-ups are critical for teaching, practicing, and improving vocal technique. Thoughtful use of exercises is essential in order to help singers develop their voices and make the most efficient use of warm-up time. Virtually all of the chapters in this book contain exercises targeting specific aspects of vocal technique. In addition, the final chapter contains sequences of suggested warm-ups.

## A resource to address vocal technique systematically

### How this book differs from others in the field

This book differs from traditional vocal pedagogy resources in that it links vocal technique to specific individual and choral goals. It addresses technical information in an understandable fashion and provides comprehensive information based on recognized pedagogical sources and vocal scientists. It also includes topics not typically found or given limited attention in vocal pedagogy books such as: improving intonation, vibrato in early music, vibrato in the choral setting, approaches to choral blend and the role of vocal technique in blending, working with changing voices (both adolescents and older individuals), as well as approaches to teaching staccato, melismas and accents. It is divided into two major sections:

**Section I: Foundations of Vocal Technique.** The foundations section covers six topics we consider to be essential for all singers:

- Posture
- Breath control
- Initiation, creation, and release of sound
- Resonance
- Vowels
- Consonants

**Section II: Enhancements of Vocal Technique.** The enhancements section covers topics that can help good singers and choral groups become superior:

- Vibrato
- Negotiation of the vocal registers
- Improving range
- Improving intonation
- Legato, staccato, melismas, and dynamic control
- Improving choral blend
- Changing voices
- Reducing tension
- Guarding singers' vocal health

The final chapter of the enhancements section outlines an approach to a productive warm-up. It contains recommended sequences of exercises to help singers improve their vocal technique in key areas. We also provide several examples of recommended warm-ups as well as a compendium of exercises relevant to the various aspects of vocal technique.

For many of our recommendations about technique, additional supporting information from authoritative sources is indicated with an arrow bullet. You will also find text boxes that include more detailed or technical treatments of certain topics. You may wish to skip these until you have read the main material of a chapter.

Throughout the book we endeavor to explain why a specific technique should be used—all too often singers are expected to accept a technique or related exercise based on faith. Yet, if conductors and teachers communicate the reason, singers would implement it more effectively and enthusiastically.

## Our philosophy about exercises

Each chapter includes exercises and examples in italics for clarification. Exercises are intentionally simple—our governing philosophy is that the focus of singers should be on the technical process and goals rather than the execution of a complicated sequence. We reiterate the need to explain the purpose of an exercise to singers. Explanations need not be technical, but singers should understand what they are trying to accomplish.

Some exercises are presented immediately below information about a specific vocal technique, but virtually all chapters contain a small set of other exercises at the end of the chapter. We also summarize exercises mentioned within a chapter at the end of that chapter. We have tried to select those exercises that will most effectively teach the relevant techniques. Included in most chapters are some exercises designed for children, but which adults may appreciate as well. Starting pitches for exercises are merely suggestions. In some cases we show exercises starting on middle-C ($C_4$) for simplicity, but the starting pitch and key should be varied as needed and desired.

Singers will benefit from multiple repetitions of exercises over time. Repetition helps to develop muscle memory that allows good vocal technique to become automatic and routine. Both massed practice (multiple repetitions within a given warm-up/rehearsal) and spaced practice (repetition over time) are important for learning and retention of good technique.

### Summary of our approach

Our approach has been to create a guide that is at once practical and grounded in vocal science. Read from cover to cover, it will give a comprehensive yet concise overview of vocal technique, with a continual focus on linking technique to the musical product. This book can also be used as a reference to a specific topic or concern, providing quick access to the best advice available.

## Bridging the rift between voice teachers and choral conductors

Many voice teachers have a firm conviction that singing in ensembles is not healthy for developing voices. This view is often based on their experiences working with conductors who know little about the voice, or conductors who ask their singers to use vocal techniques that are inappropriate because of their lack of information or because of misinformation. Voice teachers may also believe that the individual voice is lost while singing with others. Thus, they are concerned that singers must sacrifice healthy vocal production in order to fit in with a chorus.

While singers do need to learn to be flexible in the way they use their voices, we strongly believe that when conductors are cognizant of good vocal technique, each member of a choral group can sing in a healthy manner. In such an environment, choral singing can offer the benefits of musicianship training, ensemble skills, and knowledge of repertoire, while providing support and encouragement for technical singing progress.

As mentioned above, choral conductors often spend more time with singers than do voice teachers and can have a profound impact on singers' vocal production. The opportunity is great, therefore, for choral conductors to reap the rewards of applying vocal technique in the choral context and to support the work of their voice teacher colleagues. This book thus attempts to bridge and merge the disciplines of solo and choral singing. Moreover, we want to continue to open opportunities for dialogue and cooperation between voice teachers and conductors, who historically have had somewhat adversarial relationships.

## Both historic and modern resources provide guidance

We have naturally drawn on our own training and experience in writing this book, but we have also considered a number of important resources. While many books address singing, they vary in both quality and readability, with the more technically accurate and comprehensive books often being less readable. In addition, there is a vast scientific literature that is largely inaccessible to most conductors, teachers, and singers. We have organized what we believe to be the best information about vocal technique from a variety of the most accurate sources and have tried to make it understandable. These include technically knowledgeable great artists of the past and present, modern vocal pedagogy resources, and research from the field of vocal science.

**Great artists** have much to tell us about optimal methods of vocal production. One valuable resource is a collection of talks on singing by tenor Enrico Caruso and soprano Luisa Tetrazzini. This was originally published by the Metropolitan Opera Company in 1909 and republished by Dover in 1975. Both of these world famous singers have valuable bits of wisdom about singing, and we have referenced some of their best ideas about vocal technique in various chapters. For a more modern perspective, Renée Fleming's book, *The Inner Voice* (2005), provides another look at vocal technique from a great artist's viewpoint. Fleming is one of the most technically knowledgeable artists of our era.

**Modern vocal technicians and pedagogues** are another important resource. William Vennard wrote perhaps the first truly comprehensive treatise on vocal technique, grounded in both his vast experience with solo and choral singing and in scientific investigation into vocal production. His book, *Singing: The Mechanism and the Technic* (1967), is a true classic (though admittedly difficult to read!). Another important authority is Richard Miller, arguably the world's foremost modern technician, as well as an accomplished singer. He published more books on vocal technique than any other modern author, and wrote numerous articles in professional singing journals. We have also referenced the work of other modern pedagogues such as Meribeth Bunch Dayme (Bunch, 1995; Dayme, 2009), James McKinney (2005), Larra Henderson (1979), James Stark (2003), Karen Sell (2005), and Clifton Ware (1998) as well as vocal clinicians such as Fisher (1966). And we considered the work of choral pedagogues such as Ehmann and Haasemann (1982), Haasemann and Jordan (1991), Emmons and Chase (2006), Jordan (2007), Smith and Sataloff (2006), Weston Noble (2005), and Robert Shaw (Blocker, 2004). The work of pedagogues focusing on children has also been utilized (e.g., Phillips, 1996; Cooksey, 1999; Gackle, 2006).

**Modern vocal science research** has revealed much about the best methods of vocal production, often by studying and comparing trained and untrained singers, as well as through computer and physical modeling of vocal production. Increasingly, this has also included important studies of how differences in vocal technique affect the perceived quality and intensity of sound. This is exemplified by the work of Sundberg, famous for a groundbreaking article on vocal science that appeared in *Scientific American* in 1977. Ingo Titze (e.g., 2000) who has a background in physics (and, incidentally, is an accomplished bari-tenor), has also conducted fascinating research on optimal vocal production. Both Sundberg's and Titze's research have resulted in some very practical methods for improving singing. Research in the field of vocal science has increased dramatically since 1990. We reference numerous studies since that time which provide further insight into improving vocal technique.

**Perceptual studies of singing** further add to our knowledge of desirable approaches to vocal production. While we include a number of more recent studies in this area, Carl Seashore's (1938) pioneering research in the psychology of music deserves particular mention, especially when it comes to the topic of vibrato.

## A note about symbols used in this book

To indicate a given pitch, we use the standard Acoustical Society of America designation of $C_4$ for middle-C and $A_4$ for a concert-A. A note which is an octave above middle-C is thus $C_5$ and the note a full step above $C_5$ is $D_5$. C is always the first note in a transition to a higher numbered set of pitches.

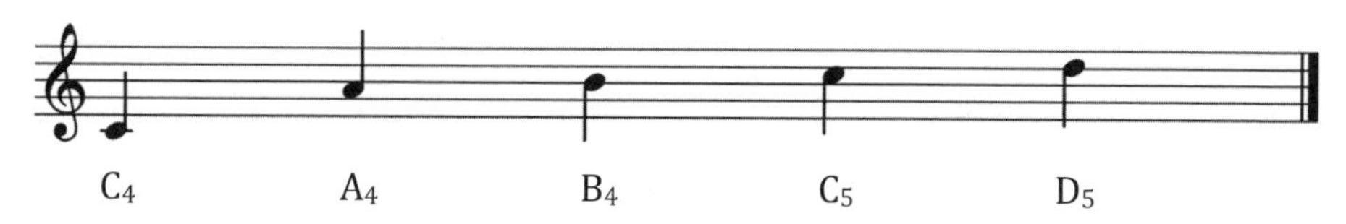


**Figure I.1 Illustration of pitch notation**

Specific vowels and consonants are shown between square brackets. For example, the vowel sound in "ghost" is [o]. We use the International Phonetic Alphabet (IPA) to illustrate vowel sounds. (Because IPA symbols for some consonants and even some vowels are not intuitive, IPA symbols for common vowels and some consonants in English, German, French, and Italian are contained in the Appendix A.) Table I.1 lists the symbols for what are often called the five basic Italian or "cardinal" vowels. Chapter 5 on vowels expands this chart. (Note that vowel symbols in IPA largely reflect the vowel sounds of the Romance languages, such as Spanish and Italian.)

| Vowel | Example |
|---|---|
| [i] | N*ee*d |
| [e] | *A*te |
| [ɑ] | F*a*ther |
| [o] | G*o* |
| [u] | Ch*oo*se |

**Table I.1 IPA symbols for cardinal (five basic Italian) vowels**

## A word about terminology

Some authors use the term "tone" to refer to the note being sung. Tone, however, can be confused with the concept of the color and quality of the sound. We think "pitch" is a better choice, even though from a technical standpoint, pitch refers to what we *perceive* the note to be (the heard fundamental frequency). This can actually be different from what the singer intends, as outlined in Chapter 4 on resonance. Nonetheless, for simplicity we will use "pitch" to refer to the note being sung.

# Section I: Foundations of Vocal Technique

# Chapter 1: Posture

Proper posture has three major benefits (Bunch, 1995):

- Breathing is easier
- Tension is reduced
- Singing is less tiring

Correct posture elevates the ribs, allowing greater lung expansion and finer control over breathing. Without proper posture, muscles that can affect vocal production must compensate to maintain body position. Tensing of these muscles degrades sound quality. Moreover, singers with poor posture tire easily because they spend too much energy on maintaining balance. Even singers who know posture is important need reminders from time to time.

## Essentials of proper posture

To help achieve good posture, align your body so that an imaginary straight line passes from the top of the head through the back of the ear, the center of the shoulder, the highest point of the hip bone, the knee joint, and just in front of the ankle. Place your feet directly beneath the shoulders (i.e., a shoulder's width apart) to help maintain balance. Keep one foot *slightly* in front of the other to counteract any tendency to rock from side to side. Weight should be evenly distributed over the feet—avoid placing too much weight either on the heels or on the balls of the feet.

Elevate the sternum (breastbone) to lift the ribs (they are attached to the sternum). This increases lung capacity (Bunch, 1995). A useful device for learning this is to "... imagine that you are a marionette, hanging from strings, one attached to the top of your head and one attached to the top of your breast bone [sternum]. This keeps the head erect and lifts the chest ..." (Vennard, 1967, p. 19)

Figure 1.1 illustrates good standing posture with both frontal and side views.

*Try standing against a wall with the shoulder blades and buttocks touching the wall (the head should not touch the wall, as this will compress the throat). This is particularly helpful for singers who round the shoulders forward, or who fail to elevate the sternum.*

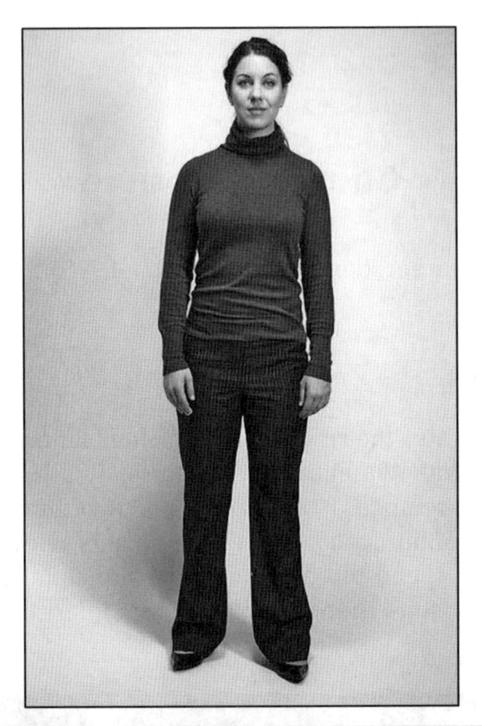

**Figure 1.1 Illustrations of good standing posture**

## Important aspects of posture

### Head and chin position

Although head position is itself critical, it can significantly affect other aspects of posture as well. If the head is aligned improperly, other parts of the body will compensate to maintain balance, leading to excess tension and expenditure of energy (Bunch, 1995).

The chin should be tilted *slightly* down, not parallel to the ground, to counteract the natural tendency to raise the chin when singing high notes (McKinney, 2005). If the chin is raised, the larynx often rises, leading to a strained or "pressed" style of production. If the chin is tilted too far down, opening the jaw is difficult.

Refrain from pulling the chin back, as this constricts the throat. X-ray studies show that pulling back the head depresses the larynx excessively (Vennard, 1967). This creates extraneous tension and results in a "woofy" sound. At the same time, avoid jutting the chin forward. This, too, distorts the shape of the vocal tract.

#### *Head turning to see the conductor*

In some choral settings singers may need to turn their heads slightly to the left or right to see the conductor. Ideally, singers should turn their bodies to face the conductor so that the head can face straight ahead. A *slight* turn of the head toward the conductor, however, should not pose serious problems. If the head is turned too much, the neck muscles will tense, consuming energy and compromising sound.

Singers must also have adequate space to allow them to see the conductor easily. Those who have difficulty seeing the conductor may resort to contorting themselves, leading to undesirable tension. Sufficient spacing is also necessary for singers to hear both themselves and others, an important factor affecting choral intonation (see Chapter 10, which treats intonation in more detail).

#### *Holding music and seeing the conductor*

Choral singers often experience head posture problems when holding music. A common cause of the problem is holding the music in a low position. Singers who do this tilt the chin down when reading music and raise the chin when looking at the conductor. Singers who hold the music fairly high only need to use their eyes to look up and down, avoiding raising and lowering the chin. The bonus is that singers will more easily see the conductor.

Figures 1.1 and 1.3 illustrate proper ways to hold a music folder in both standing and seated positions. Note how the folder is cradled in the singer's hands and wrists. The position of the folder facilitates viewing of the conductor without interfering with the path of sound. Such interference attenuates important higher harmonic frequencies, discussed further in Chapter 4 on resonance (Galante, 2011).

The way head position affects the sound illustrates how you are your instrument. You wouldn't bend a trumpet and expect it to play well, nor should you bend your vocal tract. *To demonstrate the effect of doing this on the quality of sound, sing [a] ("ah"). Move your head back and then forward, jutting out the chin. Note how the sound changes. Now try singing [a] and move your chin up and down to see how that changes the sound.*

### Relaxed shoulders

Shoulder position affects the amount of extraneous tension in the body. The shoulders should be rolled back and feel as though they have dropped into their sockets. They should not be rigid or locked.

### Arms, hands, and feet

The arms and hands should hang at the side (if singing from memory) and singers should avoid clenching the hands (McKinney, 2005). Some singers hold their hands together in front or in back. We do not recommend this practice, for it creates unproductive tension in the arms and shoulders.

When singing from music, think carefully about the weight of music folders. Consider investing in a lightweight, easy-to-hold folder. A heavy folder increases the likelihood of singers experiencing tension in the arms and shoulders, not to mention anxiety about dropping the folder.

Clenching the feet should be avoided as well—this is a surprisingly common problem, for as singers release extraneous tension in one group of muscles, they often make the mistake of transferring it to another.

### Knees

It is very important to avoid locking the knees. Locked knees inevitably lead to an undesirable swayback posture. To avoid this problem, Henderson (1979) recommends tucking in the tailbone. The resultant shifting forward of the pelvis unlocks the knees automatically. Tucking in the tailbone, however, should not be exaggerated, or it will become another source of tension. The key is that posture should give a feeling of ease and freedom.

## Common posture problems

Choral directors and teachers may observe a number of common posture problems that tire singers, disrupt breath control, and create tension (Bunch, 1995). These problems include:

- Rounded or hunched shoulders (particularly when sitting)
- Collapsed chest
- Excessively arched lower back
- Raised or excessively lowered chin

A related problem is the "overeager" posture. This includes holding the music too high, leaning forward and raising the chin.

Figure 1.2 illustrates both hunched and overeager postures, often seen in amateur singers. Notice how these problematic postures result in body misalignment.

## Avoid excessive body movement

Many people engage in a variety of body movements while singing. Such movements interfere with good vocal production, because they expend energy unproductively and introduce extraneous tensions affecting the breathing mechanisms and vocal tract. This creates strain and thus, poor tone. (We are not speaking of natural movements required when acting, or choreographed movements.)

Body movement and other indicators of inappropriate tension such as strained neck and facial muscles often fall outside of a singer's awareness. Singing in front of a mirror at home is a helpful way to create awareness of them.

> Fleming was given the following advice by Ubaldo Gardini (one of her coaches). He suggested that she "sing in the mirror. If it looks funny, it's wrong" (Fleming, 2005, p. 36). To this Fleming adds, "... singers have to ... rid themselves of the popping veins, the trembling jaws, ... and the inability to ... move the voice without moving the whole body" (p. 20).

In the choral setting, conductors should spend a few minutes during the warm-up on body awareness and provide feedback to singers. Further postural reminders can be given from time to time in rehearsals.

**Figure 1.2 Examples of hunched and "overeager" postures**

Movement is often a response to nervousness and tension, stemming from a lack of confidence in one's vocal technique. Hence, movement may be used to compensate for a missing element of technique such as breath support. To counteract this, singers can focus on positive actions that will promote good vocal technique. For example thinking, "Maintain expansion of the rib cage as notes are sung," will help maintain breath support (see Chapter 3 on breathing for more on this subject). Focus less on the negative (e.g., "don't tighten the muscles of your arms" or "don't sway as you sing") and more on what should be done. Singers should occasionally monitor themselves for signs of progress.

## Sitting posture and seat types

Choral groups spend much of their rehearsal time seated. While most aspects of standing posture also apply to sitting posture, the legs and feet are less relevant—they are no longer supporting your weight. From the hips up, though, you should feel as though you are standing (Henderson, 1979).

Unfortunately, we tend to collapse or slump our chests when our shoulders are propped up by our chairs, making it harder to keep the sternum elevated. This can have a disastrous effect upon breath support. Singers should maintain an elevated sternum when sitting, otherwise breath control will suffer (as outlined in Chapter 3 on breathing).

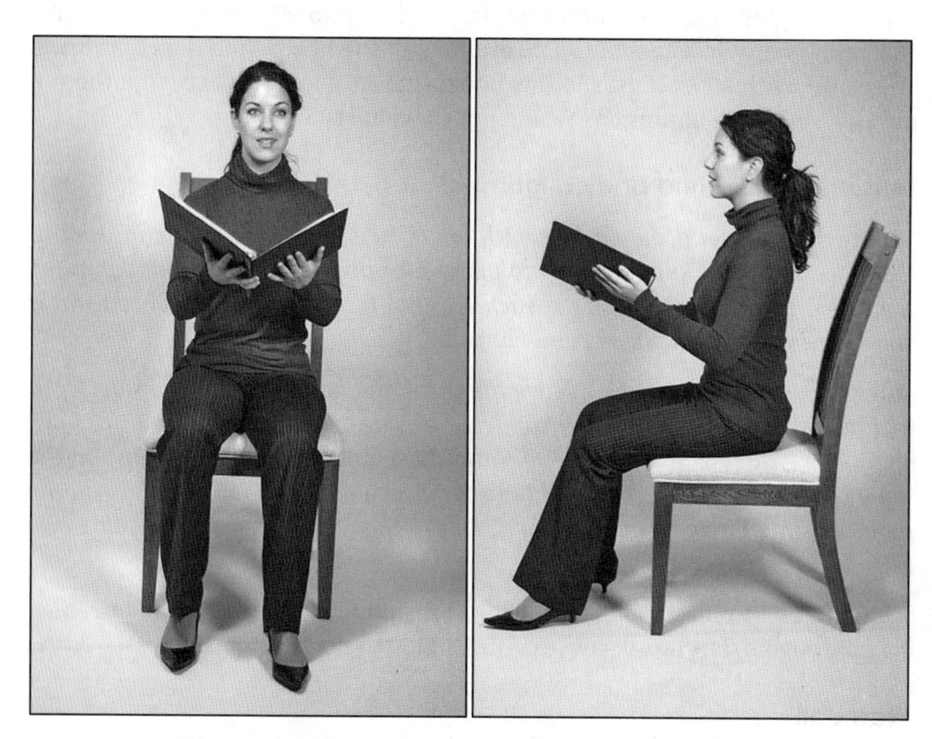

**Figure 1.3 Illustrations of good seated posture**

Some singers sit near the front edge of their seats to maintain a standing posture from the hips up, but McKinney (2005) suggests sitting well back in the seat. We think that either method can work well, as long as an erect posture is maintained. The key is to avoid slumping!

As for the type of seating, bucket seats and, more generally, seats with substantially raised fronts (e.g., some church pews) can be problematic, because they fold the body inward, interfering with proper breathing. In this situation singers should sit near the front edge of the seat. Armchairs should also be avoided, because they encourage the raising of the shoulders.

Choral conductors should ask singers to switch occasionally from sitting to standing positions during rehearsal. This will reduce the tension that accumulates from being in one position for too long.

Figure 1.3 illustrates good seated posture. Notice how the alignment of the upper body resembles proper standing posture.

## Exercises for posture

Prior to singing, a few physical exercises can help to align the body and give singers better awareness of the positioning of the head, shoulders, torso and knees. (As with all exercises in this book, singers should not attempt them if physical or health limitations would put them at risk.)

### Tension release and body alignment

*Stand with the feet a shoulder's width apart, one foot very slightly in front of the other. Bend the knees slightly to make sure they are unlocked. If you experience leg or feet tension, shake each leg and foot. If you experience arm or hand tension, shake each arm and hand.*

*Raise the arms over the head. Move the torso and head from side to side. Next, with arms down, tilt the head from side to side. Then, tilt the head forward and move it slowly in a half-circle to the back and to the front again. Do the same thing to the right. This will help to release neck tension. Finally, roll the shoulders in a circle to the back and then to the front, letting them relax into their sockets.*

See Chapter 14 on reducing extraneous tension for information about reducing pharyngeal/laryngeal, jaw, tongue, shoulder, and leg tension.

### "Rag doll"

"Rag doll" is an excellent exercise to help with both posture and relaxation.

*If standing, drop the body forward at the waist with the head and arms hanging limp. There should be no tension in the shoulders or neck. If there is tension, first move the head from side to side and roll the shoulders as described above. Avoid locking the knees. Then, slowly roll the torso up to a standing position with the sternum comfortably high and the shoulders falling into their sockets. Inhale fully (but not excessively) and sing a prolonged [a] vowel or exhale on [s].*

This exercise can also be applied to sitting posture:

*Put the knees together and drop the torso forward so that the shoulders rest on the knees (or as low as comfortable). The rest of the exercise follows the standing version.*

### An aid to proper standing posture

*Try standing against a wall with the shoulder blades and buttocks touching the wall (the head should not touch the wall, as this will compress the throat).* This is particularly helpful for singers who round the shoulders forward, or who fail to elevate the sternum.

### For kids and everyone! Neck relaxation and positioning; body consciousness

*Yes and No—raise and lower the head for yes, rotate head back and forth for no. Ask questions about the singers' weekend or day that have yes or no answers. (Adapted from Phillips, 1996)*

### For kids and everyone! Brain/body coordination

*Try a variety of motions and have the singers follow you, either changing together with you or in a delayed sequence, for example, as in "Simon Says." (Adapted from Cooksey, 1999)*

### For kids and everyone! Body awareness and physical warm-up

*Disco Dance—use funny "disco" motions such as "the sprinkler" and "starting the lawnmower." Invent your own moves.*

### Head position

*Sing [a] ("ah"). Move your head back and then forward, jutting out the chin. Note how the sound changes. Now try singing [a] and move your chin up and down to see how that changes the sound. Find a chin position that is slightly below level and neither too forward nor too backward. Singers should try this in front of a mirror at home.*

# Chapter 2: Breath Control

Breathing is *the* foundation of singing. As Tetrazzini says, "... uncontrolled breath is like a rickety foundation on which nothing can be built, and until that foundation has been developed and strengthened, the would-be singer need expect no satisfactory results" (Caruso & Tetrazzini, 1975, p. 10).

Why is proper breathing so critical? And why are phrases such as "breath support," and "sing from the diaphragm" so prevalent in the vocabulary of voice teachers, conductors and singers? The reasons are numerous—a singer with proper breathing technique will:

- Create the breath pressure necessary to sing higher notes properly
- Meter breath to handle long passages
- Modulate breath pressure to better control dynamic level
- Avoid a strained sound by not using the muscles surrounding the vocal tract to squeeze air through the tract
- Relax the breathing muscles between phrases, easing tension and producing a freer and more pleasing sound
- Have a more stable vibrato

Vennard (1967) sums up these advantages rather nicely, saying that no matter how well people sing, their singing will be further enhanced with improvement in breathing technique.

## Phases of the breathing cycle

The four basic phases of the breathing cycle in singing are:

- Inhalation
- Very brief suspension of the breathing apparatus
- Exhalation
- Recovery

## Inhalation

### How to achieve proper inhalation

The diaphragm and the external intercostals (outer rib muscles) are the two major muscles contracted during inhalation for singing (Sundberg, 1993).

The diaphragm is one of the most discussed muscles in singing. It is a dome-shaped muscle underlying the lungs, separating them from the abdominal contents. When the diaphragm contracts, it descends, creating a vacuum within the lungs (See Figure 2.1). Air then flows in and fills the lungs. As the diaphragm descends it displaces the contents of the abdominal cavity.

Based on the advice to "sing from the diaphragm," singers often mistakenly assume that the diaphragm lies in the abdominal area. As Figure 2.1 shows, the top of the diaphragm is surprisingly high, thus this advice should really be focused on the abdominal and intercostal muscles, as outlined below.

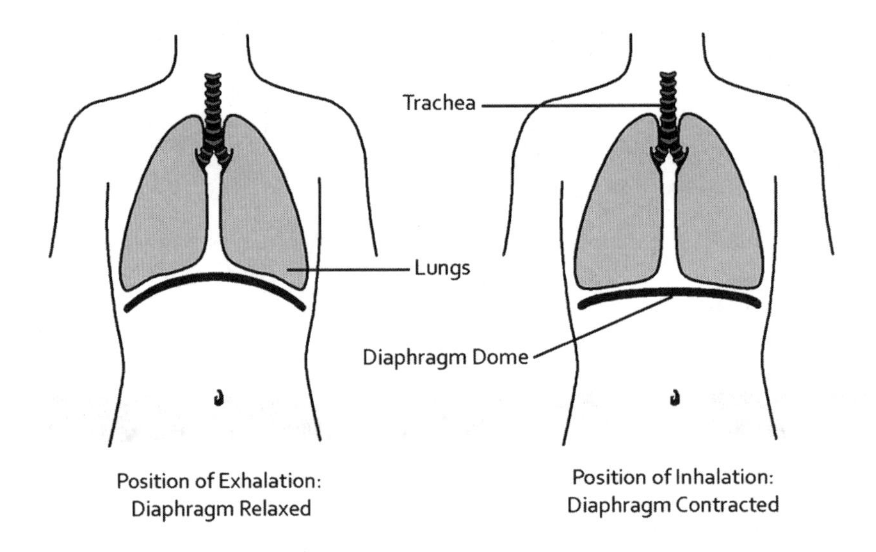


**Figure 2.1 Illustration of the diaphragm**

The diaphragm will descend fully and maximum air will be inhaled only when the abdominals are relaxed. Think of this as creating vertical space for the lungs. At the same time, think of creating horizontal space by expanding the ribs.

- Tetrazzini suggests imagining the lungs as empty sacks into which air is dropping like a weight, filling the space from the bottom up (Caruso & Tetrazzini, 1975).
- Fleming (2005) advises release of the abdominal wall outward—without pushing—so that the diaphragm can descend, allowing the lungs to fill to their greatest capacity. The chest should also expand slightly, but this is only in the final stage of inhalation when air fills the lungs "to the top."

When we speak of releasing the abdominal wall, we are not including the lower abdomen (the area from the top of the pubic bone to just below the navel). Expanding this portion of the abdomen simply pushes out the intestines and internal organs; it does not create additional room for the diaphragm to descend. Singers who push out the lower abdomen may cave in the ribs. This results in less room for the lungs to expand during inhalation and more rapid air depletion during exhalation (R. Miller, 1993).

#### *Back expansion*

The back will expand slightly as a natural consequence of rib expansion, but some singers find it helpful to focus a bit more on back expansion as a method of increasing room for the lungs to expand. Fleming (2005), for example, argues that singers should imagine their torsos as a barrel and that expansion should include the back muscles.

We think that singers who desire additional lung capacity can benefit from monitoring back expansion in addition to side and frontal expansion. A few cautions are nonetheless in order:

- Singers should not concentrate so much on back expansion that frontal expansion suffers (McKinney, 2005). Abdominal expansion is essential for proper inhalation. As outlined below, it is also crucial for enhanced control over exhalation.
- Some voice teachers advocate pushing the shoulders forward to enhance back expansion (McKinney, 2005). It should be apparent, however, that this advice encourages poor posture and additional tension. Moreover, it can cause the sternum to drop.

### Keep the sternum/chest comfortably high

Chapter 1 explains why good posture for singing includes holding the sternum in a comfortably high position. We want to re-emphasize this point: a high sternum is crucial for creating room for the diaphragm to descend and for the lungs to expand. (See Figure 2.2 which illustrates the location of the sternum.)

While singing, imagine the sternum as the center point of the chest, and strive to hold it in a comfortably high position. Experimentation will demonstrate that with the sternum in the proper position, more vertical space is created and the ribs are easier to expand, both of which aid the process of inhalation.

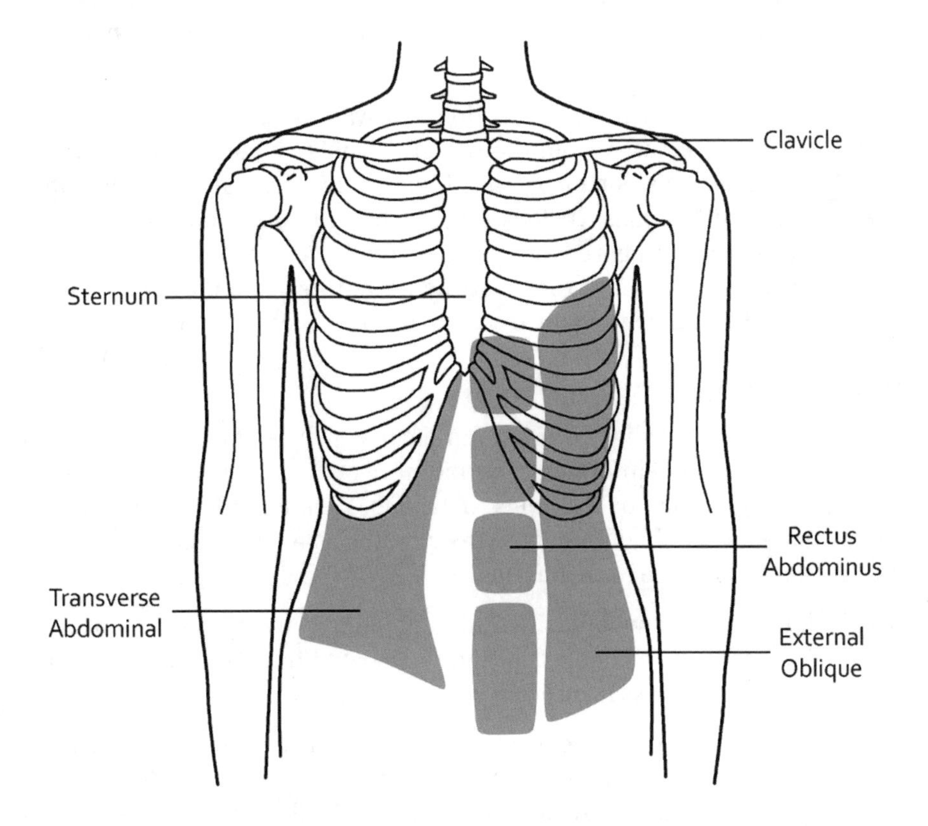


**Figure 2.2 Illustration of the clavicles, sternum, rib cage, and abdominal muscles**

### Inhalation should be noiseless

Breath intake should be noiseless. Noise indicates throat constriction (R. Miller, 1996), which inhibits tone quality.

Typical causes of constriction include one or more of the following:

- Soft palate too relaxed (See Figure 4.1 in Chapter 4 on resonance)
- Jaw open insufficiently
- Tongue contracted too far back in the throat

Singers who inhale with the space between the vocal folds partially closed will also be noisy. This may occur when singers begin to sing without proper preparation.

*Try inhaling with the tongue, mouth, and jaw in the position of the vowel that is to be sung*. This is highly efficient, and has the added benefit of avoiding an unwanted and unpleasant vowel change as singing is initiated.

*Try inhaling in a fashion associated with each of the four typical causes of constriction, followed in every case by a silent inhalation. Notice the sensations associated with each inhalation.*

### Inhalation should be visible

An expanded abdomen and ribs are clues that a singer is inhaling properly. Even advanced singers may have difficulty with proper inhalation. At a master class at a major university school of music, Renée Fleming observed a participating singer and commented that she could not see abdominal and rib expansion indicative of appropriate breathing. After she recommended some modifications to the singer's breathing technique, inhalation became visible, and the quality of singing noticeably improved.

### Avoid clavicular breathing (upper chest breathing)

Singers often engage in clavicular (collar bone) breathing, mistakenly believing that the chest must be expanded as much as possible to completely fill the lungs. Clavicular breathing is commonly known as upper chest breathing because the collar bones of the shoulders are moved in order to expand the upper chest. The clavicles are illustrated in Figure 2.2.

Other causes of clavicular breathing include:

- Singers holding in the abdomen to keep the stomach flat for the sake of appearances. (If the abdomen is held in, upper chest breathing is about the only option available.)
- Inappropriate carryover from other activities. Singers who engage in strenuous exercise (e.g., running) may unconsciously adopt clavicular breathing because this is how people often respond to being out of breath while exercising. (The solution is to carry over proper breathing technique to the exercise environment. While exercising, focus on inhaling by releasing the abdominal muscles and expanding the ribs.)

Clavicular breathing results in several problems:

- This shallow form of breathing provides insufficient air for long phrases. The volume of the upper area of the lungs is less than the volume of the lower area (see Figure 2.1).

- It does not allow fine control over exhalation. The abdominal muscles must be relaxed during inhalation, allowing a full range of contraction to create and modulate the breath pressure necessary for singing.

Sundberg (1993) is particularly dismissive of holding in the abdomen and use of clavicular breathing. He notes with amusement that some proponents cite the "technique" of barking dogs—as if singers are trying to mimic a bark!

#### *Upper chest breathing and shoulder movement*

Shoulder movement may accompany upper chest breathing (Vennard, 1967). Such movement occurs unconsciously because shoulder movement helps to compensate for the shallowness of this method by assisting inhalation. Various muscles connect the shoulders and the ribs. Raising the shoulders can lever the ribs, exerting a bellows-like effect that draws air into the lungs. Shoulder-assisted breathing will result in neck and laryngeal tension because the muscle groups involved in shoulder raising, the sternocleidomastoids and the scalenes, extend from behind the ears down to the clavicle and sternum (Fisher, 1966; Vennard 1967). Singers should be mindful of shoulder movement—even if it is not always a sign of upper chest breathing, it is a sure sign of unproductive tension.

### Take a full breath, but avoid excessive inhalation

Singers should take full breaths because a relatively high lung volume helps to maintain a low larynx position, which in turn may help to reduce mechanical stress on the thyroarytenoids, important muscles involved in pitch control (Iwarsson & Sundberg, 1998). As outlined in Chapter 4 on resonance, a high larynx position is often associated with a strained sound.

At the same time, avoid the temptation to take as much breath as possible.

> ➢ Richard Miller (1996) argues that "... the lungs should never feel crowded—only satisfied" (p. 26).

There is a very practical reason to avoid overfilling the lungs—it tends to increase the rate of exhalation (R. Miller, 1996), defeating the purpose of taking such a large breath. In addition, overblown exhalation produces a breathy, grainy-sounding, or "unfocused" tone.

*Try breathing through the nose for a while. This will slow down the inhalation phase and allow singers to feel more easily the passage of air into the lungs. Then try breathing through both the nose and mouth. Finally, breathe through the mouth. (When actually singing, breathe through the mouth unless you are humming or have a long rest period. Otherwise, breathing through the nose means the soft palate will be down, creating insufficient space in the pharynx and the risk of a nasal tone. See Chapter 4 on resonance for more information about the importance of soft palate position.)*

## Very brief suspension

Very brief suspension prior to exhalation allows a transition from using muscles for inhalation to using muscles for exhalation. In everyday breathing there is often no real suspension, but rather an immediate shift from inspiration to exhalation. But this brief pause is necessary in singing to set the stage for good breath support.

A number of authorities recommend specific exercises for suspension (e.g., inhaling and holding the breath without closing the vocal folds for several seconds, then exhaling). If nonprofessional singers engage in drawn-out suspension exercises, they tend to tense the laryngeal and neck muscles and hold the glottis tightly. This may inadvertently encourage a hard onset (glottal attack).

Nonetheless, suspension exercises are helpful for learning to maintain the inhalation position of the abdomen and ribs during suspension. This is good practice for what also needs to be done during exhalation. Conductors and teachers should caution singers to give careful attention to keeping the glottis open and to relaxing the laryngeal and neck muscles during such exercises.

## Exhalation

Following Tetrazzini's advice, we have now filled the lungs with air from the bottom up. The ribs and abdomen are expanded slightly outward and we are ready to sing. At this point, many singers have heard that they need "breath support" to sing properly. But what does this truly mean?

### Achieving breath support

Breath support involves delivering the right level of breath pressure to the vocal folds. Some authors emphasize the role of the internal rib muscles (internal intercostals) in the modulation of breath pressure (e.g., Emmons & Chase, 2006). But both rib and abdominal muscles are important. If anything, the abdominal muscles may be more important for breath support.

- In a study of perceived singing quality, Robison, Bounous, and Bailey

(1994) found that those singers judged to have the best tone and most consistent vibrato used the abdominal muscles more than the intercostals.

Note, however, that we are not advocating so-called "belly breathing." The intercostals must also be involved in breath support.

An important key to using these exhalation muscles in a way that allows fine control of breath pressure is to *resist collapsing the abdominal musculature and the ribs until the very end of a phrase* (Vennard, 1967). To do this, the inhalation and exhalation muscles must be in balance. For example, the external intercostal muscles have to slightly oppose the internal intercostals as breath is exhaled. (Technically, this is an oversimplification of the role of these and other rib muscles but the concept of muscular opposition is nonetheless correct—see Dayme [2009] and Vennard [1967].)

- McKinney (2005) says that breath support entails the delivery of sufficient air pressure to the vocal folds through dynamic tension between the muscles of inhalation and exhalation. This dynamic tension was termed by the great Italian singing teacher Lamperti as "appoggio," which comes from "appoggiare," meaning "to lean upon," or more freely translated, "to support" (Lamperti, 1877).

Richard Miller (1996) is perhaps the foremost modern proponent of appoggio. In talks on the subject he discussed the need to consciously initiate appoggio. That is, there must be a gentle activation of the abdominal muscles which the singer will feel as a slight pushing out of the abdomen but with little or no muscle wall excursion. If you place your fingers on the abdomen between the sternum and the navel, you should feel engaged muscle that nonetheless has some give, like a firm mattress (S. Beatty, personal communication, April 12, 2010).

#### *The appoggio technique also reduces tension in the vocal tract*

Great artists have noted the benefits of the appoggio technique for reducing extraneous muscle tension, and consequent strain in the vocal tract. Tetrazzini (Caruso & Tetrazzini, 1975) explicitly warns that without proper support, pressure is created in the throat. Similarly, Fleming (2005) states that proper breath support relieves throat strain.

The concept of the "throat" may seem nebulous, but it is more understandable if we think of the throat as encompassing the portion of the vocal tract from the larynx up through the back of the mouth. Many singers and speakers move air through the vocal tract in part by constricting the muscles that surround the tract. This is a compensatory response to inadequate breath pressure resulting from suboptimal methods of breathing. Problems associated with constricting the muscles surrounding the vocal tract include the following:

- Harmful tension is created, which can result in a strained sound and a tired singer.
- A resonant tone is difficult to develop. (See Chapter 4 on resonance.)
- High pitches are difficult to sing well because there is insufficient breath pressure; for the same reason, it is difficult to sing loudly (see below).
- Long notes are difficult to sustain because little breath is available.

### Upper chest breathing results in poor control over exhalation

Earlier we outlined the problems associated with upper chest breathing during inhalation. This also makes control over exhalation difficult because the muscles involved in upper chest breathing allow little control over exhalation. Exhalation in this mode of breathing is assisted mostly by elastic recoil of the lungs and upper ribs with limited assistance from the upper portion of the abdominal muscles. The middle area of the abdominals and important areas of the intercostal muscles are not activated.

- In Vennard's words, "Since phonation is expiratory, and singing especially demands fine control, we see here the prime reason why this kind of breathing is inefficient for singers" (1967, p. 27). Vennard thus advocates using the abdominal and intercostal muscles to control exhalation.

Recall that singers who use upper chest breathing often hold in their abdomens. This practice further compromises control over exhalation because contracting the abdominal muscles to hold in the abdomen limits the range of potential muscle contraction, further reducing control over breath pressure (Hixon & Hoffman, 1978).

### Specific abdominal muscles involved in exhalation

The contraction of the abdominal muscles moves the abdominal contents upward, in turn raising the diaphragm and exhaling air from the lungs (Sundberg, 1993). An understanding of the involved abdominal muscles is thus helpful. Moreover, strengthening the abdominal muscles through exercises is an excellent way to improve breath support (Vennard, 1967).

Figure 2.2 illustrates the three main abdominal muscle groups. (The illustration shows each muscle group on only one side of the body to allow illustration of all of the muscles in one drawing. Each muscle group exists on both sides of the body.)

The vertical sets of muscles on either side of the center of the abdomen are the rectus abdominus muscles. The muscles on the side of the abdomen are known as the internal and external obliques. The internal obliques are not shown in Figure 2.2 because they underlie the external obliques. Although both the rectus abdominus and obliques play a role in breath support, the internal obliques are particularly important (Sears, 1977). The transverse muscles are the most interior abdominal muscles. They wrap around the abdomen and extend back to the spine. Relaxing the transverse abdominals is crucial to allow the diaphragm to descend properly into the abdominal cavity during inspiration; contraction of this muscle also plays an important role in control of exhalation (Vennard, 1967; Dayme, 2009). The transverse abdominals also provide core support for the torso, which is essential for maintaining good posture when singing for long periods of time.

*Sit-ups are one obvious option for exercising the abdominals, but straight sit-ups are not sufficient as these primarily focus on the rectus abdominus.*

*Try this exercise for the obliques: lie on your back with knees drawn up. With your hands cradling your head, contract the abdominal muscles to raise the shoulders and head off the floor—first toward one knee and then toward the other. It is not necessary to lift more than the shoulders off the floor (i.e., abdominal crunches are sufficient). Be careful not to use your neck and upper back muscles to raise the head and shoulders; use only the abdominal muscles.*

*To strengthen the abdominal transverse muscle, try this: In a sitting or kneeling position exhale and attempt to suck in the area around the navel, compressing the waist. A more effective exercise is the pelvic tilt: lie on your back with knees drawn up and a towel under the small of the back. Attempt to tilt the pelvis up using only your abdominal muscles.*

- Fleming (2005) recommends Pilates to exercise the entire core. Yoga can also be helpful. As singers age they are particularly prone to failing to maintain core strength, which can result in poor breath support and a wavering vibrato.

### Role of the diaphragm in exhalation

Singers control exhalation with abdominal and rib muscles, not through direct control of the diaphragm. Singers should not be advised to "sing from the diaphragm" or "bounce the diaphragm" for staccato passages or those involving melismas. (See Chapter 11 on staccato, legato, accents, melismas, and dynamic control for more accurate ways to talk to singers about how to achieve these special techniques.)

The most important thing to know about the diaphragm is that there are great advantages to delaying its ascent during exhalation. Sundberg (1993) found that trained singers appear to do this and that it has two benefits: finer control over breath pressure and creation of a pull on the trachea. The pull on the trachea lowers the larynx, which increases vocal tract volume and enhances resonance. It also reduces excessive pressing together of the vocal folds at high pitches, avoiding the strained sound of pressed phonation.

Sundberg's findings raise the question of how to delay the ascent of the diaphragm. A hint appears in Henderson's (1979) fluoroscopic observations of one of her students. When the singer did not keep the abdominal and intercostal muscles engaged during exhalation, Henderson observed that the diaphragm ascended. Thus, resistance to the collapse of the abdominal and intercostal muscles may play an important role in preventing premature ascension of the diaphragm.

## Additional points about exhalation

### Breath metering

"Breath metering" involves conserving air during singing to complete musical phrases with sufficient energy. As outlined above, breath pressure must be modulated as well through "breath support." Both of these are essential components of "breath control."

Efficient metering of air requires exhaling no more and no less than what is necessary to produce the desired tone. Many singers exhale too much air, producing a breathy or grainy tone, as well as poor intonation (typically too sharp). Additionally, efficient metering is essential for singing long phrases.

- Fleming (2005) states that the key to efficient metering of air is to resist collapse of the abdomen and the ribs. Fleming further argues that a singer must not collapse the chest. She based this recommendation on her observation of great singers, and notes that this underlies the caricature of opera singers as "pigeon-chested."

In short, the appoggio technique essential for good breath support is also essential for breath metering.

## Vocal fold pressure and breath metering

Breath metering can also be affected by how firmly the vocal folds are held together. If they are loosely held together or if there is a small space between them, glottal leakage occurs (the glottis is the space between the vocal folds). Glottal leakage can make it difficult for a singer to complete a long phrase.

If the folds are held together very firmly there will be less leakage, but the singer may suffer long-term damage to the vocal folds and have undesirable resonance characteristics (unless the singer is purposefully "belting" in a healthy way; see the belting section of Chapter 3 for less hazardous methods of creating a "belt" sound). The key is to have firm closure without excessive tension in the folds. This is a critical aspect of vocal technique, discussed in detail in Chapter 3 on initiation and creation of sound and in Chapter 4 on resonance.

### *Breathiness of younger voices*

Choral directors and teachers should be particularly patient with young voices, which often have a breathy quality (particularly, girls' voices). They will develop a clearer tone with training, experience, and physical maturity. Such breathiness is associated with vocal changes during adolescence, specifically the inability of certain laryngeal muscles (the interarytenoids) to close the back third of the space between the vocal folds, a natural part of adolescent development. In some cases breathiness is also due to imitation of pop singers.

Exercises can reduce some of this breathiness. In our experience this is particularly important for middle/junior high school choral groups in which the sound balance between girls and boys can pose difficulties due to overly breathy singing by the girls (and heavy chest voice production by some boys). Chapter 4 on initiation and creation of sound contains some exercises to help both young people and adults achieve a less breathy tone.

## Higher pitches and dynamic levels require higher breath pressure

With experience, singers learn the amount of breath pressure necessary for a given pitch and dynamic level. Loud tones require high levels of breath pressure (technically known as subglottic [below the glottis] pressure). In fact, doubling breath pressure generally doubles the perceived sound level (Sundberg, 1987). Higher pitches also require more breath pressure—for example, a tenor moving from A3 to E4 at moderate loudness will need to increase breath pressure by about 150% (Sundberg, 1987). Since the vocal folds are under greater tension at higher pitches, more force is required to open them (Titze, 1989). This explains why more breath support is needed for higher pitches.

High pitches do not, however, require more airflow (Sundberg, 1987; Rubin, Lecover, & Vennard, 1967). If singers push too much air through the vocal folds at high pitches, it can result in both undesirable sound quality and poor intonation.

### Breath support is critical for leaps in pitch

Breath support is critical in leaping from a low to a high pitch. This support must be engaged *before* the move is made from the low note to the high note. Many singers mistakenly engage support muscles only as they sing the higher note. This can lead to singing under the desired higher pitch or "scooping" up to the correct pitch.

## Recovery

Recovery should be a conscious aspect of the breathing cycle. Muscles need to relax after singing each phrase so that they can recover and perform efficiently for the next. As McKinney (2005) notes, this also applies to the laryngeal muscles, the muscles involved in creating resonance (such as those of the pharynx and mouth), and the muscles involved in articulation of vowels and consonants (such as the tongue, lips, and jaw). Without a rest period (brief as it may be in singing), tension will build, resulting in undesirable sound.

In cases where passages are long without rests, and, in particular, where there is also a high tessitura (high average pitch), it may be judicious to add an eighth or quarter rest at some points of punctuation to provide needed rest and recovery, brief as it may be. In the choral setting, singers should be encouraged to take adequate time for recovery when stagger breathing.

## Breathing exercises

Proper breathing is not difficult to learn. It is, however, difficult for singers to apply knowledge of proper breathing every time that they sing. It takes much practice and repetition over time (measured in years!) before good breathing technique becomes second nature. Conductors and teachers will need to remind their singers to work on this individually as well as during rehearsals and lessons.

### Breathing while lying on the back

The following is a simple method for experiencing proper breathing technique that singers can try at home. (For choral conductors, if you have enough room in the rehearsal space, it could also be done there.) It encourages the use of the intercostal and abdominal muscles and naturally limits upper chest and shoulder breathing.

*Lie flat on the back with a book under the head to create better body alignment.*

*Think about how babies breathe when they are asleep on their backs. Their bellies rise as they take in air. Release the abdominal and rib muscles and let the belly rise and ribs expand during inhalation. The chest may expand slightly as well, but it should expand only after the abdomen has risen (good evidence that the lungs are being filled from the bottom up).*

*To better monitor the pattern of abdominal expansion and contraction, place a lightweight book on the abdomen. As you breathe, observe when the book moves. (Using a heavy book or stack of books to exercise abdominal muscles is not recommended.)*

*After spending several minutes observing and adjusting your breathing on the floor, move to a standing position and repeat, again observing the abdomen and lower ribs moving outward during inhalation.*

### Inhalation

*Try inhaling with the tongue, mouth, and jaw in the position of the vowel that is to be sung.* This is highly efficient, and has the added benefit of avoiding an unwanted and unpleasant vowel change as singing is initiated.

*Try inhaling in a fashion associated with each of the four typical causes of constriction (relaxed soft palate, insufficiently open jaw, tongue too far back in the throat, and partially closed space between the vocal folds). In each case, follow this with a silent inhalation. Notice the sensations associated with each inhalation.*

### Avoiding overfilling of the lungs

*Try breathing through the nose for a while. This will slow down the inhalation phase and allow singers to feel more easily the passage of air into the lungs. Then try breathing through both the nose and mouth. Finally, breathe through the mouth. (Normally, singers should breathe through the mouth unless humming or there is a long rest period. Otherwise, if breathing through the nose, the soft palate will be down, creating insufficient space in the pharynx and the risk of a nasal tone.)*

## The sibilant exercise to improve control over exhalation

One of the most commonly recommended exercises to increase control over exhalation is the sibilant exercise, so named because it involves saying [s] over an extended period of time (i.e., hissing through the teeth). This restricts airflow and allows concentration on metering the breath. Richard Miller (1996) suggests the following to improve control over the muscles involved in metering:

*Place one hand over the center of the abdomen, with the lower portion just covering the navel.*

*Place the other hand on the side, just below the rib cage.*

*Hiss and concentrate on not allowing the abdominal wall or the ribs to collapse until the very end. Having the hands in the above positions helps to monitor the expansion of the abdominal area and the ribs and to provide feedback that will increase control over this process.*

For an extension of this exercise, try the voiced consonant [v]. This is more like singing and requires further engagement of the support muscles (K. Brunssen, personal communication, November 28, 2011).

Another approach to monitoring the abdominal area during the sibilant or [v] exercise is to place both hands on the upper abdomen, thumbs touching lower ribs, little fingers near the waist, and middle fingers just touching (McKinney, 2005). Then:

*Release the abdominal muscles and expand the ribs to fill the lungs from the bottom up. The middle fingers should part slightly. This is a good sign that abdominal muscles are allowing the diaphragm to descend correctly. If some rib expansion is felt, this is a further good sign that the intercostal muscles are engaged. Press the abdomen gently with your fingertips. You should feel firm muscle with a small bit of give—like a firm mattress.*

*Hold this expanded position briefly and observe how it feels. Remember, the goal is to maintain this expanded position (within reason) while saying [s] or [v] and, ultimately, while singing.*

*Be sure that the vocal folds remain open while engaging in the sibilant exercise (they will need to be closed if using [v]). Closing the folds to prevent the escape of breath may negatively affect the onset of tone when singing. Keep the vocal folds open and prevent excessive escape of air during this exercise through control of the abdominal muscles and intercostals.*

*Make the [s] or [v] sound with a metered flow rate, all the while trying to keep the abdominal and rib area expanded (i.e., keeping fingers on your abdomen apart), allowing collapse only at the very end. Maintaining full expansion should be considered a goal, but this shouldn't lead to strain. There will naturally be some contraction, but the idea is to prevent ascent of the diaphragm as much as possible.*

### Snap breath

Henderson (1979) introduces an interesting variation on the sibilant exercise that may be helpful when preparing to sing passages with limited or no time for breaths.

*Take a "snap-like breath" letting the abdomen spring out quickly (but naturally) for the intake of breath, and then meter the breath on exhalation. Be sure to breathe in silently when doing this exercise, as quick breaths are often associated with constriction in the vocal tract.*

### Practice breathing in front of a mirror at home

At home, singers should practice their breathing exercises while singing in front of a mirror, when possible. Conductors and teachers can function as a mirror during rehearsal and lessons.

*Conductors and teacher should give helpful feedback to singers about their breathing. Look carefully for visual clues that indicate tension. Head movement is especially chronic in choral singers who feel the need to "cue" the beginnings of phrases with the chin or neck. Some also sway on inhalation. Shoulder movement may indicate upper chest breathing. Encourage good posture and inhalation that not only sounds silent but "looks quiet" too.*

*Singers can experiment with the effect of movement by nodding the head with every inhalation and then keeping the head still for each inhalation.*

### Physical exercises to strengthen abdominal muscles

*Sit-ups are one obvious option for exercising the abdominals, but straight sit ups are not sufficient as these primarily focus on the rectus abdominus.*

*Try this exercise for the obliques: lie on your back with knees drawn up. With your hands cradling your head, contract the abdominal muscles to raise the shoulders and head off the floor—first toward one knee and then toward the other. It is not necessary to do more than lift the shoulders off the floor (i.e., abdominal crunches are sufficient). Be careful not to use your neck and upper back muscles to raise the head and shoulders; use only the abdominal muscles.*

*To strengthen the abdominal transverse muscles, try this: In a sitting or kneeling position exhale and attempt to suck in the area around the navel, compressing the waist. A more effective exercise is the pelvic tilt: lie on your back with knees drawn up and a towel under the small of the back. Attempt to tilt the pelvis up using only your abdominal muscles.*

### Breath support

*Practice exercises with a variety of melodic patterns (e.g., slides of a fifth, arpeggiated triads) that clearly indicate whether support muscles (abdominals and rib muscles) are engaged. A lapse in support will be revealed by variation in tone quality and in some cases by breaks in phonation.*

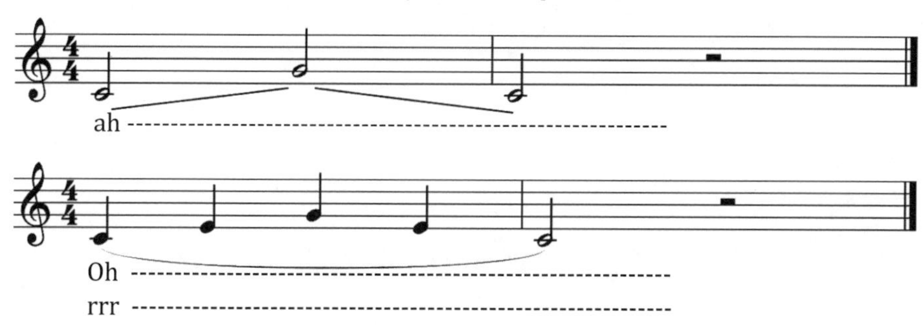


*Tongue/lip trills (rrr/brrr) will also indicate if support lapses—the trill will be interrupted or tone quality will be variable when this occurs. Trills are particularly good for development of breathing skills because they create high resistance to airflow and thus require excellent technique to maintain consistent breath pressure.*

### For kids and everyone! Maintaining breath support

Staccato Boo-Boo-Boo—*release each pitch marked staccato (see Chapter 11 for more on staccato production) and slur the remaining notes. Repeat, moving by half steps. (Adapted from Phillips, 1996)*

### For kids and everyone! Big dog

*Ask singers to "woof" like a big dog; listen to make sure the pitch is neither too low nor too high. This encourages a feeling of openness in the vocal tract as well as abdominal support. (Adapted from Phillips, 1996)*

### Don't drop breathing exercises from your warm-ups too quickly!

Breathing exercises are often the first to be dropped from both individual and choral warm-ups. Perhaps this is because we think of breathing as something we do every day, and thus easily modified to accommodate the demands of singing. We may also assume that once we have done some breathing exercises we will employ what we have learned. Nothing could be further from the truth! Developing fine control over all of the muscles involved in breath support and control takes months, or even years, to become fully automatic. Breathing practice is needed until the appropriate movements become automatic and reflexive (Bunch, 1995).

# Chapter 3: Initiation, Creation, and Release of Sound

How we initiate a pitch has a substantial effect on the quality of the sound throughout a musical phrase. If a phrase *begins* with excellent technique, it is more likely to be maintained. Conversely, if a singer uses poor technique to start a phrase, it is very difficult to make an adjustment mid-phrase. More generally, singers who understand the vocal mechanism are likely to appreciate better the issues involved in the initiation, creation, and release of sound.

Among the many benefits of proper initiation, creation, and release of sound are:

- A more clear, "focused" tone
- A tone that is not pinched, strained, harsh, or breathy
- Optimal vocal fold vibration
- Efficient sound production
- Better breath control
- Better vocal health
- Precise phrase endings

## How sound is initiated and created

Vocal science texts and some vocal pedagogy texts examine laryngeal anatomy and physiology in detail. This chapter covers the essentials necessary to understand how the vocal folds create sound, how pitch is controlled, and how various approaches to onset affect the degree of closure of the vocal folds.

Our voices are basically wind instruments. All wind instruments produce sound by sending pressurized air through a vibrator, which creates sound waves that are acoustically enhanced in one or more resonators. For example, a clarinet's sound is the result of air pressure vibrating a reed. The vibrations of the reed are selectively amplified in the body of the clarinet.

In the same way we use the abdominal and intercostal muscles to create the necessary lung pressure to activate the singer's vibrator, known as the "vocal folds." The folds are also commonly called "vocal cords," but modern scientific study has shown that they are not simply ligaments, but rather a complex structure composed of multiple layers of tissue. As a result, "vocal folds" has become the more widely used term.

Sound is initiated when a singer closes the space between the left and right vocal folds (the space is known as the glottis) and sufficient air pressure is created beneath the folds to overcome the muscular pressure on them, causing the folds to open. This opening lasts only a split second, because the quick passage of air through this narrowed area of the vocal tract creates a zone of low pressure, drawing them shut. (The passage of air through the narrowed area that creates the lower pressure is technically known as a Bernoulli Effect.) Think of this lower pressure as a vacuum that sucks the folds closed.

Closing of the folds is also aided by elastic reversion of the tissues (van den Berg, 1958). An example of elastic reversion is a rubber band returning to its original form after being stretched.

The rapid closing and opening of the vocal folds is called vocal fold vibration. The number of openings and closings per second determines the fundamental frequency of the audible pitch that is heard. For example, singing $A_4$ causes the vocal folds to open and close 440 times per second.

Vocal fold vibration creates puffs of air. The alternating compression and rarefaction (increasing and decreasing density of the air above the glottis) creates what we know as sound waves. These sound waves are modified further in the structures of the vocal tract above the vocal folds. (Chapter 4 on resonance explores how this occurs and how singers can control sound modification.)

## Components of the singer's instrument

Figure 3.1 is a simplified illustration of the components of the singer's instrument. Breath energy produced by the action of the abdominals and intercostals on the lungs is converted to sound energy by the vocal folds. The sound energy is further modified (filtered/resonated) by the vocal tract. Although sound production seems to be a linear process, research has shown that a feedback of energy from the vocal tract to the vocal folds can occur. For example, singers can assist vocal fold closure through a careful alteration of the vocal tract that feeds energy back to the vocal folds. This alteration of the vocal tract improves vocal efficiency and is illustrated by the return arrow in Figure 3.1. Chapter 4 on resonance and Chapter 5 on vowels discuss this process in more detail.

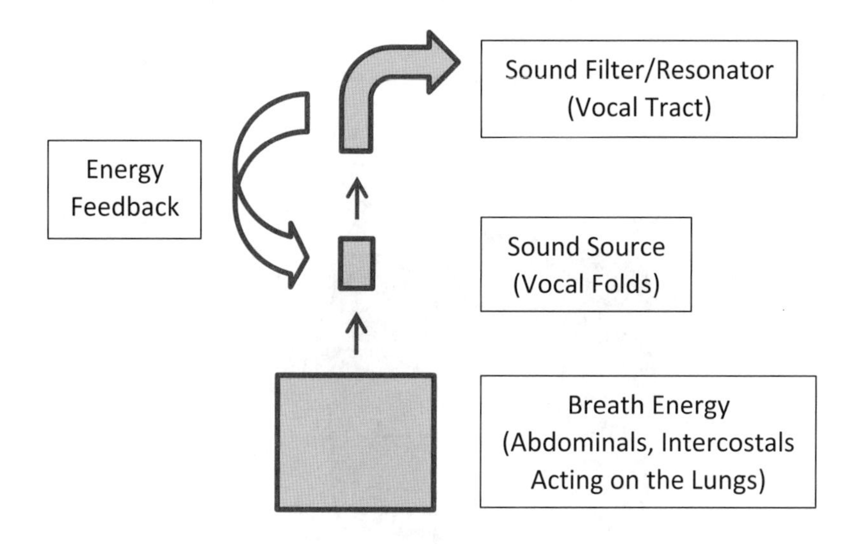


**Figure 3.1 Simplified illustration of the singer's instrument**

Figure 3.2 is a cross-sectional view of the larynx illustrating the flow of air past the vocal folds. Figure 3.3 is a side view of the larynx. Notice that the larynx is suspended from the hyoid bone by the thyrohyoid membrane, which connects it to the major cartilage of the larynx, the thyroid cartilage. The vocal folds and some of the important muscles controlling them are contained within this cartilage. The thyroid cartilage is connected to the cricoid cartilage (the cartilage at the top of the trachea) by the cricothyroid muscles, which play an important role in pitch control.

The hyoid bone is particularly important because it connects to the tongue. Tongue position and tension can thus affect the larynx, a point of significance for later chapters on tongue position and vowel formation (Chapter 5 on vowels) and tension (Chapter 14 on reducing tension).

Figure 3.4 illustrates an open glottis during normal inhalation/exhalation, a closed glottis, and the opening of the glottis during a vibratory cycle. The view is looking down from the area of the throat at the back of the mouth, with the front of the larynx at the top of the illustration. (The opening of the glottis during the vibratory cycle is so fast that it cannot be seen with the naked eye. This is a simplified illustration of what might be seen with stroboscopic video.)

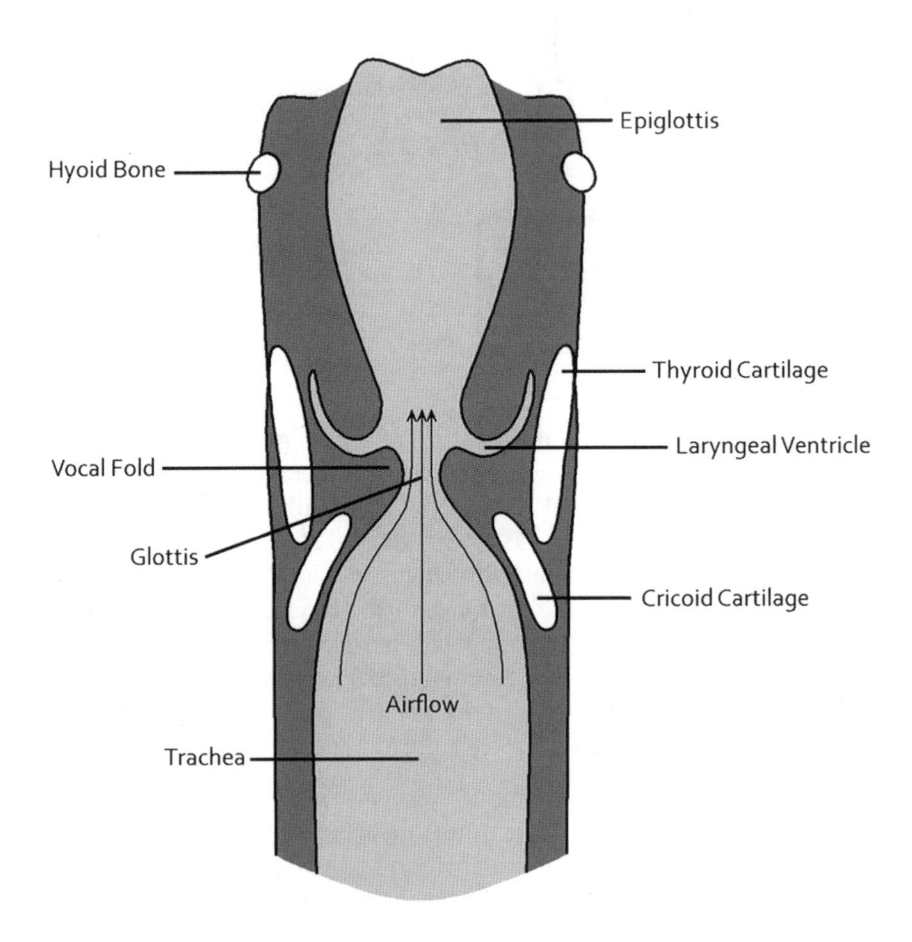


**Figure 3.2 Illustration of the larynx (cross-section, posterior view)**

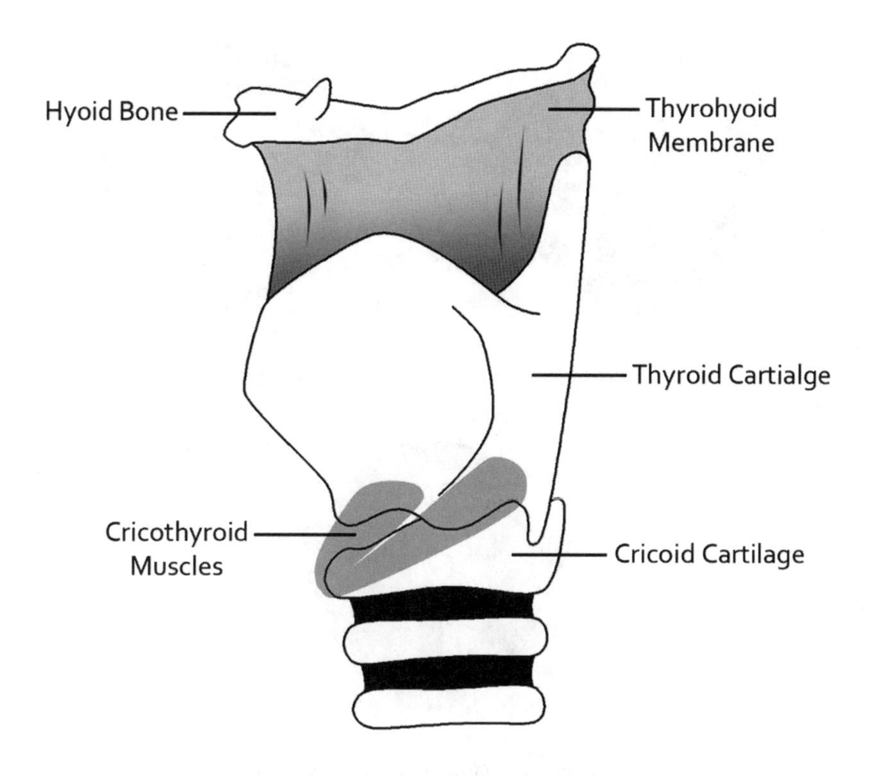


**Figure 3.3 Side view of the larynx**

The vocal folds are surprisingly small. An X-ray study found the vocal folds to average 14.9 mm for sopranos, 16.6 mm for contraltos, 18.4 mm for tenors and 20.9 mm for basses (a range of 9/16 in. to 13/16 in.; Roers, Mürbe, & Sundberg, 2009). This small mechanism can produce amazing sound, but it can be damaged with improper vocal technique and harmful health habits over time. (Factors affecting vocal health are addressed in Chapter 15.)

## Muscles affecting pitch

Some of the muscles that control the vocal folds have a direct effect upon pitch and tonal quality. Muscles affect the frequency at which the folds vibrate by:

- Altering the thickness of the folds. A thick fold vibrates more slowly (i.e., at a lower pitch) because of its greater mass per inch.
- Altering the tension of the folds. A slack fold vibrates more slowly than a tense fold.

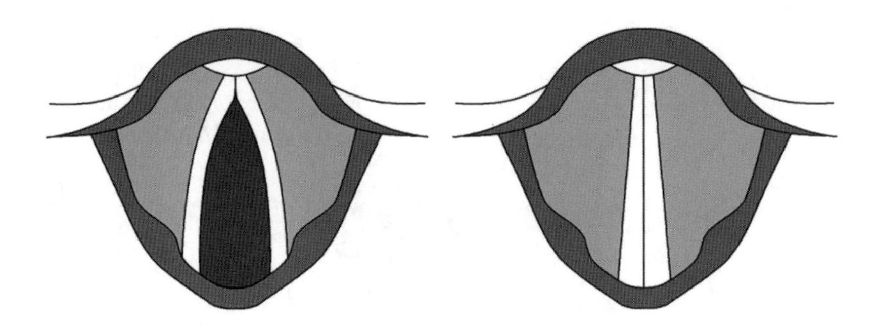

Glottis Open During Normal Inhalation/Exhalation; Glottis Closed

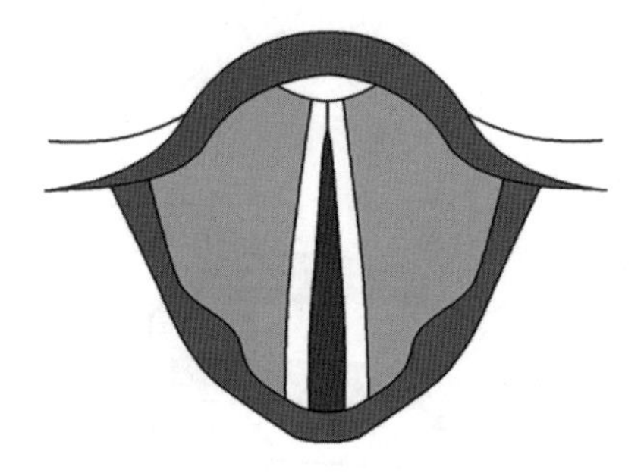

Glottis Open During a Vibratory Cycle

**Figure 3.4 Illustrations of the glottis**

### More on Vocal Fold Vibration

Titze (2000) has shown that the "myoelastic-aerodynamic theory" ("myoelastic" for the elastic reversion of the vocal folds and "aerodynamic" for the Bernoulli effect) is too simple to account fully for continuous vocal fold vibration. He and his colleagues have demonstrated that other factors likely contribute to sustained vibration, among them a wave-like motion in the vocal folds and a zone of low pressure that develops momentarily above the glottis, aiding their closure.

Two major sets of muscles affect pitch: the cricothyroid and thyroarytenoid muscles. Note, however, that singers do not have direct, conscious control over them to control pitch. Nonetheless, these muscles can be controlled indirectly (see the text box on biofeedback). Other muscles may also be involved in pitch control, but they are not well understood and are the subject of ongoing scientific research.

The role of the cricothyroid muscles is clear: contracting these muscles stretches and thins the vocal folds by pulling down on the thyroid cartilage (which is hinged at the back), tilting it forward (see Figure 3.5). This raises the pitch (fundamental frequency). Think of the violin, whose thinnest strings create the highest pitches because the strings with the lowest mass per inch vibrate more quickly.

The role of the thyroarytenoid muscle (also known as the vocalis muscle), the innermost layer of the vocal folds, is more complex and less well understood (see Figure 3.6, an illustration of a cross-section of the vocal fold area of the larynx). Contraction of this muscle in lower portions of a singer's range can lower the pitch by thickening the vocal folds. However, in other circumstances, such as with ascending pitch, contraction of this muscle can stiffen the vocal folds, causing them to vibrate more rapidly.

Although both muscle groups tend to be involved to some extent at all pitch levels in most singing, greater involvement of the cricothyroids is crucial for singing high pitches easily and efficiently. While conscious control of the relative involvement of the cricothyroids is impossible, indirect control is feasible through methods described in Chapter 4 on resonance and Chapter 9 on range extension.

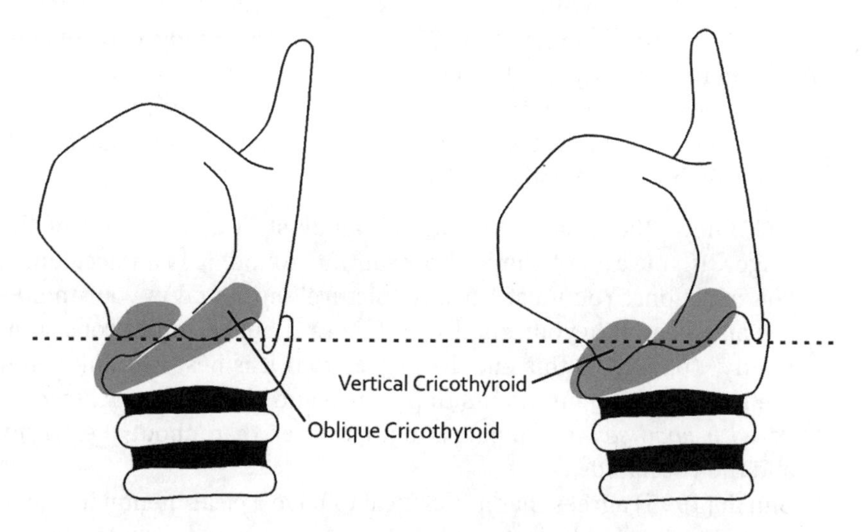


**Figure 3.5 Illustration of tilting of the thyroid cartilage by the cricothyroid muscles**

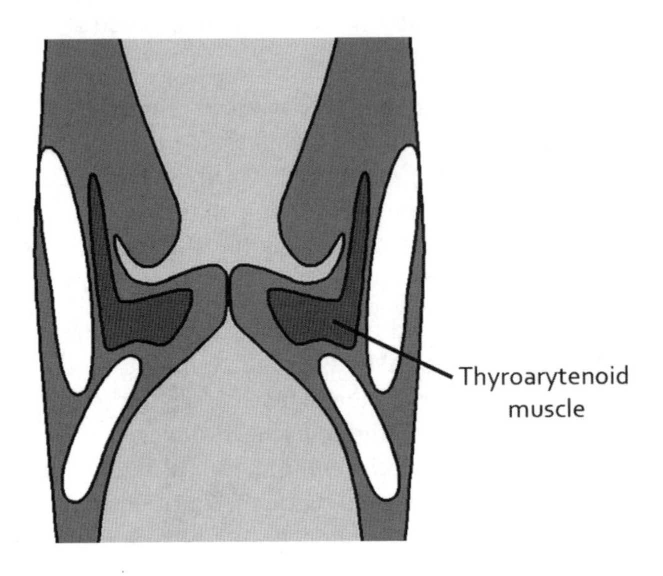


**Figure 3.6 Illustration of the thyroarytenoid muscles (cross-sectional view)**

## Controlling pitch and tone through mental images

How do we control pitch without conscious control over the muscles affecting the tensioning and thinning of the vocal folds? Surprisingly, control over pitch and even tone quality is achieved by thinking about the sound that we want to produce, and then making that sound. Psychologists call this a "mental representation," and view it as critical to the development of musical ability (Lehmann, Sloboda, & Woody, 2007).

- McKinney (2005) says, "Beautiful sounds start in the mind of the singer. If you cannot think of a beautiful sound, it is an accident if you make one. You must learn to 'picture' the sound in your mind's eye and 'hear' it in your mind's ear before it can become a consistent reality" (p. 78). To this end, he argues that it is best to think about the kind of sound one wants to produce and *the sensations associated with good sound* (emphasis ours) rather than about the larynx and the vocal folds.
- Bunch (1995) agrees that it is critical to have a clear mental image of the desired sound before singing. This image should include thought about the desired type of onset (whether normal, pressed, or breathy), the pitch, and the dynamic level. The vocal muscular sys-

tem should be pretuned in response to this mental concept just before singing. Without advance thought, the singer may enter under the pitch or "scoop up" to the correct pitch.

**Biofeedback helps singers gain control over laryngeal muscles and vocal tract configuration**

While conscious control over most laryngeal muscles is impossible, psychological research has shown that control over unconscious physiological processes can be gained through biofeedback. For example, one can gain some control over blood pressure through biofeedback, even though direct conscious control is not possible (Nakao, Yano, Nomura, & Kuboki, 2003). Physical sensations (kinesthetic feedback) associated with given pitches and beautiful tones are examples of biofeedback for singers.

Auditory feedback is important as well, particularly for pitch control. Nonetheless, auditory feedback has limitations—because bone conductance emphasizes lower frequencies, singers do not hear accurately the spectral qualities of their own sound (Ware, 1998). In addition some of the sound they hear is reflected sound. Because of this, singers need feedback from teachers and conductors about their sound and must learn to correlate that with how good singing feels. With training and experience, dependence on auditory feedback is reduced somewhat, but not eliminated (Mürbe, Pabst, Hofmann, and Sundberg, 2002). The ability to rely more heavily on kinesthetic feedback and muscle memory can be particularly important in choral settings where the presence of other singers, differences between performance venue acoustics and rehearsal space acoustics, and accompanying instruments can mask singers' ability to hear their own voices.

A further example involves development of the singer's formant, as outlined in the Chapter 4 on resonance. (The singer's formant is an amplified set of high frequency overtones in the range of 2500–4000 Hz. depending upon voice type.) With proper technique, as outlined in Chapter 4, singers will start to produce this formant occasionally and will recognize it by hearing a "ring" in the voice. Over time, a singer will subconsciously adjust vocal production and produce this formant more consistently by listening for the ring. Learning to produce the singer's formant can be accelerated with visual feedback such as that provided by inexpensive computer programs such as *VoceVista* (D. Miller, 2008), which display the amplitudes of the various harmonic frequencies produced by a singer.

## Good hydration is critical for proper vocal fold vibration

When our bodies are not properly hydrated, the mucus coating of the vocal folds becomes more viscous, making it more difficult for the folds to vibrate. A number of well-controlled, experimental studies have shown that higher breath pressure and greater phonatory effort are necessary to achieve vocal fold vibration when a singer is dehydrated (e.g., Verdolini-Marston, Titze, & Druker, 1990; Verdolini, Titze, & Fennell, 1994). Higher pitches are particularly difficult to sing in this situation. Chapter 15 on vocal health addresses hydration in more detail.

## Sound quality is affected by firmness of vocal fold closure

The only internal (intrinsic) muscles of the larynx over which we have conscious control are those that open and close the space between the vocal folds. The posterior cricoarytenoid opens the vocal folds. The lateral cricoarytenoids and the interarytenoids are two muscles involved in closure. The lateral cricoarytenoids bring the vocal folds together, but action of the interarytenoids is necessary to close the posterior (back) portion of the glottis (Ware, 1998). Closing the vocal folds with just the right amount of tension is an important key to quality sound.

- If the glottis is closed too firmly, the sound will have a strained, pressed quality.
- If the folds are held together too lightly or slightly apart, the sound will have a breathy quality as air escapes through the folds.
    - Similarly, Titze (2000) states that the vocal folds will not be in an optimal mode of vibration unless the folds are brought together appropriately.

Proper closure is also important for creating the right amount of subglottal pressure, which as noted earlier must increase with increasing pitch and loudness. Cottrell (2010) argues that glottal resistance is an integral aspect of breath support. Without sufficient resistance even a singer with the best appoggio technique cannot properly control subglottal pressure, with the result of a breathy sound or breaks in the voice. An exercise to experiment with glottal resistance is included at the end of this chapter.

### Glottal tension and the "closed quotient"

Recall from Chapter 2 on breathing that the firmness of vocal fold closure (glottal tension) is an important aspect of breath metering. A measure correlated with the firmness of vocal fold closure is the "closed quotient," or the percentage of time the vocal folds are closed during each vibratory cycle. If the folds stay closed for a high percentage of time, tonal quality is generally enhanced. Improved sound occurs because the vocal tract resonates best during the closed phase of the vibratory cycle (Rothenberg, 1981; D. Miller, 2008). During the open phase there is a damping of important higher frequency harmonics. When the glottis is open, some sound energy is sent down into the trachea and absorbed (Sundberg, 1995).

The closed quotient can be too high, however. This is created by excessive glottal tension and can result in a pressed sound.

Howard (1995) has demonstrated that training improves the closed quotient of singers. Teachers and conductors can train their singers through use of onset exercises outlined at the end of this chapter. These are particularly helpful for developing the right degree of glottal tension. Also helpful are exercises that assist glottal closure by placing a resistive load on the vocal folds. These include nasal consonants like [m] that seal the mouth and force air through the more constricted nasal passages. For more details see the next section of this chapter concerning onset and the text box on nasal consonants/singing through straws.

## Method of initiating sound affects glottal tension

How we initiate sound strongly influences whether the folds are held together with the right degree of tension during the subsequent phrase. There are three basic approaches to sound initiation, which we refer to as "onset." These include the following:

- **Coordinated Onset** involves closing the glottis simultaneously with the flow of air. This onset method is normally preferred.
- **Glottal Onset**, sometimes called a hard attack, involves inhaling, closing the glottis, and then beginning to sing. (People involuntarily close the glottis when they lift a heavy object.) Glottal tension is eased just enough to cause the vocal folds to vibrate and produce sound. Many untrained singers inadvertently use this onset method.
- **Breathy Onset** occurs when singers inhale and then start to exhale while leaving the glottis open. Shortly thereafter, they close the glottis just enough to bring the vocal folds into vibration.

### Using nasal consonants and singing through straws to assist vocal fold closure

Research (e.g., Titze, 2006) has shown that creating resistance to airflow assists the vocal folds in closing. The results are a clearer tone and easier, more efficient singing. Singing nasal consonants such as [n], [m] and [ŋ] ("ng") can be a helpful warm-up as they offer resistance to airflow.

Titze, Finnegan, Laukkanen, and Jaiswal (2002) have also shown that singing through straws is an excellent way to provide resistance to airflow and is helpful for improving vocal fold closure at high pitches. A standard-size straw works well, but singers should experiment with different diameters. *Sing through a straw, holding it with one hand to prevent tensing the lips to hold the straw. Use glides of a fifth, arpeggiated triads and scales.*

Research shows that the beneficial effects of such warm-ups, particularly singing through a straw, continue during singing of repertoire.

## Coordinated onset should be used for most singing

In most cases a coordinated onset should be used to initiate sound. As noted above, this involves controlling the timing of breath exhalation and the closure of the glottis so that they occur simultaneously. To assist in achieving a coordinated onset, the abdominal and intercostal muscles must be engaged just prior to singing so that there is sufficient breath support for the onset of sound.

Studies have shown that singers who use a coordinated onset actually start the flow of breath milliseconds before full closure of the folds, but we suggest concentrating on coordinating the closing of the glottis with the flow of air to prevent breath from escaping prior to closure.

When singers use coordinated onset and have learned to relax laryngeal tension, the result is what Sundberg (1987) has called "flow phonation." This creates a clear sound that is neither breathy nor pressed. Exercises at the end of the chapter address methods of achieving coordinated onset.

### Unconscious physical movement makes coordinated onset difficult

Unconscious movement is a common roadblock for singers working for consistent, coordinated onset. (We are not speaking here of necessary movement in rib and abdominal muscles, natural movement in musical theatre, or *conscious* use of arm/hand gestures to assist learning to use coordinated onset.) Many amateur singers move their heads or upper bodies when inhaling or beginning sound. These movements can cause singers to revert to their habitual mode of an undesirable onset (i.e., pressed or breathy).

### Summary of steps to achieve a coordinated onset

To encourage a coordinated onset, singers should observe the following sequence:

- Imagine both the pitch and vowel to be sung
- Create the space necessary for both the pitch and vowel (see the Chapter 4 on resonance and Chapter 5 on vowels)
- Open the glottis
- Inhale without extraneous movement
- Engage the breath support muscles
- Exhale and close the glottis at the same time

As mastery of this process occurs, the detailed steps should not require conscious attention. Singers can then simply think to themselves: "Imagine, Inhale, and Sing" (D. Edwards, personal communication, November 30, 2011).

## Glottal onset (hard attack) should be used selectively

Several problems are associated with a glottal onset. First, a glottal onset bursts open the vocal folds, creating an almost grunt-like noise before the sound of the desired note. Second, a glottal onset leads to a pressed sound ("pressed phonation"). Third, when singers use glottal onset, the amplitude (loudness) of the fundamental frequency is substantially less than with flow phonation (Sundberg, 1987). In fact, a singer who uses a coordinated onset and achieves release of laryngeal tension will have a fundamental frequency up to two and a half times louder than what is achievable with pressed phonation. Coordinated onset is also necessary to achieve a balanced timbre (though resonance of higher harmonic frequencies is also necessary as outlined in Chapter 4 on resonance).

Understanding these issues is particularly important for sopranos, who depend upon a strong fundamental frequency to create high sound levels at high pitches (see Chapter 4 on resonance). Sound intensity above roughly $D_5$ is determined solely by the intensity of the fundamental frequency, unless the singer also exhibits what is called the "singer's formant" (Titze, 1992). (Chapter 4 on resonance discusses the singer's formant.)

The benefit of flow phonation for increased sound level for other voice categories is less clear. Their sound level depends more upon the amplitude of higher harmonic frequencies and they may be able to produce a higher sound level through pressed phonation. Nonetheless, a pressed sound is typically not as pleasing, precisely because it tends to overemphasize higher frequency overtones and thus lacks a balanced timbre. (Of course in some cases a somewhat pressed sound achieves a desired tonal color, as in pop/musical theatre belting and in some gospel choirs. See the section on belting in this chapter.)

- Sundberg (1993) found that singers who have a pressed or strained sound (resulting from vocal folds that are held together too tightly) need a higher subglottal pressure to produce the same level of sound achieved with a lower subglottal pressure by using flow phonation. Thus, pressed phonation is also less efficient than flow phonation.

Singing with a glottal onset can be an unconscious habit most likely to occur on passages beginning with a vowel. It often occurs when singers do not think about coordinating breath with vocal fold closure. When asked to sing a passage, singers with this habit simply close the folds and engage the breathing muscles to sing.

Encouraging singers to be aware of their use of a glottal onset, and following the exercises we have outlined at the end of this chapter, will go a long way toward eliminating this problem.

### Potential for harm

Continued use of a hard glottal onset at high dynamic levels can potentially harm the vocal folds. A hard glottal onset creates tremendous friction between the vocal folds, similar to coughing or clearing the throat (Bunch, 1995). In some cases nodes or polyps on the vocal folds may develop. While some singers can use pressed phonation for many years without apparent problems, ultimately there is a price to be paid.

- Caruso also recognized that improper attack could damage the voice, noting that singers who do this may sing well initially, but soon find their voices failing, putting an early end to their careers (Caruso & Tetrazzini, 1975).

### Uses of a soft glottal attack

A soft glottal attack is helpful in English songs when emphasis is desired, but it should be used sparingly. For example, when singing "her eyes," it is helpful to use a soft glottal when singing "eyes" to make the two words distinct.

Occasional soft glottals are also useful in musical theatre and popular music, because they can add to the clarity of diction. In German, a soft glottal should be used for words beginning in a vowel within a phrase. If a phrase begins with a vowel, a coordinated onset is more appropriate.

## Breathy onset is generally undesirable

Breathy onset can result from a simple failure to coordinate airflow and closure of the vocal folds (i.e., exhaling air prior to closure of the folds), or it can be due to air flowing too fast and/or under so much pressure that the folds do not come together properly (Bunch, 1995).

Breathy onset is generally undesirable for a number of reasons. It can cause intonation problems, most frequently singing sharp, due to the excessive airflow. Another problem associated with a breathy onset is poor tonal quality due to the noise generated by the onset and a lack of complete vocal fold vibration, which leads to a dearth of higher harmonic frequencies. The excessive amount of air emitted also impedes the singing of long passages.

Although breathy onset should be generally avoided, the choral texture can occasionally benefit from a breathy onset. For example, it can be a useful device when a very soft or light entrance (what might be called a "feathered entrance") is needed.

## Onset and younger singers

Adolescent singers may have a breathy quality due to an inability to close the posterior one-third of the vocal folds (see Chapter 2 on breathing). The onset exercises at the end of this chapter will help resolve some of this breathiness, but not all breathiness can be eliminated in some adolescents until they have further matured.

Keep in mind that many younger singers model their vocal technique on popular music, jazz, or theatre singers who often start a phrase with either a breathy or glottal onset. The quality of sound produced by many popular recording artists is not a desirable model for developing solo and choral singers. Singers should be aware that considerable editing and technological wizardry is employed to create the finished sound we hear on the radio or recordings. Singers should always endeavor to find their own sound possibilities, and to be conscious of their onset as part of their singing journey. It is counterproductive for young singers and teachers of young singers to have preconceived notions about what their voices should sound like.

## Ending sound—inhaling is a simple approach to release

The most important principle for ending sound is that when breath stops, the sound will stop, accomplishing the task without affecting sound quality. The easiest way to stop the breath without closing the glottis is to inhale at the end of the phrase. With a fresh breath often needed immediately for the next phrase, this is a natural method of release.

Other methods of release will create undesirable effects:

- Closing the glottis is very common but it strangles the sound, produces noise, and alters pitch. Sometimes this is referred to as a glottal release, the release equivalent of the glottal onset.
- Closing the mouth is a frequently observed method of release on a vowel, but this creates a change in the vowel and thus an undesired diphthong. Perceived pitch alteration may also result, as the vowel sound is compromised by movement.
    - McKinney (2005) cautions against letting breath support sag toward the end of a long, sustained note. This too affects pitch and quality of the sound.
- When the final note of a phrase involves a vowel, some singers open the glottis while continuing to exhale, creating a breathy sound at the end of the vowel—the release equivalent of a breathy onset. This too is undesirable except when planned as a special effect.

Proper release also requires knowing *when* to release. This is crucial in a choral setting, where everyone must release at the same time. Singers must count time precisely and conductors must be clear about the proper point of release. It is surprising how few singers, particularly those in amateur choral groups, know when they are supposed to release. Conductors should communicate clearly to their ensembles where the release should occur. For example:

- Put final consonants on the rest that follows.
- When a phrase ends on a vowel, inhale on the rest that follows.

## Belting

Belting is often used in popular and musical theatre singing and in gospel choirs, show choirs, sacred harp singing, and some music of other cultures. It is not desirable in "classical" solo and choral singing. More generally in a choral setting, if some singers are belting and others are not, blend difficulties will arise. Singers who are belting will have a fundamental frequency that is lower in amplitude than the other singers, but a higher level of certain harmonic frequencies (Sundberg, Thalén, & Popeil, 2011).

Belting is a controversial subject in vocal pedagogy. We want to say at the outset that we are not opposed to belting if it is done in a healthy manner and is used in musical genres that call for this method of production. We are, however, opposed to "raw" or "untutored" belting that involves excessively strong compression of the vocal folds at the extremes of a singer's range. This is the type of belting that can create hoarseness short term and do more permanent damage long term, including causing vocal nodules (Bunch, 1995; Reid, 1983). Periodically we hear news stories about the latest rock singer who has diminished vocal capability and/or has undergone surgery because of this approach to singing.

"Raw belting" involves continued exclusive use of the thyroarytenoid muscles as pitch ascends—with very little/no use of the stretching/thinning muscles (cricothyroids). This is what is meant by carrying "chest voice" too high. It is characteristic of early Broadway belters such as Ethel Merman and many modern rock singers.

Wells (2006) describes a more refined, healthier approach to belting that is used by a number of contemporary Broadway belters. The following are some characteristics of a more refined approach to belting:

- Mixed use of thyroarytenoid and cricothyroid control—i.e., mixed voice but likely one with more emphasis on thyroarytenoid control (see types of mixed voice in Chapter 8 on registers). Unlike raw belting, modern belt sound is not properly produced by carrying exclusively chest voice into the upper portions of a singer's range. By using a mixed voice approach to belting, modern female belters can extend their range up to $G_5$ (Wells, 2006).
- An elevated larynx, but we would argue that it should not be excessively elevated.
- Stronger compression of the vocal folds against each other than with "classical" or "bel canto" singing, with a concomitantly higher closed quotient. It is important however to avoid excessive compression.

Note that both the elevated larynx and higher level of vocal fold compression contribute to the intense, brassy sound that is distinctive of the belt. The elevated larynx raises the frequency of the major vocal tract resonances, creating a perception of a brighter sound (see Chapter 4 on resonance), and the tight compression increases the amplitude (sound level) of higher harmonic frequencies. Tight compression of the folds also reduces the amplitude of the fundamental frequency, which contributes further to perceptions of brightness.

Also contributing to this brighter belt sound is a reduction in pharyngeal resonance (which is lower frequency, or "darker" resonance) and brightening of vowels. See Chapter 4 on resonance and Chapter 5 on vowels for more information about controlling pharyngeal resonance and the distinction between dark and bright vowels.

### Singers who only belt should also explore other methods of production

Singers who only belt should also explore other methods of production to broaden their tonal palette. Raw belters should also do this to protect their voices and learn use of mixed voice for belting. It is also worthwhile to explore classical methods of production to experience reduced phonatory effort relative to belting. Belting requires more effort because greater breath pressure is required for vocal fold vibration when the folds are pressed tightly against each other (see, for example, Sundberg, Thalén, & Popeil, 2011).

Singers who only belt can be encouraged to expand their methods of production by learning to access their upper register ("head voice"). They should use sirens and other exercises that work from the top of the range down (where it is very difficult to achieve phonation while belting). See Chapter 5 on vowels, Chapter 8 on registers and Chapter 9 on range for more exercises to assist acquisition of head voice and increase upper singable pitches. Singers who generally belt may be resistant to changing their production, feeling that their voices sound weak when they are not belting. Encourage them to explore other ways of strengthening their sound, including appropriate breath pressure, use of resonance, and correct approaches to vowel formation.

### A healthy approach to the belt sound

Singers of repertoire requiring a belt sound who use an "untutored" belt can benefit from learning to produce a belt sound in a way that is less hazardous to vocal health. In addition, there are times when the classically trained solo singer or choral ensemble will want to create the sound of belting for particular musical genres. For example, most show choirs are expected to have the ability to both belt and sing with good classical technique. Here are some things for conductors and teachers to consider when asking their singers to belt:

- Singers should understand what they are being asked to do. A brief explanation will be helpful in allowing singers to attempt switching between a classical mode of production and belting. Remind them that when belting, the folds are pressed together more firmly, breath pressure must be greater, and the larynx will rise. Safe belting does not involve use of chest voice for high pitches, but rather a mixture of chest and head voice.
- Belting should occur in small quantities and should not be requested in the extremes of the upper range. Conductors should carefully place repertoire that requires belting in rehearsals so that it can be balanced with repertoire that is less vocally taxing. A piece that requires belting could be followed with a straightforward piece, allowing singers time to think about and adjust their technique back to their classical mode of sound production.
- Not all belts are created equal! Singers can create a belt sound with less tension by modifying vowels to those that are brighter (hump of the tongue is more forward—see Chapter 5 on vowels), with substantial breath pressure to produce an intense sound. This approach may reduce the need for extreme pressure on the vocal folds and an excessively raised larynx that can jeopardize healthy vocal production. Further manipulation of vowel formation using less pharyngeal space can be particularly helpful in achieving a belt-like sound in the upper register and/or for those singers who cannot belt. (See Chapter 3 on resonance for a discussion of factors influencing pharyngeal space.)

## Exercises for development of coordinated onset and release

### Experiencing different methods of onset

Richard Miller (1996) suggests the following sequence of phrases to help singers experience the different methods of onset, and particularly, to help them learn a coordinated onset. (He suggests speaking them; we suggest singing them):

*Ha, Ha, Ha, Ha—linger on the "h." This gives singers the sense of a breathy onset.*

*Uh, Uh, Uh, Uh—close the glottis and then sing, lingering on the explosive initiation (almost like a grunt). This gives singers the sense of the glottal onset.*

In between these two extremes is the coordinated onset:

*[a], [a], [a], [a]—we find images such as pulling a tissue gently from the box, or*

*a scarf from out of a magician's hat to be helpful. Performing these physical actions as you sing each "ah" is particularly helpful. An extension of this might be to imagine that the tissue box is located just above the navel and performing the gesture as each "ah" is sung.*

### For kids and everyone! Onset/connection of breath with sound

*Fffff-ah—begin by inhaling slowly, then exhale on [f] over four beats moving seamlessly into [a] on as indicated. Also try ascending and descending scales after the initial [f]. Try changing the first consonant to [s], "th", "wh" and/or changing the vowel that follows. (Adapted from Cooksey, 1999)*

### Good onset, good phrase!

*To build upon the concept that a good onset affects how a phrase is sung, sing the same note on [e] three times with the goal of a coordinated onset. (Your first two attempts may be breathy or glottal, but by the third try you will hopefully achieve a coordinated onset.). Immediately following the third attempt, sing a simple five-note ascending and descending scale. Once your onset is consistently coordinated, sing the exercise without the "false starts." Notice how a supported, free sound can continue through a phrase. Use a variety of vowels, particularly [i], which is one of the most difficult vowels to sing with a coordinated onset.*

### Encouraging coordinated onset

The following sequence provides another method to encourage a coordinated onset. Choose a pitch in the middle of the singers' range. As an advanced exercise, choose a pitch in the upper portion of the range. Singers should:

- Imagine both the pitch and vowel to be sung
- Inhale without extraneous movement
- Engage the breath support muscles
- Exhale and close the glottis at the same time

### Sustained notes to experiment with glottal resistance

Cottrell (2010) recommends use of sustained tones with small changes in pitch during warm-ups to allow experimentation with both breath pressure and glottal resistance as a means of improving tonal quality. We would add that this technique also allows experimenting with how both factors affect dynamic level. The following exercise is adapted from Cottrell. *In measures three through six, experiment with breath pressure only, keeping glottal resistance constant; then experiment with glottal resistance only to see how this adjustment affects dynamic level.*

### Quiet head and body

*Inhale and exhale as suggested in Chapter 2 on breathing. Try to keep the body relaxed without any unnecessary tension.*

*Add a simple vocal exercise (e.g., triad or scale passage), being conscious of the head and body during the breath cycle, onset, and release.*

Teachers and conductors should monitor their singers to check periodically for any extraneous motion. Such motion is often unconscious and thus outside of the awareness of singers. Calling their attention to the problem can help them to self-monitor.

### Coordinated release

*Sing an ascending triad and then a descending triad on any vowel. On the top note of the ascending triad, stop the tone by closing the glottis to get a sense of a hard release. Then sing the ascending triad and stop the tone on the top note by breathing in. This is the coordinated release. The added bonus is that you have already inhaled to sing the descending triad. Be sure to initiate the top note of the descending triad with a coordinated onset. Repeat, moving up by half steps.*

# Chapter 4: Resonance

Superior resonance is an important attribute of the accomplished solo singer. Some assume that superior resonance is not as important for choral singers because a larger group can achieve sound intensity by sheer force of numbers. Nevertheless, not all choral groups are large, and moreover, this assumption overlooks the importance of sound *quality*. A choir whose individual singers have good resonance will invariably have a more pleasing sound. Furthermore, knowing the factors affecting resonance will enable conductors to alter tonal color as needed.

Improving and controlling resonance allows both solo and choral singers to:

- Deliver a rich tone
- Sing efficiently
- Sing in tune
- Achieve thrilling dynamic contrasts
- Negotiate the higher and lower pitches of a singer's range

## Superior resonance improves tonal quality and vocal efficiency

From an artistic perspective, superior resonance creates a richer tonal quality and allows singers to produce higher sound levels with less effort. Take, for example, a trumpet mouthpiece. By itself, the mouthpiece produces a low-intensity buzz, much like the vocal folds (Fleming, 2005). But the hollow body of the trumpet resonates at select frequencies to produce a rich tone at a much higher sound level. Similarly, the hollow physiological structures of the vocal tract (the larynx, the pharynx and the mouth) resonate to produce an improved tone and higher sound levels. These structures also act as an acoustic filter, dampening some frequencies.

Recent research indicates that the vocal tract does more than simply amplify and filter sound—when configured properly, the resonating structures of the vocal tract can actually feed energy back to the vocal folds, assisting vibration (e.g., Titze, 2008b). We should note, however, that when we speak in terms of amplification, we are saying that a singer who has good resonance is more efficient in converting breath energy to sound—the vocal tract does not amplify sound in the way that an electronic amplifier increases sound level.

How the vocal tract structures are shaped and the firmness of the vocal tract tissues affect the quality of resonance.

- As Fleming (2005) puts it, "What makes a voice what it is, is a combination of sound from the vocal folds and the blending, or balance, or processing through the resonance tract" (p. 18).

For generations, voice teachers and singers have recognized the role that superior resonance plays in the creation of excellent timbre and vocal projection. Singers who lack this may seem soft and sweet, but the voice will sound "feeble, small, [and] poor" (Marifioti, 1922, p. 110).

## Resonance involves selective amplification

When the vocal folds are brought together and breath is exhaled, the folds vibrate in a complex manner, producing:

- **The fundamental frequency ($F_0$).** This frequency is associated with the note being sung. For example, A below middle-C ($A_3$) involves vocal fold vibration at a frequency of 220 cycles per second, abbreviated as "220 Hz." (Hz is an abbreviation for Hertz—it honors the German physicist Heinrich Hertz.)
- **Harmonic frequencies.** These higher frequencies are multiples of the fundamental frequency. For example, when $C_3$ is sung (fundamental frequency of 131 Hz), overtones are generated at 262, 393, 524, 655, 786, 917, etc., vibrations per second. The energy associated with the overtones declines substantially as frequency increases. Without amplification of some of these overtone frequencies, a singer would mostly produce a fundamental frequency lacking the richness imparted by higher harmonics. Enhanced resonance provides the necessary amplification.

Figure 4.1 illustrates a few harmonics generated by $C_3$. Note that the fundamental frequency is also considered to be the first harmonic, thus the first overtone is actually considered to be the second harmonic. Our nervous system interprets the fundamental frequency and associated harmonics as a single pitch. The harmonics emphasized by one singer versus another are perceived as variations in timbre.

**Figure 4.1 First five harmonics generated from singing $C_3$**

Singers differ in the amplitudes (sound level) of the fundamental and harmonic frequencies produced by vocal fold vibration (Sundberg, 1987). They also differ in the physiological structure of their vocal tracts above the vocal folds. These structural differences affect the frequencies that are amplified and degree of amplification. While physiological differences cannot be changed, all singers can learn to adjust and enhance their voices by learning to alter their vocal tract configurations. Mastering control of the vocal tract will improve timbre and efficiency because singers with superior resonance require less breath pressure to achieve an equivalent level of perceived loudness.

## Structure of the vocal tract

To improve resonance, it helps to have a basic understanding of the major components of the vocal tract (see Figure 4.2 for an illustration):

- Larynx
- Oral Pharynx (throat)
- Mouth

The **larynx** contains the vocal folds and the muscles and cartilage that control them. It is suspended from the hyoid bone, which is also connected to the tongue. This connection explains why tongue position and tension can affect laryngeal function. (Suspension of the larynx from the hyoid bone can be seen in Figures 3.2 and 3.3 in the preceding chapter; the connection of the hyoid bone to the base of the tongue can be seen in Figure 4.2.)

The **oral pharynx** extends from the epiglottis (the flap of tissue that folds over the top of the larynx to prevent food from entering the lungs) to the back of the mouth. It is a particularly important resonator within the vocal tract.

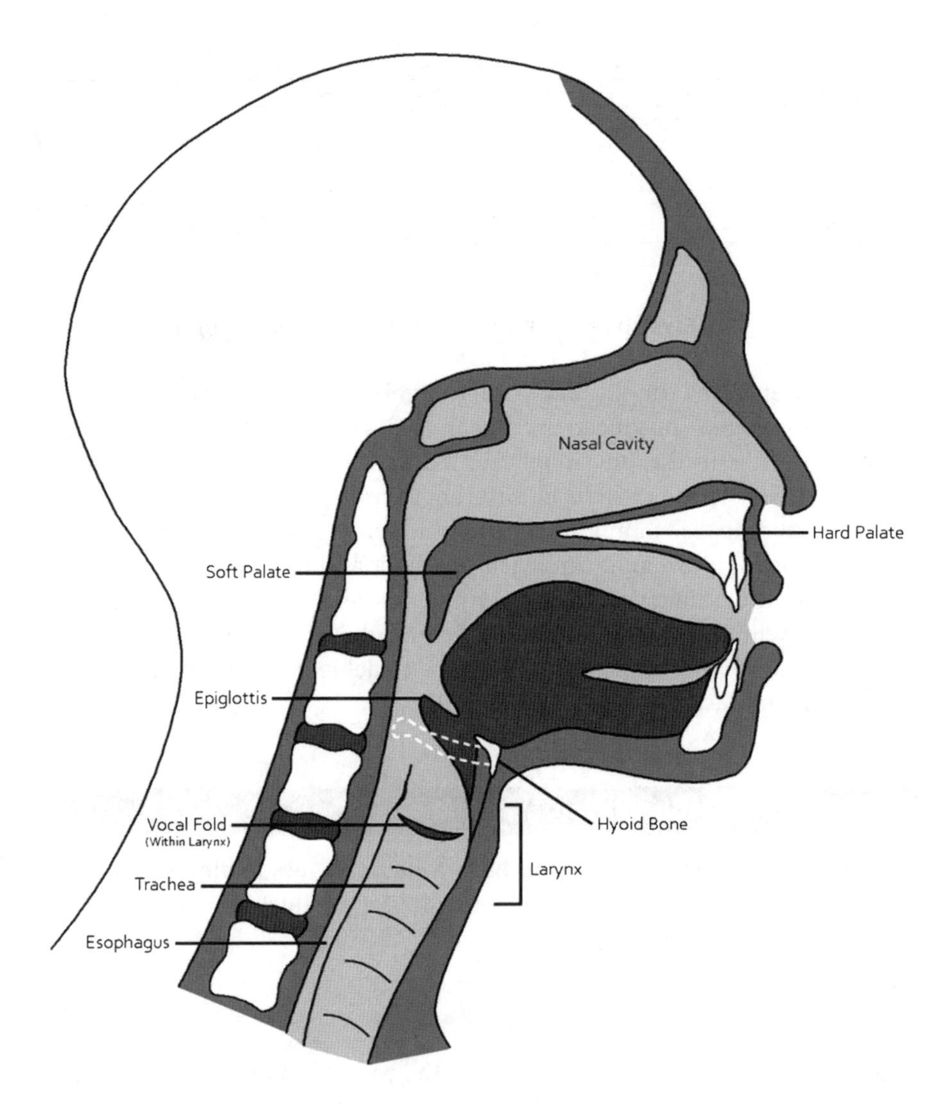


**Figure 4.2 Illustration of the vocal tract**

The **mouth** is also an important resonator. As shown in Figure 4.2, the tongue occupies the majority of the mouth. Changes in tongue position affect the size and shape of the cavity, which in turn alters the frequency of resonation. When singing vowels, the tip of the tongue should rest against the lower front teeth (the lower incisors). The bottom portion of the tongue tip should just touch the gum line, as illustrated.

The texture of the interior tissues of the cheeks also affects the resonating characteristics of the mouth. When these tissues are firmed (through use of the zygomatic and buccinator muscles as well as a jaw position), their ability to reflect sound waves increases resonance properties of the mouth (Fisher, 1966). The mechanics of this are discussed in greater detail below.

The **nasal pharynx** is important for the production of nasal vowels (e.g., French nasals) and nasal consonants (e.g., [m], [n]). For most singing it is not a resonator and should be largely closed off. Closure is accomplished by raising the soft palate, as outlined below. See the text box later in this chapter for further discussion of the role of nasal resonance.

## Resonance and formants

The vocal folds generate many harmonics, but only some are amplified. The vocal tract cavities resonate most strongly within certain ranges of frequencies known as *formants*. Formants are thus the resonances of the vocal tract.

Note that formants are "certain ranges of frequencies." Formants are not fixed frequencies; they can be adjusted by altering the shape and volume of the vocal tract cavities. The amplification ability of the associated cavities can also be changed with the right adjustments. Formant frequencies and amplified harmonics have a significant impact on tonal quality and perceived loudness.

The harmonic frequencies that are the most amplified are the ones that are near the formant frequencies. A harmonic does not have to coincide exactly with the formant in order to be amplified because the vocal tract walls are not hard surfaces resonating over a very narrow range. When a harmonic is in the vicinity of a formant, vocal tract resonance feeds energy back to the vocal folds, assisting their vibration as mentioned above.

Certain formant frequencies are a function of the vowel being sung. The somewhat broad resonance of the formants allows singers to be understood, yet still achieve amplification. See the accompanying text box for examples of how the formants of the vocal tract amplify certain harmonic frequencies.

Topics relating to formants are among the most difficult to understand in the fields of vocal science and vocal pedagogy. Nonetheless, gaining an understanding of formants is essential to understand how to:

- Alter vocal tract configurations to change tonal quality at will
- Alter the amplitude of various harmonics
- Modify vowels to improve production of pitches at the upper end of a singer's range
- Cope with register transitions

Authorities differ in formant enumeration and labeling (listing anywhere from three to five major formants). Our experience and review of the literature suggests that there are four to five significant formants. The first three are as follows:

- The lowest formant ($F_1$) is the resonance of the pharynx, as it is the largest cavity in the vocal tract. $F_1$ is particularly responsive to lowering of the jaw. As the jaw opening increases, the frequency of $F_1$ rises. It probably seems counterintuitive that creating a larger space in the pharynx *increases* a resonance frequency. The reason is that a greater jaw opening reduces the volume of the pharynx closest to the larynx and increases space closest to the mouth (Sundberg, 1977). The reduction in volume closest to the larynx leads the pharynx to resonate at a higher frequency as the jaw is lowered. $F_1$ is normally between 250 Hz and 800 Hz ($B_3$ to $G_5$), depending upon the vowel that is sung. For example, $F_1$ is highest when singing [ɑ] as the jaw is most open for this vowel. $F_1$ can rise above 800 Hz with further jaw opening. A soprano singing [ɑ] can have a first formant at 1400 Hz with a highly open jaw and a slight smile.
- The next highest formant ($F_2$) is the resonance of the mouth, the second largest cavity in the vocal tract. Its frequency and amplitude is affected by the shape, volume and firmness of the tissues of this cavity. $F_2$ is normally between 800 Hz and 2200 Hz. ($G_5$ to $D_7$–flat), with the frequency of resonance varying in accordance with tongue position and to some extent with lip shape. For example, $F_2$ is at its highest frequency when the highest point of the tongue (the arch or "hump of the tongue") is forward and the mouth opening is wide, as with [i]. In contrast, when singing [u], the highest point of the tongue is toward the rear of the mouth and the mouth opening is narrow, which lowers $F_2$, explaining why [u] sounds "darker" than the other vowels. Rounding the lips also contributes to $F_1$ formant lowering because it increases the length of the vocal tract. Chapter 5 on vowels addresses these topics in greater detail.
- The source of the third formant ($F_3$) is not as clear. Some vocal scientists say that it relates to the amount of space between the front of the tongue and the lower incisors (Sundberg, 1987; Zemlin, 1988). Others argue that it is one of the resonances of the larynx (see below under the discussion of the singer's formant). Since tongue position affects the larynx, the two perspectives are not incompatible. $F_3$ normally ranges from about 2200 Hz to 3000 Hz ($D_7$–flat to $F_7$#). $F_3$ is highest with [i] and lowest with [u]. [i] is thus the "brightest" of all vowels because the associated $F_2$ and $F_3$ formant frequencies are highest.

The formant frequency ranges listed above are approximate over the various voice categories. Women's formants tend to be 10–15% higher than men's, and there are individual differences as well.

As noted above, formant frequencies are also affected by total vocal tract volume. In addition to lip shape, larynx position affects the formants. If the larynx is comfortably low, the total size of the vocal tract increases, thereby lowering all formant frequencies and mellowing tone (Sundberg, 1987).

### The vowel being sung largely determines $F_1$ and $F_2$

The particular frequency of the first two formants is largely dependent on the vowel being sung. (See Chapter 5 on vowels for a more in-depth discussion.) The changes in jaw, tongue, and lip position associated with different vowels alter the shape and volume of the vocal tract, naturally affecting the frequencies at which it resonates. The amplitudes of these formants are affected by how well singers shape the resonating tubes/cavities. Appendix B contains illustrations of $F_1$ and $F_2$ frequencies for [i], [ɑ], and [u].

Although the third formant is highest with [i] and lowest with [u], it does not vary according to the vowel being sung as much as do the first two formants. For example, $F_2$ varies according to the vowel by over one and a half octaves. In comparison, $F_3$ varies by roughly a third of an octave. Thus, $F_3$ has limited significance in determining what vowel is heard by the listener, but it does make some contribution to vowel timbre.

Both [i] and [u] have a low $F_1$. The major difference between these two vowels is that $F_2$ is high for [i] and low for [u]. [ɑ] has the highest $F_1$ frequency and its $F_2$ is between [i] and [u]. For acoustic reasons, as the $F_1$ frequency increases, the sound intensity of a vowel becomes greater. This is why [ɑ] sounds louder than other vowels for a given level of vocal effort.

### Singer's Formant

When the vocal tract is configured appropriately, the frequency of $F_3$ rises and creates a cluster with the higher frequency formants, $F_4$ and $F_5$, known as the singer's formant. This clustering can create substantial sound intensity at higher harmonic frequencies (e.g., Sundberg, 1974). See Appendix B to view the clustering of these formants in tenor and soprano formant graphs.

The singer's formant is often called the "ring" of the voice. Most untrained singers do not have this formant (nor do they have strength in other important formants). However, this capacity can be developed through techniques outlined in subsequent sections on adjusting vocal tract structures, as well as the exercises described at the chapter's end.

### Examples of formant amplification of harmonic frequencies

Here are some examples of the role formants play in amplification of harmonic frequencies:

- For tenors singing in their lower register (chest voice), the second harmonic ($H_2$) is amplified by the first formant and the fourth harmonic ($H_4$) is amplified by the second formant (basses amplify higher harmonics with the formants). The first formant dominates and accounts for much of the sound level in this register (Neumann, Schunda, Hoth, & Euler, 2005). Titze and Worley (2009) appropriately note that formants should not be exactly tuned to harmonics but rather be close proximity to them. Exact tuning of formants to match harmonics creates excessive vowel distortion.
- As tenors approach their upper register, some choose to reinforce the second harmonic with the first formant by lowering the jaw and allowing the larynx to rise. If tenors adopting this strategy do not lower the jaw and allow the larynx to rise, their second harmonic frequency will pass beyond the first formant and create acoustic instability, which can be manifested by a cracking voice or a sudden change in pitch. Reinforcing the second harmonic by the first formant in the upper range is characteristic of belting.
- Other tenors cope with increasing pitch by allowing the second formant to play a more important role where it amplifies the third harmonic ($H_3$). They do this by raising the second formant frequency through arching the tongue toward the front of the mouth ("fronting the tongue"). Luciano Pavarotti was a master at this technique (D. Miller, 2008). This issue is revisited in the section on vowel modification in Chapter 5.
- Women singing in their lower register also tend to reinforce the second harmonic with the first formant. Because the transition from lower register to middle voice occurs at roughly the same pitch as parallel men's voices, women adopt either the belting resonance strategy or the second formant strategy outlined above for tenors. At $D_5$ and above, belting is difficult for both resonance reasons and vocal fold limitations (see Chapter 8 on registers). Above $D_5$, they depend upon the first formant to amplify the fundamental frequency. Sopranos have to lower the jaw substantially and exhibit a slight smile for this to occur. This is essentially a vowel-modification strategy that is discussed further in Chapter 5.

The singer's formant is thought to be generated in small cavities of the larynx just above the vocal folds, an area known as the epilarynx tube. The epilarynx tube extends from the vocal folds about two to three centimeters into the laryngeal vestibule and includes portions of the laryngeal ventricles (Titze & Worley, 2009; see Figure 4.3).

The frequency of the singer's formant varies little by the vowel or pitch being sung, but does vary by gender and voice type (it is highest in sopranos). This formant (or the most prominent formant of the $F_3$, $F_4$, $F_5$ cluster) falls in the range of 2500 to 3200 Hz for male voices, around 3200 Hz for contraltos and mezzos, and up to 4000 Hz for sopranos (R. Miller, 1996). Formant graphs for a tenor and soprano in Appendix B show very clearly that the most prominent formant in the singer's formant region is at a substantially higher frequency for the soprano than for the tenor.

If the singer's formant has high amplitude, the voice can carry above musical instruments, or even a large orchestra. The orchestra's sound energy declines rapidly with increasing harmonic frequencies. Specifically, the orchestra's amplitude in the 2500–4000 Hz range will be lower than that of a singer who can effectively produce the singer's formant. Vennard (1967) believes that even slight production of the singer's formant can be very helpful, because the outer ear chamber of the listener is resonant in this range. The amplitude of the singer's formant does not need to be extremely high to increase the perceived volume of the singer's voice.

- Hunter and Titze (2005) concur that human hearing is most sensitive in the area of 3000–4000 Hz. They note that singers using proper vocal technique to achieve the singer's formant can achieve sound levels 15 decibels (dB) higher than those not using such technique.
- An increase of just 6 dB is perceived to be twice as loud as a reference sound (Warren, 1970). Thus, with proper technique, singers can achieve dramatically increased volume levels.

### *Singer's formant and choral blend*

Some have argued that the singer's formant is not desirable in choral singing on the basis that it can be destructive to blend if only some singers have this formant. It is true that in a nonprofessional group there will be a mixture of singers who do and do not exhibit a singer's formant. A conductor who perceives a vocal color that is standing out excessively due to a high-amplitude singer's formant can ask the singer to be more sensitive to surrounding singers and reduce the volume. Alternatively, a conductor can work with other singers to enhance their singer's formant just as conductors should work with all singers in an amateur/developing ensemble to enhance the amplitude of their first and second formants. Certainly the singer's formant can be very helpful when a chorus is singing with an orchestra. In any case this should rarely be a problem because studies show that both male and female singers decrease the amplitude of the singer's formant somewhat when attempting to blend in a choral setting compared to a solo setting. This is particularly true when singing softly (Rossing, Sundberg, & Ternström, 1986a, 1986b). See Chapter 12 for more discussion of choral blend issues.

## Desirability of balanced resonance

### Balanced resonance creates a desirable tonal quality

For most singing, a balanced tonal color is desirable—neither too bright nor too dark. In other words, singers should achieve a reasonably balanced production of the important formants—$F_1$–$F_5$. On the one hand, if resonance is largely in the pharynx, with little mouth resonance and no singer's formant, the sound will be quite dark. On the other hand, if there is little resonance in the pharynx and strong mouth resonance emphasizing the high end of the $F_2$ formant frequency range, the sound will be quite bright. The key is to understand how to alter the vocal tract to manipulate formant frequencies and their amplitudes as outlined in subsequent sections of this chapter.

### Balanced resonance is important for intonation

The resonating chambers of the vocal tract affect not only tonal quality but also perceived pitch.

Marafioti (1922) credits Edward Scripture as the first to demonstrate through scientific experimentation that good resonance is important for good intonation.

- Winckel (1967) adds that a singer whose voice is rich in overtones (harmonics) will have greater intonation stability.
- Dayme (2009) states that a singer lacking in resonance of high harmonic frequencies will be perceived by listeners as being flat, even though the fundamental frequency is accurate. By the same token, a singer who lacks resonance of low harmonic frequencies will be perceived by listeners as being sharp.

### Balanced resonance contributes to higher perceived vocal loudness

Perceived vocal loudness is often thought to be equivalent to sound pressure level measured in decibels. Sundberg (1994) states, however, that higher perceived loudness is related to a balance in the amplitudes of lower and higher harmonic frequencies. Similarly, Skinner and Antinoro (1970) found that our auditory mechanisms perceive sounds with many overtones as louder than those at the same fundamental frequency lacking these overtones.

## Adjusting the larynx

The larynx influences resonance in two ways:

- The length of the vocal tract is affected by the vertical position of the larynx. When the larynx is in a comfortably low position, the vocal tract is longer and thus has more total volume. This lowers all formant frequencies, contributing to a mellow tone.
- Certain structures in the larynx can resonate to create the singer's formant.

### Controlling the vertical position of the larynx

The muscles that determine the vertical position of the larynx are important to understand. Many untrained singers raise the larynx unconsciously as they sing higher pitches, raising all formant frequencies and resulting in a pressed sound. (Only do this when purposefully belting.)

> ➢ McKinney (2005) reviewed various studies that examined the relationship between laryngeal position and sound quality. He found that among expert auditors the tone quality created by a comfortably low larynx is preferable to that obtained with a high larynx. A high larynx tends to produce a "tight, edgy sound" (p. 129).

Various muscles above and below the larynx affect its vertical position. Muscles above the larynx relate to swallowing, while those below the larynx are associated with inhalation and yawning. The dynamic balance between these muscle groups determines the position of the larynx (McKinney, 2005).

When the muscles above the larynx (swallowing muscles) are contracted, the larynx will tend to rise.

*Test this by gently placing a finger on the larynx (Adam's apple) and then swallow.*

When the muscles below the larynx (yawning muscles) are contracted, the larynx is pulled downward.

*Now initiate a yawn (but avoid a full yawn) and feel the larynx descend.*

### Resonance and the concepts of "chest voice" and "head voice"

The resonance which occurs in the vocal tract is known as *cavity resonance*. Two other resonance phenomena contribute to the vibrations felt in the chest and head, *sympathetic resonance* and *conductive resonance*.

An example of sympathetic resonance is the vibration of a piano string that is an octave higher than the one that is struck. Similarly, the sinuses, for example, can resonate sympathetically in response to sound that is resonating in the mouth and pharynx.

The violin operates, in part, according to the principle of conductive resonance—the vibrations of the string are transmitted to the body of the violin through the bridge and sound peg via direct contact. In like manner, vibrations of the vocal folds and the vibrating tissues surrounding the vocal tract transmit sound conductively through the bones, cartilage, and tissues to other areas of the body.

The chest vibrates at lower frequencies, hence when singing at low pitches with thyroarytenoid control ($D_4$ and below) we feel vibrations there, particularly if we are using flow phonation, which produces the highest fundamental frequency amplitude (Sundberg, 1987). In fact, feeling chest vibration at $D_4$ and below is a good test to see if a singer has achieved flow phonation. Recall that this is important to achieve a balanced timbre and to avoid both breathy and pressed phonation.

The cavities of the head, particularly the sinuses and nasal passages (the facial mask), vibrate at higher frequencies; hence when singing higher pitches with more cricothyroid control we feel vibrations there. (The head has smaller cavities than the chest.)

The terms "chest voice" and "head voice" refer to where vibrations are felt in the low and high range of a singer's voice, respectively. Most importantly, these resonances in the chest and head are not heard by the listener; rather they are experienced by the singer. The chest and head (other than the mouth, pharynx and nasal passages in the case of nasal consonants) are not important resonance cavities for singing. Thus, to speak of head resonance as a singer's goal is meaningless.

#### *The start of a yawn and good inhalation technique encourage a low larynx*

Vennard (1967) recommends singing in the position of an incipient yawn to cause the larynx to descend by reflex action.

- McKinney (2005) concurs that singers should try to maintain an *approach* to a yawn, while avoiding a full yawn.
- Vennard also suggests placing a finger gently on the larynx as an exercise. Feel it drop upon an approach to a yawn and monitor its position as singing begins so that it does not rise excessively. This is an excellent method to monitor laryngeal position.
- As noted in Chapter 2 on breathing, Sundberg (1993) has observed a phenomenon he calls "tracheal pull," which results from good inhalation technique. The diaphragm descends, pulling on the trachea, and in doing so causes the larynx to further descend.

### Creating resonance in small chambers of the larynx to produce the singer's formant

Small resonating chambers in the larynx may resonate at the high frequencies of the singer's formant. The ventricles (the pockets just above the vocal folds) are one possibility. However, the predominant view in the last 15 years holds that the entire area just above the folds (the *epilarynx tube*) resonates in the right circumstances. This area includes the ventricles and is illustrated in Figure 4.3.

A comfortably low larynx and an open pharynx are vital to achieving the singer's formant. Sundberg (1977) has calculated that the ratio of the area of the cross-section of the pharynx to the cross-section of the epilarynx tube must be at least six to one to achieve the singer's formant. A comfortably low larynx creates a narrow epilarynx tube. The next section discusses methods for enlarging the pharynx.

## Adjusting the oral pharynx

The oral pharynx extends from the epiglottis (which covers the larynx during swallowing) to the soft palate at the back of the mouth. Enlarging the pharynx improves its resonance characteristics (Vennard, 1967).

The pharynx can be enlarged by:

- Lowering the back of the jaw
- Raising the soft palate (See Figure 4.2. The soft palate is down in this illustration to show the opening to the nasal passages. Illustrations of the vocal tract shape for various vowels in Chapter 5 show the soft palate in the raised position during singing.)

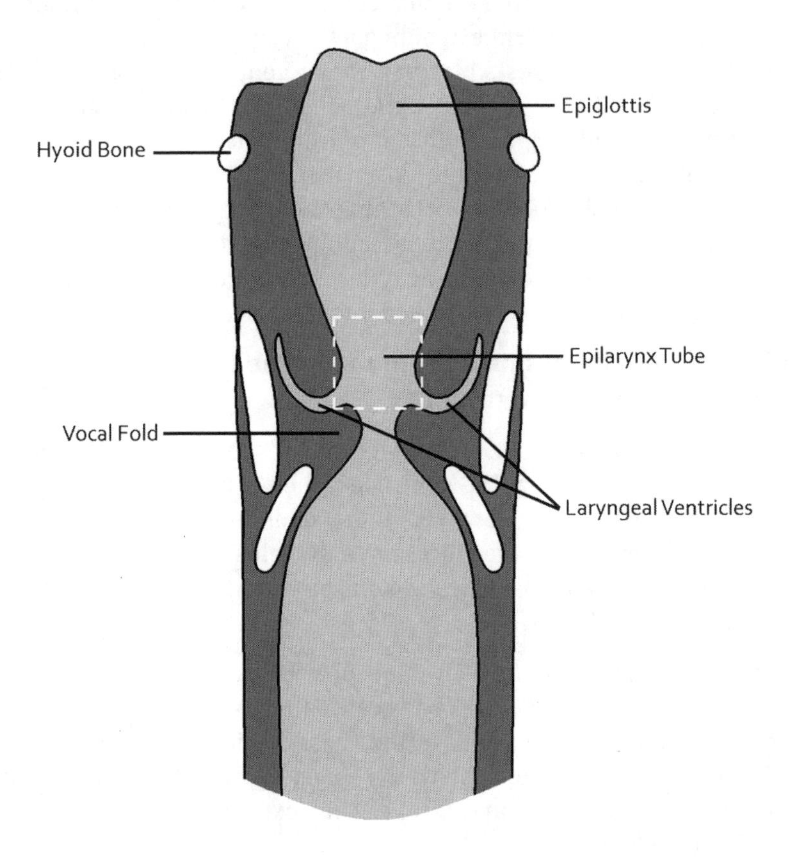


**Figure 4.3 Cross-sectional illustration of the larynx with a focus on the epilarynx tube and the ventricles**

## Raising the soft palate

Raising the soft palate is critical for improving the resonating qualities of the pharynx. For centuries great singers have recognized the importance of this vocal tract adjustment (e.g., Caruso & Tetrazzini, 1975), but it eludes many singers. Most amateur singers and even some trained singers have limited control over the relevant muscles. We want to call special attention to two of the exercises at the end of this chapter that can teach singers to accomplish this "lift."

- Bah, Gah, Kah, Pah, Tah—plosive consonants followed by a vowel to raise the soft palate
- Hang-ah to raise the soft palate

These exercises must be practiced for some time until control is gained, as this skill does not develop overnight.

*For now, imagine that you have been surprised and as a result quickly inhale a breath through both the mouth and nose. You should feel the soft palate lifting as you do this.*

Raising the soft palate helps to increase pharyngeal volume, but this lift is important for other reasons as well:

- Raising the soft palate increases the firmness of the pharynx walls. Firmer tissues improve the resonating properties of a tube or cavity and reduce the absorption of sound waves. As Fisher (1966) says: "If the walls of the cavity are irregular in contour and spongy in texture, short [higher frequency] waves become trapped or absorbed in the 'pockets' or irregularities and are not reflected" (p. 93).
  - Consistent with this, Vennard (1967) notes that hard walls of a resonator make a tone more brilliant.
- A raised soft palate is important for accurate intonation. Otherwise high pitches tend to sound flat.
- A raised soft palate closes the nasal port and blocks most of the breath from escaping into the nasal passages. This avoids an undesirable nasal tone. Also noteworthy is that it prevents a nasal antiresonance which diminishes the amplitude of the first formant (House & Stevens, 1956).
  - As Dayme (2009) says, "The relaxed soft palate . . . leads to an ugly, hypofunctional vocal production with too much nasal resonance" (p. 123).

## Lowering the back of the jaw

While lifting the soft palate is important, the jaw must also be lowered in the back to create sufficient space (Fleming, 2005). The combination of releasing the jaw at the back and raising the soft palate further stretches the walls of the pharynx.

In addition to its direct effect on pharynx expansion, releasing the jaw at the back pulls the tongue out of the pharynx, further increasing its volume (Vennard, 1967). This is particularly important for [ɑ], but it applies to other vowels as well.

When opening the jaw, be careful not to jut it forward to obtain space—the jaw should open down and slightly back. Some singers open the front of the mouth as opposed to releasing the jaw in back. This is to be avoided. Singers can use a mirror at home to ensure they are doing this properly, and conductors/teachers can watch singers during rehearsals and lessons to assist them in making necessary corrections.

Choral singers are often told to "drop the jaw" or "open the mouth," but they sometimes open the jaw and/or mouth excessively in response to such instruction. The exercises section includes a method to help determine if the jaw has been properly released. (Also see Figure 5.6 in Chapter 5 on vowels for two pictures of an excessively open mouth and jaw.)

Singers should experiment with the range of motion of the jaw, both up and down, forward and back, and side to side, including circular motions, to get a sense for what a comfortably open position feels like. This experimentation may also relieve jaw tension, a common affliction of singers. (See Chapter 14 on reducing tension for additional methods of relieving jaw tension.)

## An open pharynx and low larynx help create the singer's formant

The combination of an open pharynx and a low larynx supports the creation of the singer's formant. Vennard (1967) explains that certain muscles, referred to as the anterior pillars and the posterior pillars, need to be stretched. The anterior pillars form an arch over the back of the tongue when stretched, while the posterior pillars form an arch to the rear of the throat. Lowering the larynx and jaw aids the stretching. Particularly when the posterior pillars are stretched, the voice will exhibit the singer's formant—the ring of the voice that aids its carrying power.

- The stretched pillars are an indication that the pharynx has been opened and that the larynx is in a comfortably low position. As noted above, Sundberg (1977) found that the cross-sectional area of the pharynx must be at least six times larger than the cross-sectional laryngeal area above the glottis for the singer's formant to occur. Raising the soft palate and lowering the jaw are key aspects of creating an open pharynx. By keeping the larynx in a comfortably low position, the laryngeal area above the glottis is narrowed (Sundberg, 1987).
- Sundberg (1974) also found that lowering the larynx widens the ventricles, thereby strengthening the singer's formant.
- McKinney (2005) adds that the *beginning* of a yawn helps to create this condition.

## Adjusting the mouth

Recall that the mouth is a smaller cavity than the pharynx, causing it to resonate at the higher frequencies of the second formant. Good mouth resonance helps to create tonal brilliance.

Resonating qualities of the mouth are affected by:

- The zygomatic majorus muscles (which lift the cheeks) and the muscles controlling the upper lip. When the zygomatic muscles raise the cheeks, the soft palate is also raised, increasing space at the back of the mouth and in the oral pharynx.
- The jaw. A properly released jaw helps create mouth space in addition to pharyngeal space. Furthermore, it helps to stretch the cheeks, creating firmness in their interior tissues.
- Position of the tongue. This has a substantial effect upon the frequency of the second formant.

### Creating an "inner smile"

Many writers have spoken about singers needing an "inner smile." This can be thought of as the creation of horizontal and vertical space in the mouth. It is particularly important for resonance of the second formant. We want to be clear, however, that we are not advocating a "spread sound" created by an excessive exterior smile, which exaggerates higher frequency harmonics.

Renée Fleming's voice professor at the Crane School of Music, Patricia Misslin, would remind her to raise her cheeks slightly in order to attain this "inner" lift (Fleming, 2005).

> - Henderson (1979) has a wonderful explanation of the inner smile. To get the feeling of an inner smile, she suggests closing the mouth but not the teeth, keeping an open feeling in the oral cavity. Then smile as though you were smiling at someone across the room but you did not want other people to notice you doing so. This produces a slight lifting under the eyes and creates the sensation of a dome in the oral cavity as it helps to lift the soft palate.

Another way to feel the sensation of an inner smile is to express surprise with a slight gasp.

**Why nasal cavities and sinuses do not contribute to desirable resonance; avoid asking singers to "place the tone in the mask"**

For nasal vowels, such as certain French vowels, the nasal pharynx is an important resonator. Some singers, conductors, and voice teachers think nasal and sinus resonance is important for other vowels as well. Thus, they speak of "placing the tone in the mask." But nasal and sinus cavity resonance is unimportant in most singing in English and other Western European languages (Vennard, 1967; R. Miller, 1996). Moreover, a nasal tone is objectionable for nonnasal vowels.

Although the nasal passages and sinuses resonate due to sympathetic and conductive resonance, this adds nothing to the sound heard by the audience for nonnasal vowels. In an experiment by Wooldridge (1954), singers whose nasal passages were blocked with cotton sounded the same as they did normally (on nonnasal vowels). Vennard (1967) replicated these findings. In his replication, he also half-filled the maxillary sinuses with water, and again observed no difference in sound.

To avoid producing a disagreeable sound, little breath should pass into the nasal cavities for nonnasal vowels. With nasality, the first formant is diminished in amplitude (House & Stevens, 1956), in part because of anti-resonance in this frequency range in the nasal tract and in part because vertical space in the pharynx is diminished. Simply put, too much air directed into the nasal cavities destroys resonance.

Considering all of this, it is best to avoid asking singers to "place the tone in the mask." The risk of doing this is an objectionable nasality.

### *A modest exterior smile is helpful*

Renée Fleming's mother (a singer herself) gave her a sound piece of advice — smile and look like you are enjoying yourself (Fleming, 2005). Forming an inner smile encourages a small exterior smile, which brightens the tone. Exposing a *few* front teeth reduces absorption of higher frequencies by the upper lip. Conductors and teachers who smile slightly will incite their singers to smile and brighten their tone subconsciously. Besides, audiences appreciate singers with a slight smile (unless it conflicts with the mood of the music).

- Vennard (1967) has a suggestion for finding the appropriate degree of exterior smile. He suggests smiling such that the edges of the four upper teeth are visible when singing the vowel [ɑ].
- McKinney's (2005) advice is to have a pleasant expression, as if one were beginning to smile, or even a slight smile.

### *Avoid an excessive exterior smile*

Artists and vocal technicians alike warn against an excessive exterior smile:

- An excessive smile can produce a harsh sound due to too many high harmonic frequencies (Bunch, 1995). With an excessive smile, the teeth are more exposed. This hard surface at the outlet of the mouth emphasizes high harmonic frequencies excessively, which can create too bright a sound, devoid of mellowness (Vennard, 1967).
- Tetrazzini concurs that a slight smile is desirable, but that too wide a smile produces "the white voice" (Caruso & Tetrazzini, 1975, p. 29–30).
- McKinney (2005) argues that pulling the lips off the teeth into a forced smile tightens the pharynx near the soft palate, emphasizing high harmonic frequencies and thus creating too bright a sound. He notes that this is common among pop singers who want to enhance diction, but it comes at the price of tonal quality. Other methods of creating a bright sound, such as those outlined in the healthy belting section of Chapter 3 and in the text box on vowels in musical theatre in Chapter 5, are preferable.

## Effect of the tongue on mouth resonance

The position of the tongue alters the space in the mouth, and thus, the frequencies at which this cavity resonates. In fact, the tongue plays a major role in differentiating vowel sounds because it affects the frequency of the second and, to a lesser extent, the third formant.

For example, the vowel [i] is a "bright vowel" because the second and third formants associated with it are at the highest frequencies of all vowels. The hump of the tongue is high and toward the front of the mouth, creating a small space that resonates at higher frequencies.

*Lower the hump of the tongue to create the [a] vowel (keeping the mouth opening unchanged, for purposes of this illustration) and the volume of space within the oral cavity is increased. Note how the tone is somewhat "darker," because the larger space resonates at a lower frequency.*

Some tongue resting positions create poor quality resonance. Generally, singers should form vowels with the tongue tip resting against the bottom of the lower front teeth. See Chapter 5 on vowels for more detailed instructions.

### Images to help create space in the mouth

The following images can help singers to create mouth space. As a bonus, the first one also helps to increase pharyngeal space:

*Place the mouth, jaw, and throat in a position as if you were attempting to swallow a medium-size boiled egg. This exercise unhinges the lower jaw, raises the soft palate, and creates an inner smile simultaneously.*

*Imagine opening the mouth as though biting into an extra thick sandwich or taking a bite of an apple. These images help to shape the mouth.*

## Resonance and "placement"

Some vocal authorities, voice teachers, and singers talk about "placing" the tone. The desirability of "forward placement" is often stated.

- For example, in a book on choral singing Kemp (2009) says, "All singing should have resonance on the hard palate, forward placement" (p. 72).

Although images can be helpful for singers, some images are confusing and misleading—and "forward placement" is one of them. "Forward placement" is misleading because resonance occurs in the mouth as a whole, not on the hard palate by itself. Singers may respond too literally to advice about placing tone. Aiming breath at the hard palate or even in front of the mouth can lead to tonal distortions, including unwanted nasality (Marchesi, 1932).

This confusion about resonance and placement has historical roots dating to the 16th century (Stark, 2003). Manuel Garcia, the great 19th century singing teacher, initially adopted placement as a pedagogical tool as well. However, most singers are unaware that Garcia later reconsidered and concluded that the concept of placement is a bad idea. Cornelius Reid, one of the premier singing teachers of the middle to late 20th century, reports that Garcia published a retraction of his views in the *London Music Herald* in 1894. In his retraction Garcia said the following:

> *I used to direct the tone into the head . . . I condemn that which is spoken of nowadays, viz., the directing of the voice forward, or back and up. Vibrations come from puffs of air. All control of the breath is lost the*

*moment it is turned into vibrations, and the idea is absurd that a current of air can be thrown against the hard palate for one kind of tone, the soft palate for another, and reflected hither and thither (cited in Reid, 1950, p. 169).*

Nonetheless, the placement concept endures. Realizing this, Vurma and Ross (2002, 2003) have endeavored to find the acoustical correlates of "forward placement." While there are a few differences between their two studies, both find a higher second formant frequency and a strong singer's formant with "forward placement." This suggests singers should use a more forward/higher hump in the tongue together with a comfortably low larynx, a lifted soft palate and a released jaw to create an open pharynx. Thus, very clear advice can be given about producing desired tonal quality without resorting to potentially misleading ideas about sound placement.

## Exercises for enhancing resonance

### The "surprise" breath to feel a lifted soft palate

*Imagine that you have been surprised and as a result quickly inhale a breath through both the mouth and nose. You should feel the soft palate lifting as you do this.*

### Bah, gah, kah, pah, tah—plosive consonants followed by a vowel to raise the soft palate

When a plosive consonant such as [p] is followed by a vowel, air pressure increases in the vocal tract, forcing the soft palate higher than normal and sealing off the nasal passages. Singing "pah," for example, makes it easier to understand what a singer should feel when the soft palate is elevated (Fisher, 1966). It may help to look into a mirror at home and shine a flashlight at the back of the throat, to watch the soft palate rise during this exercise. This provides visual feedback to confirm the feeling of the raised palate.

### "Hang-ah" to raise the soft palate

An exercise that combines [ŋ] (the ng in "ring") with [ɑ] (as in "father") will also help in learning to raise the soft palate. *For example, sing "hang-[ɑ]" to create a nasal sound that resolves to a nonnasal tone as [ɑ] is sung.* To sing this, the soft palate must be lowered to produce the [ŋ], and it can be felt lying against the tongue in the back of the mouth. By concentrating on the feel of the muscle pulling the soft palate up, it is possible to gain control over this important shaper of resonance (Fisher, 1966).

Note that both this exercise and the exercise with plosive consonants help more generally by focusing singers' attention on improvement of pharyngeal space (K. Brunssen, personal communication, November 28, 2011).

### Reducing nasality

Once singers have gained control over the soft palate, they can use the following to help with reduction of nasality in their tone: *gently hold the nose just below the bridge between the thumb and forefinger. Sing [i] and reduce vibration as much as possible (N. Jordan, personal communication, April 7, 2010).*

### Tetrazzini's exercise for lowering the jaw

Tetrazzini (Caruso & Tetrazzini, 1975) recognized the need to lower the jaw in the back and suggested the following method for assuring proper release:

*Place fingers below the temples in front of the ears, feeling the separation in the jaw bones as the jaw is opened. This separation confirms that you have unhinged the jaw correctly. The mouth should not be opened excessively while doing this.*

### "Aiming" sound to create pharyngeal space

Sometimes it is helpful to think about "aiming" sound to find pharyngeal resonance. However, it is important to note that this is merely a physical/image device for singers to discover resonance space in the pharynx. While singers sometimes talk about "placement," sounds cannot in fact be aimed, placed, or projected, as noted earlier in this chapter.

*Try putting one open, cupped hand just above the nape of the neck. "Aim" higher pitches toward the hand to create and access the most resonant space.*

### Using a pencil to help create an inner smile

To encourage an inner smile, sing vowels with a pencil between the front teeth.

*Place the pencil just behind the lower canine teeth and let the top teeth contact the pencil naturally. Keep the tongue in contact with the base of the lower incisors. Vocalize in the middle of the range on all primary vowels.*

Notice the sensation of vertical space in the mouth created by the jaw lowering and the soft palate rising when the front of the mouth is closed on the pencil. Singers who have difficulty creating jaw and mouth space properly will almost immediately hear a difference in their tone.

### "Fah" and "vah" to help develop an inner smile

Henderson (1979) suggests singing vowels preceded by [f] and [v] to help develop an inner smile *(e.g., sing "fah" and "vah")*. Singers will find that it does indeed help to create space in the mouth.

### "Surprise gasp" to create an inner smile

*Another way to feel the sensation of an inner smile is to express a happy surprise with a slight gasp.*

### Image exercises to improve mouth resonance

*Place the mouth, jaw, and throat in a position as if you were attempting to swallow a medium-size boiled egg. This exercise unhinges the lower jaw, raises the soft palate, and creates an inner smile simultaneously.*

*Imagine opening the mouth as though biting into an extra thick sandwich or taking a bite of an apple, without excessive exposure of the teeth. These images help to shape the mouth.*

### Alternating between [i] and [u]

*Alternate [i] and [u] on one pitch, stretching the lips outward in a "Cheshire cat" smile for [i] and pulling them into pucker for [u].* The key is to create consistent resonance at the two extremes. (Note that ordinarily these extreme positions should not be used in actual singing.) This will encourage flexible, relaxed facial muscles and help balance resonance between bright and dark vowels.

### For kids and everyone! Tuggedy tah

*On one pitch sing "tuggedy, tuggedy, tuggedy, tuggedy, tah," sustaining the final "tah." Keep an open jaw and use the tip of the tongue to quickly pronounce the t's. Maintain a resonant sound throughout. (Adapted from Cooksey, 1999)*

# Chapter 5: Vowels

Good vowel production is the essence of creating beautiful sound. Every vowel is created in a unique way and imparts a slightly different timbre to the voice. Proper production of each vowel is important for:

- Better resonance
- Intelligibility
- Consistency in tone quality
- Intonation
- Blend

Each vowel requires a slightly different configuration of the tongue, jaw, and lips to create the right resonance space. Many singers (particularly choral singers) do not understand how each vowel should be created. Often, they fail to differentiate the vowels sufficiently, resulting in a lack of tonal color variation and reduced intelligibility. Vowels are just as important for intelligibility as are consonants.

## Tip of the tongue should rest at the base of the lower front teeth

Many singers do not know where to place the tip of the tongue when forming vowels, leading to inconsistencies in vowel formation. Regardless of the vowel, *the tip of the tongue should rest against the lower incisors, just above the gum line*. We should note, however, that the portion of the tongue in contact with the teeth will vary slightly depending upon the vowel. For example, when singing [i], more of the tongue will contact the teeth. In the choral setting, a common understanding of the tongue resting position is critical for uniform production of vowels and, thus, for blending.

### Resting the tongue-tip on the gum creates a dull sound

The tongue should not rest on the gum (though the bottom of the tongue will be in contact with the gum line). At rest on the gum, the tongue will be too far in the back of the mouth, reducing the volume of the pharynx, affecting pharyngeal resonance. Furthermore, resting on the gum will cause tension in the tongue which can affect the larynx, as the tongue and the larynx share a common connection with the hyoid bone.

- Vennard (1967) concurs that the tip of the tongue should touch the lower front teeth and, further, that the tongue should not *press* against the teeth. This too will result in tongue tension and poor tonal quality. To avoid this error, remember that touching the lower front teeth is a *resting* position.

Many singers are also unaware of the importance of *immediately* returning the tip of the tongue to its resting place after completing the formation of a consonant. Singers must devote a substantial amount of attention to this over time before it becomes second nature. Until this practice becomes automatic (without conscious attention during vocal exercises and during practice) many singers let the tip of the tongue move to a position related to the preceding consonant, leading to intermediate vowel sounds. This has negative consequences for vowel differentiation, tuning, and, in the choral setting, blend.

The importance of leaving the tip of the tongue resting against the base of the lower incisors is easy to demonstrate:

*Place the tip of the tongue at the base of the incisors. Sing [a] and experiment with tongue position. Move the tip of the tongue forward over the lower teeth and then backward and down to the gum line below the lower teeth. The vowel sound will change.*

*Flick the tip of the tongue up and down to hear yet a different change in the sound of the vowel.* This illustrates what happens to the many singers who leave the tip of the tongue part way up after singing a consonant, with disastrous effects upon intelligibility and tonal quality of the subsequent vowel.

## Accurate vowel production

Articulating vowels in a consistent manner is important for communication, and in the choral setting it is even more important than in solo singing. In the choral setting the use of disparate vowels leads to blend and even intonation problems.

Accurate vowel production depends on proper:

- Degree of tongue elevation
- Point of tongue elevation
- Amount of jaw opening
- Lip shape

Figure 5.1 illustrates how vowels vary with respect to all of these factors. The chart includes the major English vowels, as well as Italian, Spanish, and

Latin vowels. French and German use many of these vowels, but there are also some special vowels in these languages (see Appendix A). Figure 5.1 also uses the International Phonetic Alphabet symbols to represent the vowels.

The sounds associated with some of the most important IPA vowel symbols are presented in Table 5.1. Cardinal vowels (the five basic Italian vowels) are shown in a bold, blue font.

| Vowel | Example |
|---|---|
| **i** | Need |
| I | Hid |
| **e** | Ate |
| ɛ | Met |
| ae | Cat |
| ʌ | The emphasized form of the neutral vowel ("uh"), but one that is challenging to sing in a pleasing manner. As in "love." |
| ə | The deemphasized form of the neutral vowel, known as the "schwa." As in the last syllable of "Christmas." |
| **ɑ** | Father |
| ɔ | Ought |
| **o** | Go |
| U | Book |
| **u** | Choose |

**Table 5.1 Vowel sounds associated with IPA symbols**

We do not believe that most amateur singers need to know the complete International Phonetic Alphabet. It is useful, however, for all singers to know the symbols for the major vowels. Indeed, it is often helpful to write the IPA vowel symbol to be sung above the staff or above the lyrics. Conductors, teachers, and professional singers should have a more detailed knowledge of the IPA symbols contained in Appendix A.

Figure 5.2 illustrates how the position of the highest point of the tongue (the hump of the tongue) is most forward for [i] and moves back in the mouth with elevation declining as vowels approach [ɑ]. The height of the hump increases again as one sings vowels from [ɑ] to [u], but the hump of the tongue for these vowels is more toward the back of the mouth. In addition, the shape of the mouth opening is associated with where the tongue is elevated. There is more of a lateral opening when the tongue is elevated in the front (as in [i]) and a more rounded opening when the tongue is elevated in the back (as in [u]). This explains why the vowels from [i] to [ae] on the vowel chart are often referred to as "front vowels" or "lateral vowels," and vowels from [ɔ] to [u] are referred to as "back vowels" or "rounded vowels."

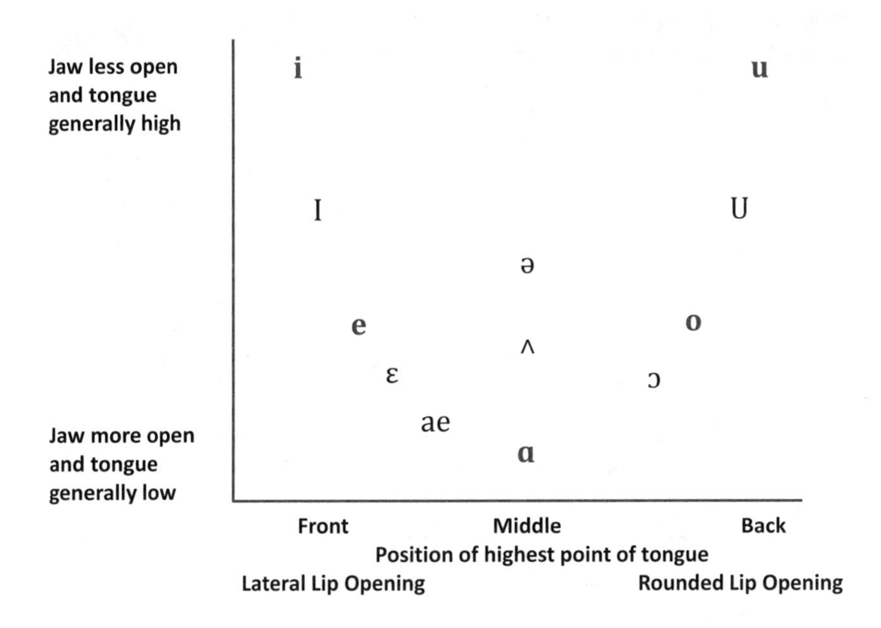


**Figure 5.1 Vowel Spectrum: Tongue position and mouth opening for important vowels**

## The Vowel Spectrum

We refer to the progression along the U-shaped curve from [i] to [u] as movement along the "Vowel Spectrum." Vowels next to each other on the Vowel Spectrum are produced similarly. It is easier for singers to develop a sense of how a vowel should feel if they can relate it to a close-by vowel because they do not have to deal all at once with the multiplicity of variables that differentiate the vowels.

*Try the following exploration of the Vowel Spectrum, using Figure 5.2 as a guide to tongue and jaw position: Place the tip of the tongue at the base of the lower teeth. Start by singing [i] in the middle of the range with a slight smile. The hump of the tongue should be elevated forward in the mouth. Then, open the jaw a pinky finger's width between the molars and sing [e], with the hump of the tongue moving back somewhat and decreasing slightly in height. Allow the hump of the tongue to move back further and reduce in height to sing [a], allowing the jaw to open a little more. Next, increase the height of the hump and round the lips to form [o] while closing the jaw slightly. Finally, increase the height of the hump of the tongue a bit more (with the hump still toward the back of the mouth), round the lips a touch more, and close the jaw to the starting [i] position to sing [u]. While an oversimplification, this device encourages singers to come to a unified understanding of vowel formation.*

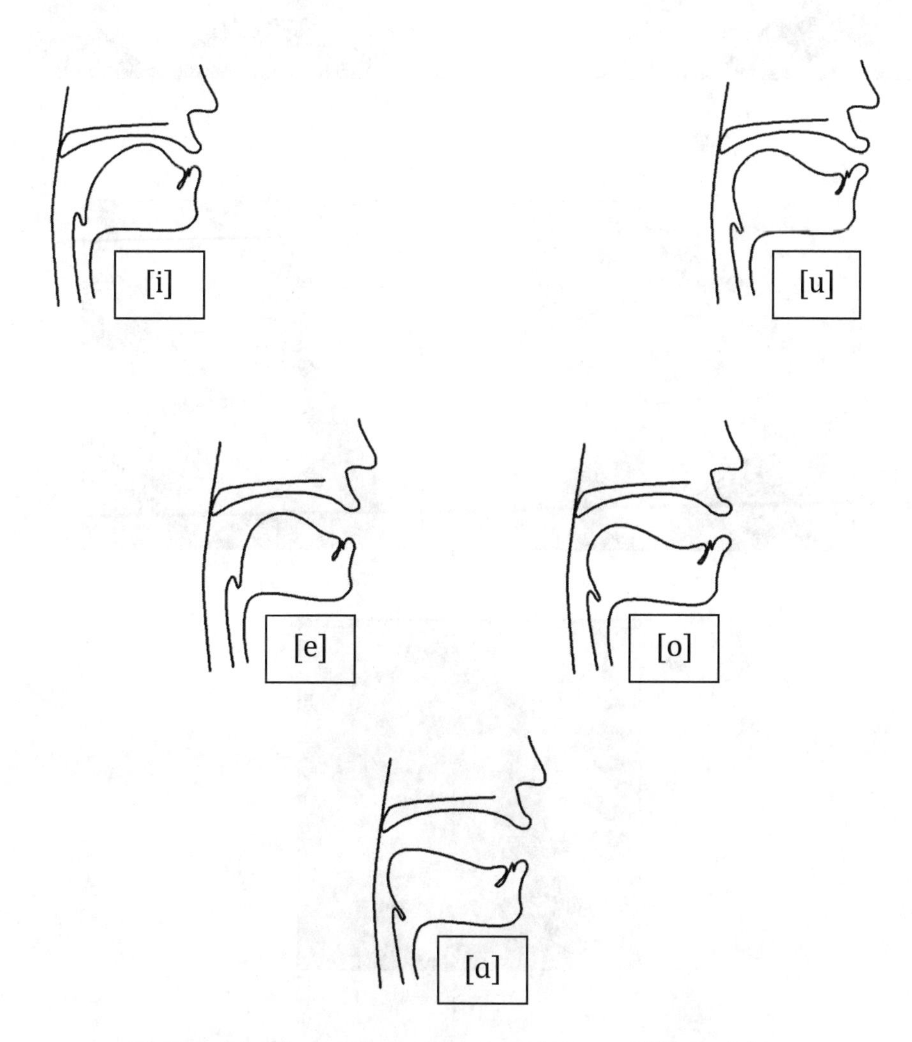


**Figure 5.2 Illustration of tongue, jaw and lip positions for the cardinal vowels**

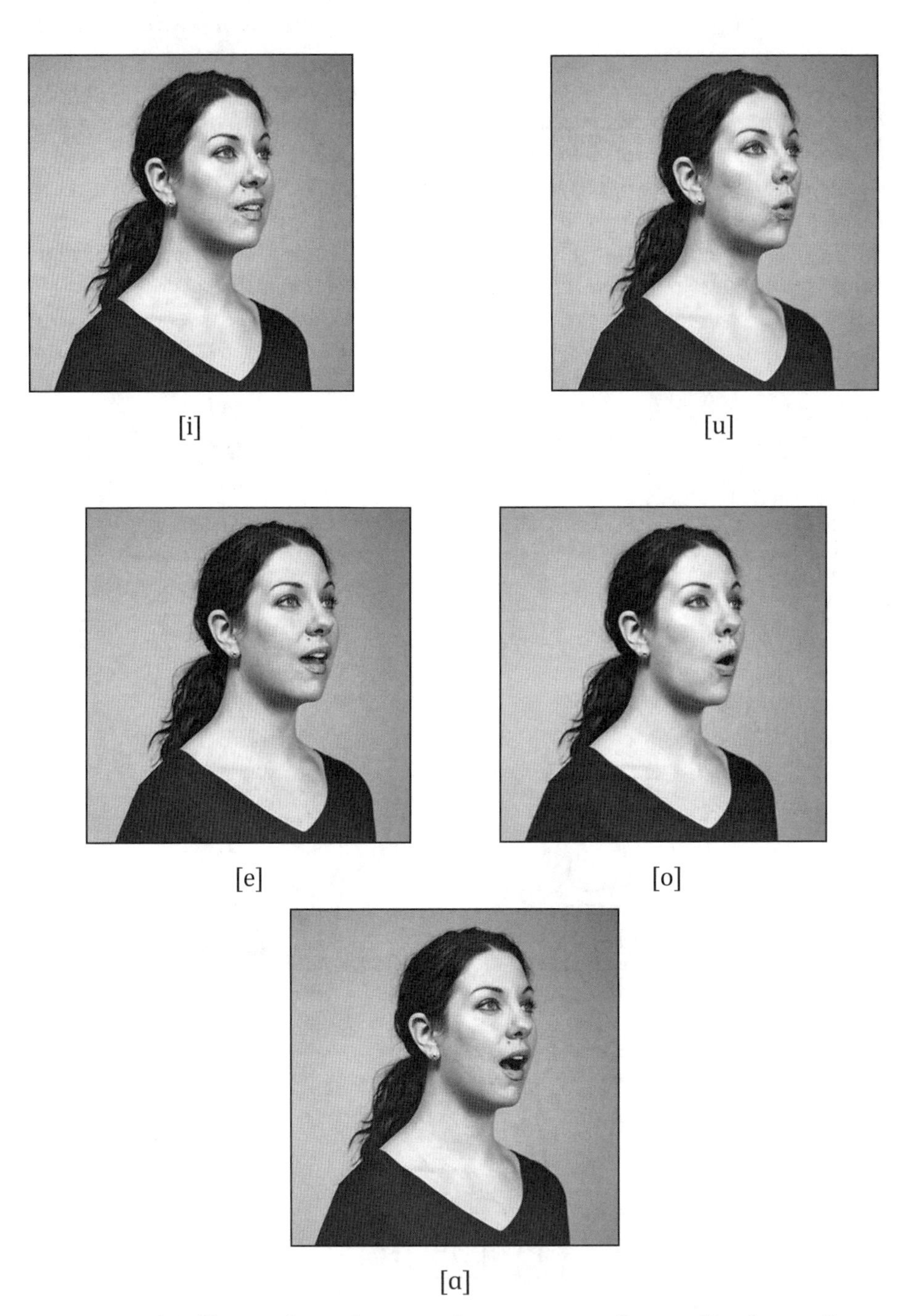


**Figure 5.3 Illustration of external appearance for cardinal vowels**

A major difference between Figures 5.1 and 5.2 and the charts of some vocal authorities is the amount of jaw opening as the vowel moves from [i] to [e] versus from [e] to [ɑ]. In our view the jaw should open more from [i] to [e], with less additional opening required from [e] to [ɑ]. If the jaw is not opened enough from [i] to [e], space at the back of the mouth will be insufficient, reducing resonance and creating a shallow or brassy sounding [e]. This slightly greater jaw opening also creates a more resonant [ɛ], which is often a dull-sounding vowel. (Note: we are speaking here of singing in the middle of a person's range.) Figure 5.3 depicts the exterior appearance for the five cardinal (basic Italian) vowels.

A small additional release of the jaw is needed from [e] to [ɑ]. If the jaw is lowered too much in the middle of a singer's range, there is a danger of failing to keep the soft palate raised, with resulting poor intonation (flatting of the pitch). Singers transitioning from [e] to [ɑ] should concentrate more on tongue position and less on lowering the jaw.

A somewhat closed jaw and rounded lips are necessary to create a resonant [u] vowel. This helps to lower the first and second formants and thus emphasize the lower first and second formant frequencies characteristic of this vowel.

Some singers move their jaws excessively when transitioning from one vowel to another. Excessive jaw movement wastes energy and creates tension, but more importantly, it alters the sound of the vowel as it is being sung, due to changes in the first formant that result from jaw movement.

Be alert to the following commonly observed problems at the end of a long-duration vowel or a long run on the same vowel:

- Closing the jaw (changes the first formant frequency)
- Moving the tongue (changes the second formant frequency)
- Allowing the soft palate to lower (reduces first formant amplitude and introduces nasality; can cause flatting of the pitch)

These problems change the resonating space, which can affect intonation, blend, and resonance quality.

*Try singing each vowel on the same note, moving along the Vowel Spectrum from [i] through [u], then moving from [u] back to [i]. Pay close attention to tongue and jaw position.*

*Choose two vowels and go back and forth between them on a single pitch. Work to make the transition feel very smooth—a quick, efficient change of jaw and tongue position should be made as necessary. This exercise works best if the vowels used are contiguous on the Vowel Spectrum chart in Figure 5.1.*

Conductors and teachers should be aware that the exterior appearance of a singer is not wholly indicative of the vowel that will be produced because vowel differentiation is largely a function of interior space created by tongue and jaw position. While singers may look different on the outside, all singers need to form vowels using the principles of vowel formation shown in the Vowel Spectrum chart. Figure 5.3 illustrates the exterior appearance for the five cardinal vowels for one particular singer.

## Vowel consistency for intonation and choral blending

Conductors and teachers should use vocal exercises to encourage consistent vowel production by both choral singers and soloists, as this is important for intelligibility and intonation. Intonation can be affected because perceived pitch is affected by overtone frequencies; singing a vowel improperly can cause singers to seem out of tune. Discussions of problematic vowels appear in the following section and general exercises for vowels are at the end of the chapter.

Blend is enhanced when choral singers share an understanding of how each vowel feels and sounds. Remember that vowels are distinguished largely by their first and second formant frequencies ($F_1$ and $F_2$). If some singers in a choral group are singing a given vowel differently from other singers, then their formant frequencies will differ.

For example, when singing [ɑ] in the middle of their range, some singers may sing the vowel properly, others may sing something closer to [ɔ], others may sing something closer to [ae], and still others may sing something closer to [ʌ]. This creates dissonance among the formant frequencies, with negative consequences for blend.

- Reviewing the literature, Aspaas, McCrea, Morris, and Fowler (2004) conclude that the tuning of vowel formant frequencies among choral members is one of the most important aspects of choral blending.

See Chapter 12 for further discussion of methods to achieve choral blend.

## Problematic vowels

### Beware of a puckered [u]

[u] is a particularly problematic vowel. Most inexperienced singers make one or more of the following errors:

- Rounding the lips insufficiently, creating a shallow and somewhat nasal sound
- Creating insufficient mouth space and consequent lack of resonating space
- Placing the hump of the tongue too far forward for this back vowel

Some choral conductors remedy these problems by asking for an excessive, forward lip puckering, but this can create an opening that is too narrow, and reduce interior space in the mouth as the cheeks are pulled in by the tensing of the lips necessary to create a pucker. Forward puckering may be useful as an effect, but as a rule, it should be avoided, for the resulting sound has a "hooty" quality and lacks resonance.

Since [u] has the lowest first and second formants of all vowels, many singers find it difficult to achieve a resonant sound on this vowel. Further narrowing of the mouth opening will lower the first formant even more, compromising tone quality and pitch. Figure 5.4 illustrates a puckered [u].

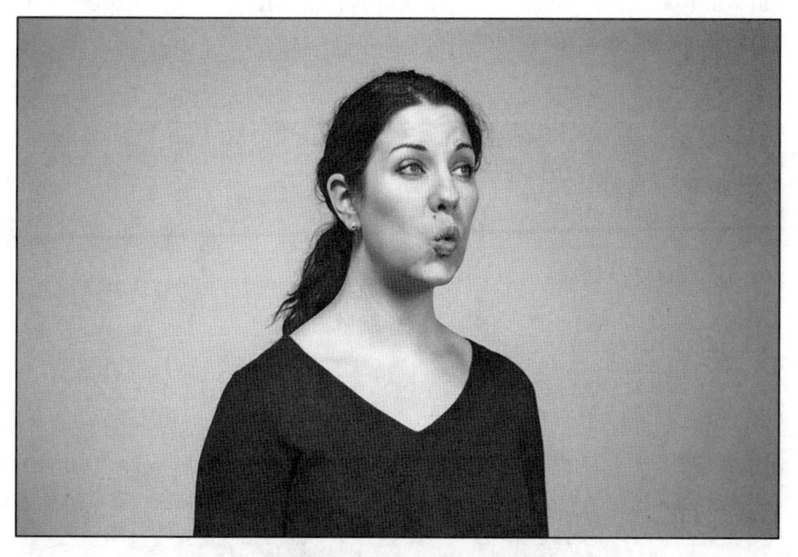

**Figure 5.4 Puckered [u]**

Singers should practice moving smoothly from [o] to [u], slightly closing the jaw and slightly rounding the lips in the transition from [o] to [u]. Avoid excessive closing of the jaw. The key is to maintain the resonance of [o] in the transition to [u]. Also try moving back and forth between [i] and [u] as suggested in Chapter 4 on resonance. This is useful because the jaw opening is the same for [i] and [u].

## Beware of making [i] too dull

The vowel [i] sounds too bright to some conductors trying to achieve a blended sound. As a result, they ask singers to modify the vowel to [I], but this modification makes words with the [i] vowel harder to understand and less resonant. An even more problematic modification is to ask singers to sing [i] in the mouth space of [u], which creates a hooty sounding [i]. (We are not speaking of singing IPA [y] in, for example, French or German, which is approximated by singing [i] in the space of [u]). Vowel modification toward a darker sound is a poor solution to the blending problem (see Chapter 12 on blending) and may create intonation problems in the middle of the range due to formant frequency alterations. A better solution is consistent production of vowels by all singers in a given section. Figure 5.5 illustrates singing [i] in the space of [u].

We are not suggesting that vowel modification of [i] to [I] is never appropriate. As outlined below in the section on vowel modification, it is certainly desirable in the upper range of a section. For example, modification will be necessary above $E_5$ for sopranos, or sopranos will find the note difficult to sing and the sound will be too brassy.

**Figure 5.5 [i] in the space of [u] (puckered [i])**

## Avoid an excessive mouth opening for [ɑ]

Some singers think that [ɑ] requires a wide open mouth, but the key is lowering the jaw in the back, not opening the mouth excessively in the front.

Singers are particularly prone to making this mistake when singing high pitches at high dynamic levels. Figure 5.6 illustrates two examples of excessive mouth opening. Note the tension apparent in both.

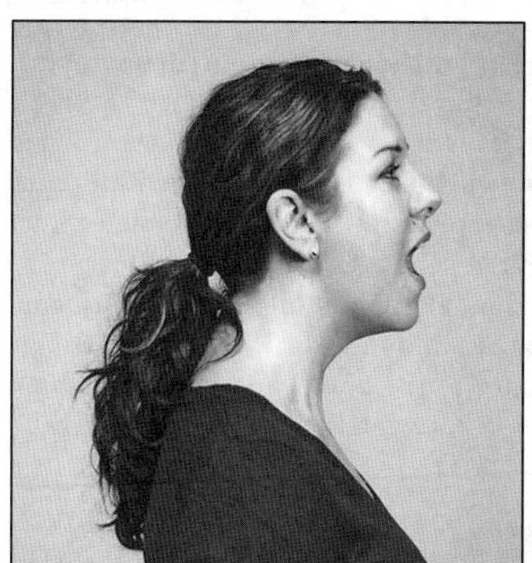
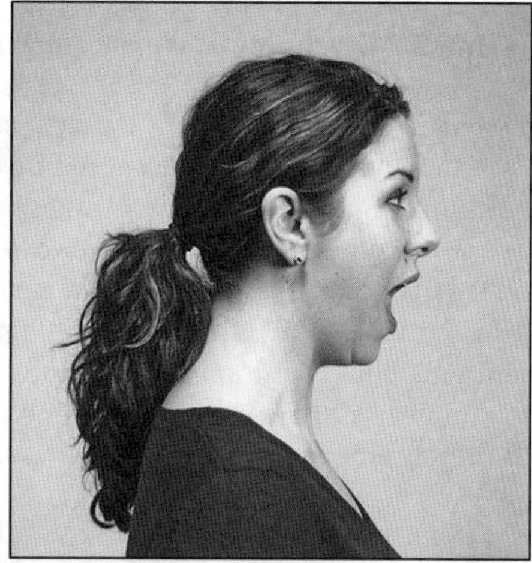

**Figure 5.6 Examples of excessive mouth opening and tension when singing [ɑ]**

## The neutral vowel "uh"

Neutral vowels have a dull, lifeless sound when sung improperly. In the choral setting they also pose problems for blend, as singers can form these vowels quite differently.

There are two neutral vowels of significance:

- [ʌ], as in "but," is the accented (stressed) form
- [ə] is the unaccented (unstressed) form, commonly referred to as a "schwa" (e.g., as in the second syllable of "people")
  - Vennard (1967) argues that the neutral "uh" vowel is a muddy, dull vowel, lacking in resonance. He even goes further to describe [ʌ] as a vulgar sound. It does not occur in Italian, German, or French as a stressed vowel.

To brighten the sound of the accented version [ʌ], modify it toward [ɑ]. For example, the word "love" when spoken often involves use of the neutral vowel, but when sung, [ɑ] should be employed.

Many English words contain [ʌ]. Because it is so problematic in singing, Table 5.2 shows examples of words that contain this vowel.

| come | love | sun | done | fun |
|---|---|---|---|---|
| blood | son | but | the | us |
| just | cut | shut | tough | fluff |
| unto | thus | dove | just | must |

**Table 5.2 Examples of words containing the stressed neutral vowel [ʌ]**

The unaccented form ([ə]), the schwa, does have its place in singing when used appropriately on unaccented final syllables. Very common with French (e.g., prier*e*) and German (e.g., lieb*e*), it appears in the final syllable of English words like "angel." In these words the schwa helps to deemphasize the final syllable. If this final syllable is sung using [ɛ] as in "angel" or [ɑ] as in "Christmas," it will have too much emphasis and the word will sound strange to the listener. To impart some resonance to the vowel and avoid making it too neutral, singers should use something between the schwa and [ɑ] (or [ɛ] as the case may be).

## Perceptions of vowels as "bright" versus "dark"

Some vowels seem "brighter" than others. Perceived brightness is largely a function of the second formant frequency, though it is also affected to some extent by the first and third formant frequencies. Vowels with high second formant frequencies are perceived as brighter than those with lower second formant frequencies. [i] is the brightest followed by [I], [e], [ɛ], [ae], and [ɑ].

The "darkest" vowel is [u], followed by [U], [o] and [ɔ]. Note that these vowels all have virtually the same second formant frequency, which is quite low (Figure 5.7). What differentiates these vowels is their first formant frequency—[ɔ] has the highest first formant frequency and [u] has the lowest first formant frequency. Thus, [ɔ] is the brightest of this set of darker vowels.

## Vowels in musical theatre and popular music

Intelligibility is particularly important in musical theater and popular genres. (Diction is also important in "classical" music, but in classical genres the beauty of the sound is of slightly greater concern.) Popular and musical theatre vowels should be pronounced more as if the vowels are spoken, which generally means that there should be more mouth resonance than pharyngeal resonance. For example, for [u] the jaw should be a bit more closed in the back to reduce pharyngeal resonance, plus there should be special attention to vertical space in the mouth. In addition, the lips should be less rounded. All of this creates a brighter sound that is less operatic. [e] sounds brighter as well if the tongue is a bit higher and elevated more toward the front of the mouth—in essence a modification of [e] toward [i].

Kayes (2004) recommends that musical theatre singers should employ a technique known as "vowel medialization." This involves moving the hump of the tongue more forward for back vowels ([ɑ], [ɔ], [o], [U], [u]). There is also some moving of the hump forward for the front vowels, but to a much lesser extent. Vowel medialization thus provides the sought after brighter musical theatre sound by raising the second and third formant frequencies, particularly for the normally darker back vowels. Singers should be careful, however, not to overdo medialization as there is the potential for loss of intelligibility.

## Modification of vowels for higher pitches

Most singers must modify vowels as they sing higher pitches. Vowel modification at higher pitches:

- Prevents dangerous crossovers of the fundamental and certain harmonic frequencies with $F_1$ that destabilize vocal fold vibration (Titze, 2008b; Titze, Riede, & Popolo, 2008). When this crossover occurs there can be a break in the voice, a sudden change in tonal quality, and/or a sudden alteration in pitch.
- Reinforces vocal fold vibration by altering formant frequencies at higher pitches, leading to less strain and lower vocal effort. This occurs due to a favorable feedback of energy to the vocal folds when a formant is reinforcing an important harmonic frequency (Titze, 2004).
- Allows singers to maintain a relatively low larynx.

Another benefit of vowel modification is that it helps to prevent front vowels (particularly [i]) from sounding too bright or brassy at high pitches. As long as the vowel is not modified too much, it will remain understandable, particularly given the context of the lyrics. Moreover, in the choral setting those sections not singing in the upper portions of their range will be singing the vowel in the normal manner.

Figure 5.7 illustrates the average formant frequencies in the Vowel Spectrum and how the first and second formants vary according to the vowel (approximate average frequencies are shown based on a variety of studies). The chart averages over men and women, but the formants are actually somewhat higher for women and lower for men. (The chart shows higher $F_1$ and

$F_2$ frequencies at the origin to show the correspondence of formant frequencies with the Vowel Spectrum chart of Figure 5.1.). Refer to Figure 5.7 to better understand the recommendations below for vowel modification.

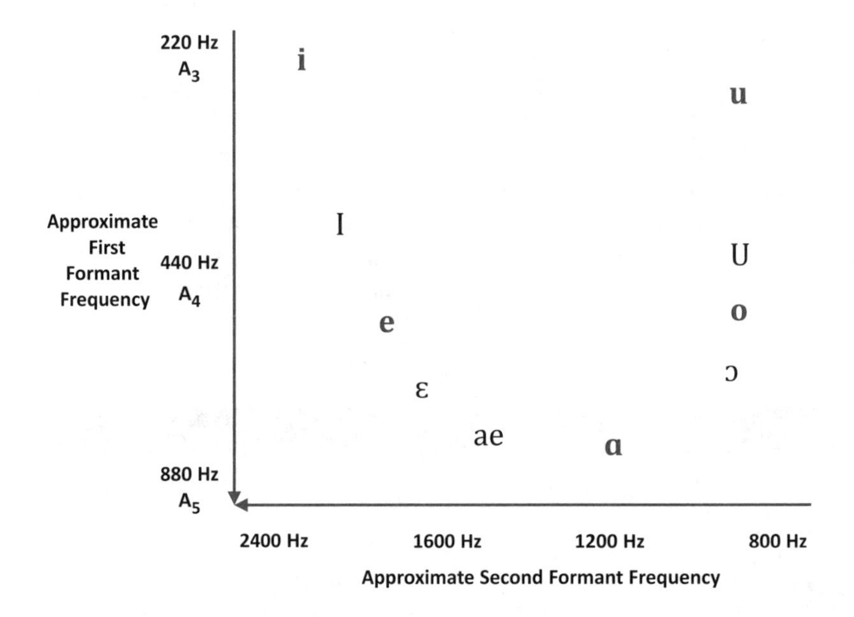


**Figure 5.7 Approximate formant frequencies for common English vowels (frequency scales inverted to follow the Vowel Spectrum chart)**

## Vowel modification for men—Moderate $F_1$ vowels and second formant tuning

Men typically resonate a higher harmonic frequency with $F_1$ through much of their range. For example, tenors typically resonate $H_2$ (the second harmonic) using the first formant. Some tenors continue to use this strategy by lowering the jaw and letting the larynx rise as they ascend to higher pitches. Lowering the jaw allows $F_1$ to rise as $H_2$ rises with increasing fundamental frequency. Allowing the larynx to rise also contributes to an increase in the first formant's frequency through shortening of the vocal tract. Both actions help to prevent $H_2$'s frequency from crossing above $F_1$'s frequency, which would create vocal instability.

This approach to negotiating higher pitches is essentially a belting strategy. But this approach has important limitations. First, it assumes that a belt sound is desirable, which will depend upon the type of music being performed. Second, unrefined belting at high pitches can have serious implications for vocal health. Third, there are limits to male singers' ability to raise $F_1$ to prevent the $H_2$ crossover. (Women can raise $F_1$ higher because their formant frequencies are naturally higher.) Take for example, the vowel [e] with a first formant of roughly 600 Hz. The second harmonic of the note, F4, is about 700 Hz, which is well above $F_1$. A tenor, bass, or baritone singing [e] on the note, F4, can lower the jaw and modify toward [ɑ] to compensate, but there are limits, particularly as pitch ascends further. As noted by Titze and Worley (2009), male belters often break into falsetto when $F_1$ can no longer be raised.

Vocal science research has revealed an alternative approach to vowel modification for men that is likely to be more successful (e.g., Neumann et al., 2005; Schutte, Miller, & Duijnstee, 2005; Titze & Worley, 2009). This involves three components:

- At high pitches men should limit jaw opening by avoiding vowels such as [ae] and [ɑ]. This will keep $F_1$ lower than $H_2$ so that phonation will not be disrupted by a crossing of $F_1$ by $H_2$. Studies of professional artists show that in the first passaggio, where vowel modification usually begins, there is a sudden reduction in the frequency of $F_1$ that avoids the destabilization problem. This is accomplished by reducing jaw opening. (A passaggio is a transition between one mode of vocal production and another—see Chapter 8 on vocal registers.) As these artists' pitch rises further, $F_1$ begins to rise again as the jaw is opened more, but $F_1$ always stays well below $H_2$.
- At high pitches, also avoid the vowels with low first formant frequencies, particularly [i] and [u]. Otherwise the fundamental frequency can cross over the first formant, creating instability. Avoid the crossover by modifying [i] and [u] to [I] and [U] respectively. These vowels may even need some modification just below the first passaggio.
- Use the second formant to resonate $H_3$ for back vowels and to resonate $H_4$ for front vowels (which naturally have a higher second formant.) This is accomplished by shifting the arch of the tongue forward—a "fronting of the tongue" (D. Miller, 2008). Increase the amount of forward shift and the height of the arch more as pitch increases.

To summarize, successful vowel modification for men involves the use of mid vowels ([I], [ɛ], [e], [ɔ], [o], and [U]) that require a moderately open jaw plus fronting of the tongue to track higher harmonics with the second formant. Singers should also maintain a comfortably low larynx position as the pitch ascends.

## Vowel modification for women—modification toward [ɑ] in the upper register

As pitch ascends above roughly $C_5$ and women enter the upper register (head voice), women must raise the first formant to keep it slightly above the fundamental frequency. Otherwise, the fundamental will cross above the first formant and disrupt phonation. Women who properly raise the first formant have a powerful voice in their upper register because the first formant resonates the fundamental frequency (Sundberg, 1987). This assumes, however, that they are using flow phonation so that the amplitude of the fundamental is strong.

The first formant is raised by additional jaw lowering as pitch ascends. (Spreading the lips with a slight smile also helps to increase $F_1$ since that raises all formants by shortening the vocal tract. Singers must be careful not to overdo this, though.)

As a practical matter, this formant resonance strategy allows a vowel to shift slightly along the vowel chart in the direction of [ɑ]. Note that singers should *not* sing [ɑ] itself. The modification through appropriate jaw lowering is *in the direction of* [ɑ].

*Try singing [i], for example, in the standard jaw position. Then allow the jaw to open while retaining the tongue position for [i].* The resultant sound is [I], the next vowel toward [ɑ].

Modifying toward [ɑ] also applies to the back vowels. Open the jaw while singing [o] and the sound will transition to [ɔ].

## Vowel modification for women—easing the transition from chest voice to mixed voice

Some female voices experience difficulty in transitioning from their lower register (chest voice) to the middle register (more appropriately called "mixed voice"; see Chapter 8 on registers for further discussion of these terms and transitional issues).

From a resonance standpoint, this problem is similar to the one experienced by men transitioning to their upper register because the pitches are in the same area. This is generally an easier pitch area for women, however, because the thyroarytenoid muscle is not pushed as close to its limits as it is in men.

If female singers are having difficulty with this transition, teachers and conductors can suggest that they also use the mid-vowel strategy with a fronting of the tongue (as outlined for men) to assist entry into middle voice.

### Avoid excessive modification—but sopranos are an exception

Excessive modification sounds artificial, so it is rare that one would modify the vowel more than one or two positions along the vowel chart. Nonetheless, at the very highest pitches (roughly $A_5$ and above) sopranos must modify all vowels to [ae] or [ɑ].

To understand why, examine Figure 5.7. Notice that the normal frequency range for the first formant is between 250 and 850 Hz. At very high pitches (e.g., $A_5$ [880 Hz] and above) all vowels sound similar. Even with a lowered jaw, the fundamental frequencies of all vowels except [ae] and [ɑ] are above the first formant.

If sopranos try to sing the written vowel at such high pitches, it will still sound close to [ɑ]. Sopranos who attempt to produce vowels in the upper portion of their range other than [ae] or [ɑ] will experience strain and vocal instability. The tone will be strident, and moreover, their efforts will be wasted. Thus, sopranos should not be asked to vocalize or sing repertoire on vowels other than [ae] or [ɑ] at high pitches, and [i] and [u] specifically should be avoided.

Of course, this means that sopranos will experience a loss of vowel differentiation at high pitches, but the result is superior tone and less dynamic variation from pitch to pitch (Joliveau, Smith, & Wolfe, 2004). Intelligibility is obtained from:

- The context of the lyrics
- Surrounding consonants
- In the choral setting, other vocal parts that are not forced into such extensive vowel modification

### At what pitch should vowel modification start?

We are hesitant to suggest an arbitrary pitch at which vowel modification should commence for a given voice type. The point at which vowel modification needs to occur will vary from singer to singer because of differences in physiological structures. As a general rule, *slight* modification using second formant vowel modification principles should begin as one enters the first passaggio. However, it may be desirable for men to modify the low $F_1$ formant vowels [i] and [u] slightly before entering this passaggio.

- For most sopranos and tenors this would be in the vicinity of $E_4$.

- For mezzo-sopranos (second sopranos or first altos in a choral group) and baritones (first basses or even second tenors in a choral group), this would be in the vicinity of $D_4$.
- For contraltos (second altos) and true basses (second basses) this falls in the vicinity of $C_4$.

Women should begin modification toward [ɑ] as they approach their second passaggio.

- For most (lyric) sopranos this would be in the vicinity of $E_5$
- For mezzo-sopranos (second sopranos or first altos) this would be in the vicinity of $D_5$.
- For contraltos (second altos) this falls in the vicinity of $C_5$.

*To assist learning vowel modification for women in the higher range, start in the lower/middle range and slide up the octave allowing the jaw to open as necessary. Allow the vowel to shift/modify without predetermining its final jaw opening. Slide up and down on various vowels—observe how the vowel sound changes and how much opening is needed. Be sure to monitor breath support as pitch ascends.*

*To assist learning vowel modification for men, start on [ɑ] in the lower/middle range. Slide up an octave modifying toward [ɔ] as the passaggio is entered. As the pitch ascends, gradually move the tongue arch forward but otherwise maintain the vocal tract in the position of [ɔ].*

## Avoid the practice of "covering" throughout the vocal range

As we noted in our discussion of [i], it is undesirable to ask singers to create [i] in the space of [u] (or even in the space of [ɑ] except for an occasional, special effect). This is an extreme example of a more general vocal strategy known as "covering," in which more subtle modifications are used to darken vowel color. This strategy is sometimes used in choral settings to create a more uniform sound—i.e., a sound with less variability in the darkness and brightness of vowels.

The term "covering" is appropriate, because the epiglottis folds over the glottis as vowels move from [i] to [u] along the Vowel Spectrum. The tonal result, as aptly stated by Fleming (2005), is to put a lid on the sound. To this we would add that if done excessively or in the middle of a singer's range, the resulting sound will strike the listener as overly dark and may make text difficult to understand. In contrast, preserving vowel integrity (with allowance for modification at high pitches) produces a broader, more pleasing tonal palette with better intelligibility.

The generalized use of formant frequency tuning at all pitches is a related strategy. Coffin (1980) developed a complex system of vowel modification depending upon pitch, to more closely match the frequency of the first or second formant to a nearby harmonic frequency of the note being sung. Formant tuning tends to result in a boost in sound level. This system is most commonly used by solo singers in opera settings, but it is not appropriate for most other singing. Except for what is necessary to sing the higher pitches of a singer's range, formant tuning is undesirable for two reasons:

- Vowel distortions in the lower to middle pitches of a singer's range make singing less enjoyable for audiences. Carlsson and Sundberg (1992) tested the preferences of expert listeners for three types of formant tuning versus constant formant singing across an octave from C3 to C4. In 98% of the comparisons between formant tuning and constant formant singing, constant formant singing was preferred. Clearly, extreme approaches to vowel modification are not desirable from an audience perspective.
- Complex systems of modification make singing more difficult.

## Diphthongs, triphthongs, and glides

Diphthongs, triphthongs, and glides are combinations of two or more vowels in succession. With diphthongs and triphthongs, the first vowel should receive the most duration. With a glide, the second of the two vowels receives the most duration.

### Diphthongs are combinations of two vowels

In words like "died," the vowel sound is actually made up of *two* distinct vowel sounds, [ɑ] and [i]. The first vowel of a diphthong should be sustained ([ɑ] in this example), shifting to the second vowel (in this case [i]) at the last moment. Table 5.3 lists common diphthongs, along with the primary vowel to be sung.

| Diphthong | Example |
|---|---|
| ɑi | night , died—sing [ɑ] primarily |
| ɑu | down—sing [ɑ] primarily |
| ɔi | voice—sing [ɔ] primarily |
| ou | low—sing [o] primarily |
| ei | day—sing [e] primarily |

**Table 5.3 Examples of diphthongs**

Some languages, such as Italian, Latin, and Spanish, use mostly pure vowels with few diphthongs. German has a number of diphthongs, most notably [ɑi] as in *dein*, which should be sung primarily on the [ɑ] vowel.

## Triphthongs are combinations of three vowels

Combinations of three vowels are known as triphthongs (Table 5.4). In most English words involving triphthongs, the third vowel is the schwa. As with diphthongs, the word should be sung on the first vowel, shifting to the second two vowels just as word is being completed.

| Triphthong | Example |
|---|---|
| eiə | prayer—sing [e] primarily |
| ɑiə | tire—sing [ɑ] primarily |
| ɑoə | hour—sing [ɑ] primarily |
| ɔiə | royal—sing [ɔ] primarily |
| ouə | lower—sing [o] primarily |

**Table 5.4 Examples of triphthongs**

## Glides

A glide involves two vowels, typically moving swiftly through the first vowel and singing the second vowel with greater duration. There are occasional glides in both Italian (e.g., *pianto* and *guanto*—[iɑ] and [uɑ]) and English (e.g., you, few, and new [iu]).

Sometimes singers fail to recognize that words such as "new" and words that start with a [y] involve a glide. While [nu] may be acceptable in speech, in singing this sound will be too dark—[niu] is preferable.

## Avoiding problems with diphthongs and triphthongs

Diphthongs can be very tricky for amateur choral singers because of a tendency to shift to the second vowel too quickly, producing a poor sound. The same is true for triphthongs where the first vowel should receive the longest duration.

This problem originates from habits carried over from speaking where the shift from one vowel of a diphthong or triphthong to another is quite rapid. It is often helpful for singers to write in the primary vowel that should be sung. Sometimes, singers may even want to cross out the word written in the lyrics and write it in the way it needs to be sung. This advice also applies to vowels that need to be sustained prior to the final consonant. Writing the vowel above the staff with a line extending to the consonant at the cutoff point can remind the singer not to move to the consonant too quickly. This is particularly important for consonants that are semi-vowels (e.g., [m] or [n]), precisely because they *can* be sustained (but should not be, unless a particular effect is desired).

When a diphthong is followed by a consonant, think of the second vowel as being attached to the consonant to allow the first vowel to retain its purity and to avoid anticipating the second vowel.

Singers also need to avoid inadvertent singing of diphthongs when a pure vowel is called for. It is not uncommon for singers to make a final pure vowel into a diphthong. For example in Italian *vivace* has the final vowel [ɛ]. English singers may inadvertently add [i] to the end of this word by closing the jaw while still singing the [ɛ] vowel, resulting in an unwanted diphthong. If singers keep the jaw open, the integrity of the vowel is preserved.

## Altering the tonal color of vowels

Understanding the principles outlined in this chapter allows alteration of tonal color when desired. For example:

- For a darker tone for an [i] vowel, place the lips in the position of the [ɑ] vowel but sing [i]. However, as noted above, reserve this only for special effects. Avoid singing [i] in the space of [u] for reasons outlined above.
- A brighter sounding [ɛ] can be obtained by shifting the vowel slightly toward [e].

### If back vowels sound too dark

If [u] seems too dark or sung from the throat, more room in the mouth can brighten it. Reducing lip compression will also help.

If [o] seems too dark or muffled, sing something closer to [ɔ] instead, shifting toward a brighter vowel.

The word "Gloria" is a good example. English singers often sing [o], when in fact it should be sung as [ɔ] when using Italianized Latin (Church Latin). Singing [ɔ] helps to enliven the sound. However, when singing Germanic Latin, [o] is the correct vowel.

### If the tone is too dark in general

McKinney (2005) provides a nice summary of factors that can lead to an excessively dark tone. We consider the following to be his most important points:

- Lowering the jaw excessively in the middle of the range. Try singing [ɑ] and quickly lower the jaw to imitate a full yawn. You will readily hear a darkening of the tone.
- Depressed larynx. This can result from opening the jaw excessively, but it can also stem from deliberate attempts to create more vocal tract space, to artificially lower one's range. A depressed larynx is most often an affliction of male singers, particularly baritones, who want to sing the lower notes required of bass choral singers.
- Insufficient oral space. Remember that the mouth is the resonating cavity that reinforces some of the higher harmonic frequencies.
- Flabby pharyngeal walls. This can be caused by insufficient lifting of the soft palate.
- Tongue pulled back.

Some singers perceive, inaccurately, that their sound is richer and resonant with a darker form of production. In reality, the sound can be lacking in resonance and be out of tune, in part because the formant frequencies are depressed. The problem is that what they perceive internally as a rich sound is not heard by the audience. Teachers and conductors should give feedback to such singers to help them balance mouth and pharyngeal resonance. This is also important for accurate vowel production.

### If the tone is too bright in general

McKinney (2005) asserts that a too-bright sound stems from overemphasized resonance in the mouth and insufficient resonance in the pharynx. This problem can result from:

- Insufficient pharyngeal space due to neck/throat tension. Remember that constrictor muscles can squeeze the pharynx. See Chapter 14 on tension for an illustration of these muscles and approaches to relieving tension.
- A clenched jaw in an excessively closed position.
- Larynx rising too high. This usually results from carrying chest voice too high—the larynx rises as the thyroarytenoid muscle is used excessively at the highest pitches. It can also result from insufficient breath support and use of the constrictor muscles surrounding the vocal tract to assist air flow.

- Excessive smile. This creates a wide aperture which emphasizes higher frequency harmonics.

To this we would add that when the hump (arch) of the tongue is excessively forward and/or excessively elevated for all vowels, the sound can be too bright because of a high second formant. *Put your hand next to your ear and point your index finger up. Sing [a] in the middle of the range. While sustaining the vowel, move your finger slowly around to a point in front of the nose, allowing the sound to brighten by increasing elevation of the hump of the tongue. Continue singing and bring the finger to the back of the head, shifting to a darker tone by depressing the hump.* This exercise helps to illustrate physically the possibilities of vowel color. Generally the goal is to have a color that is neither too dark nor too light—"opposite the ear!"

## A summary philosophy of vowel formation

The chapters on both resonance and vowels can be summarized in the following philosophy of vowel formation:

1) All vowels should be formed in the context of a comfortably low larynx, an open pharynx, and good mouth space.
2) The tip of the tongue should rest against the base of the lower incisors for all vowels in the Vowel Spectrum. After formation of consonants it should immediately be returned to its resting place for the subsequent vowel.
3) Vowel integrity is essential. This means that, with the exception of pitches in the higher portions of a singer's range, vowels should be formed with tongue, lip, and jaw positions as shown in the Vowel Spectrum chart. This creates a broad tonal palette reflective of true differences in the sound of the various vowels. Vowel integrity also preserves intelligibility. Singers should not be asked to create different vowels with the same jaw and/or lip positions. Each vowel has a unique quality.
4) The tongue and jaw should not move during the singing of a vowel because doing so alters the vowel and its associated formant frequencies.
5) Proper vowel modification is essential for singing higher pitches with ease and freedom. Without appropriate modification singers will have a strained sound and poor intonation.
6) Within choral sections, singers should use a common approach to vowel modification. With different approaches to modification there can be adverse consequences for blend.

## Vowel exercises

### Experimenting with tongue position

*The following exercise will help to convince singers to control tongue placement: Place the tip of the tongue at the base of the incisors. Sing [a] and experiment with tongue position. Move the tip of the tongue forward over the lower teeth and then backward and down to the gum line below the lower teeth. The vowel sound will change.*

*Flick the tip of the tongue up and down to hear yet a different change in the sound of the vowel.*

### Tongue position vocalise

*Sing consonants that require tongue movement before a vowel such as [a]—e.g., la, da, ta, na. Pronounce the consonant quickly and rapidly, returning the tongue to the resting place at the base of the lower incisors. Maintain vowel integrity throughout the exercise.*

### Vowel Spectrum

*Sing [i], [e], [a], [o], [u] sustaining one pitch. Progress through the Vowel Spectrum, listening to and feeling for consistency of tone and pitch.*

*Try moving carefully from one vowel to the next and then back to the first vowel, e.g., [i e i], while making sure jaw opening, tongue, and lip positions are as described in this chapter. Maintain resonance throughout. Avoid exaggerated motions—a quick, efficient change of jaw and tongue position should be made as necessary. Change pitches as desired staying in the middle range. Singers should watch themselves in a mirror when practicing. Conductors should monitor singers during vocal exercises.*

*Continue to use the Vowel Spectrum progressing [i] through [u] and in reverse through a variety of melodic patterns, always working for consistency of sound, vibrato and pitch.*

### Experimenting with vowel color

*Put your hand next to your ear and point your index finger up. Sing [a] in the middle of the range. While sustaining the vowel, move your finger slowly around to a point in front of the nose, allowing the sound to brighten by in-*

*creasing elevation of the hump of the tongue. Continue singing and bring the finger to the back of the head, shifting to a darker tone by depressing the hump. This exercise helps to illustrate physically the possibilities of vowel color. Generally the goal is to have a color that is neither too dark nor too light—"opposite the ear!"*

### Beautiful [e]

*Beware of the [e] vowel. Insert the little (pinky) finger between the back molars while singing to encourage just enough space for resonance.*

### Resonant [u]

*Singers should practice moving smoothly from [o] to [u], slightly closing the jaw and slightly rounding the lips in the transition from [o] to [u]. Avoid excessive closing of the jaw. The key is to maintain the resonance of [o] in the transition to [u]. Also try moving back and forth between [i] and [u] as suggested in Chapter 4 on resonance, because the jaw opening is the same for [i] and [u].*

### For kids and everyone! Diphthongs

*Sing the phrase, "I like my bike." Each word of this phrase contains a diphthong. Sustain the first vowel of each [a] and move to the second vowel only just before changing syllables. Use a single pitch for the whole exercise, and then move to a variety of melodic patterns. (Adapted from Phillips, 1996)*

### Vowel modification

#### Women

*Start in the lower-middle range and slide up an octave allowing the jaw to open as necessary. Allow the vowel to shift/modify without predetermining its final jaw opening. Slide up and down on various vowels and observe how the vowel sound changes and how much opening is needed.*

#### Men

*Start on [a] in the lower-middle range. Slide up an octave modifying toward [ɔ] as the passaggio is entered. As the pitch ascends, gradually move the tongue arch forward but otherwise maintain the vocal tract in the position of [ɔ].*

# Chapter 6: Consonants

Consonants certainly deserve as much attention as vowels, for they are an integral part of communicating the message of song. Successful enunciation of consonants can, however, be a challenge for two major reasons:

- Singers often compromise the preceding and subsequent vowels when they do not form consonants efficiently. We call this "vowel pollution."
- Singers often pay consonants insufficient attention because they focus on the vowels out of a desire to create beautiful tonal quality.

Singers need to learn how consonants are best formed, including which muscles and structures should be involved (and which should not).

## The articulators

The primary players in the pronunciation of consonants are the lips, teeth, tongue, the ridge just behind the top front teeth (technically known as the alveolar ridge), and the hard palate. Proper jaw position is also important. Singers should use only the articulators that are necessary to form a consonant and nothing more; otherwise, vowels preceding or following the consonant will be compromised.

## Sing consonants quickly and efficiently

In the vast majority of situations, consonants should be formed quickly and precisely, with the tongue returning rapidly to its resting place with the tip just above the gum line against the lower front teeth. As noted in the preceding chapter, this practice helps to ensure vowel integrity. Production of vowels between consonants is compromised by intermediate tongue positions that occur if the tongue returns too slowly to its resting position.

The jaw also needs either to move quickly to the best position for the subsequent vowel or, whenever possible, not change its position. Vowel shape and resonance space must be guarded! A lazy tongue or jaw risks distorting the sound of the vowel, affecting intonation, and/or losing resonance.

Sometimes an unintended vowel sound (such as a schwa) can occur when consonants are sung too slowly. Consonant clusters are particularly troublesome in this respect. For example, singing [bl] in the word "blow" too slowly may cause the word to sound like "buh-lo."

- McKinney (2005) cautions that when the initial consonant of a word is sung too slowly, it may be sung flat, forcing a singer to "scoop up" to the proper pitch on the subsequent vowel.
- This problem often occurs at the beginning of a phrase. McKinney (2005) suggests envisioning the initial consonant on the same pitch as the subsequent vowel as a solution. We would add that it is desirable to inhale with the vocal tract (pharynx space, mouth space, and tongue) in position for the vowel and pitch to be sung, whether or not a word starts with a consonant.

Excessive tongue tension/tongue rigidity makes it difficult to sing consonants quickly. Solutions to excessive tongue rigidity appear in Chapter 14 on tension.

## Be mindful of consonants; exaggeration is generally undesirable

Some vocal authorities suggest that consonants be exaggerated to make their sound level closer to that of vowels (e.g., McKinney, 2005). But exaggeration of jaw movements, in particular, can affect resonance, vowel integrity, and tonal quality. Moreover, exaggerated movement of any articulator can create unwanted noise and tension.

Our perspective is that singers simply need to understand how consonants are best formed and to be mindful of the need to execute them. This is particularly important for final consonants, which are most likely to be overlooked.

Proper use of the tongue, lips, and jaw is usually sufficient to bring out important consonants.

- As Alderson (1979) says, "Consonants are only a fraction as loud as vowels . . . but their high frequency energy is particularly adapted to human ears, so that crisp diction fairly crackles in a good acoustical setting" (p. 175).

### Final consonants

As noted above, singers often pay insufficient attention to final consonants (e.g., "t" in "it"). Without proper emphasis, a word with a final consonant may be confused with other words, or not understood at all. For example, if the "t" in "mist" is not pronounced, it sounds like "miss." Thus, in *Brigadoon's* "Heather on the Hill," the meaning of the phrase "when the mist is in the gloamin" could be misunderstood.

- McKinney (2005) states that a lack of attention to final consonants can cause the pitch to go flat. This occurs because the shift from vowel to consonant, if done too slowly, will alter the vowel being sung. Because the jaw is closing in the transition from many vowels to certain consonants, the effect will be to lower the first formant frequency, making the pitch sound flat. Additionally, singers may relax breath support too soon on a voiced consonant such as [m], also causing the pitch to go flat.
- One might think that an Italian singer such as Caruso would concentrate mostly on beautiful vowels, yet he felt very strongly about good diction and titled one of his talks on singing, "Good Diction a Requisite" (Caruso & Tetrazzini, 1975). Caruso believed that no singer can be considered to be an artist based on beautiful tone alone—clear enunciation is essential. He even went so far as to say that a singer with a small voice or less than ideal tonal quality may be more pleasurable to hear than a singer who has a big voice with poor diction.

## Sometimes consonants should precede the beat

Phrases begin sometimes with a consonant cluster or an unvoiced consonant. If these consonants are formed on the beat singers may be perceived as late. Formation of these consonants just before the beat will avoid this problem and give the subsequent vowel fuller duration. Robert Shaw applied the principle of anticipatory consonants extensively in his choral conducting (Blocker, 2004), but it is also applicable to solo singing. It is especially desirable in rhythmic music.

- Henderson (1979) argues that forming consonants just before the beat prevents singing from seeming lethargic and contributes to the sensation of a continuous, legato style of singing.
- Appelman (1986) says that "every consonant must be slightly anticipated by a proper preparation of the articulators" (p. 238). This makes it possible for the vowel to be produced *on* the beat.
- Richard Miller (2004) recommends the use of anticipatory consonants largely for unvoiced consonants that carry no pitch (for example, [s] and [p]; see the section on voiced and unvoiced consonants

for more examples). Voiced consonants should be placed on the beat because they carry pitch.

We concur with Miller's perspective—that unvoiced consonants, but not voiced consonants, be anticipatory. We would, however, consider anticipatory timing of consonant clusters as well because of their longer duration.

An anticipatory consonant can also be used expressively when you want to draw it out for effect. For example, drawing out [l] in "love" and [st] in "star" can focus audience attention on these important words.

- Sundberg and Bauer-Huppmann (2007) studied lieder recordings by eight internationally recognized artists. They found that in most instances consonants and subsequent vowels were timed so that the vowel onset occurred at the same time as the accompaniment, supporting the concept of anticipatory consonants. Nonetheless, in some instances consonants were drawn out, presumably for expressive purposes as outlined above. And, in a few cases, vowel onset occurred before the beat, again likely for expressive purposes.

## Avoid adding "uh" or "ah" to final consonants

Some singers have been trained, or have learned by observing others, to add an emphatic "uh" or "ah" at the end of a final consonant (a shadow vowel) to ensure that it is heard. We believe this is a poor technique under normal circumstances because it produces inaccurate articulation of the consonant and a distracting, unpleasant sound. In an ensemble, singers who do this will also cause blend problems because they are still making sound after the cutoff. Consider, for example, the word "died" ([daid]) when it is sung with a distinct schwa at the end—daid-uh. Such shadow vowels are most common when [g], [d], and [b] are the final consonants

- To avoid this problem, Vennard (1967) reminds us that singers need to stop the vocal folds from vibrating a moment before the formation of the consonant is complete. This means that breath must cease at the correct point to avoid a shadow vowel.

Nonetheless, there are a *few* circumstances where adding a shadow vowel is a helpful tool, particularly when singers are having difficulty with a particular consonant. For example, for the phrase "and died," elision is inappropriate ("andied") as both the [d] at the end of "and" and the [d] at the beginning of "died" need to be heard. Asking singers to add a slight schwa in between the two words can focus their attention on the problem, and most will simply emphasize the consonants properly. In the choral setting, adding a slight schwa will also help the group to form the consonants at the same time, creating better ensemble. By the same token, when singers are not enunciating a final consonant clearly, addition of a shadow vowel can help focus their attention on the problem. Once this is done, however, the shadow vowel should be dropped.

## Problematic consonants

A number of specific consonants cause problems for singers. These are often consonants that require substantial movement of the jaw, tongue, and/or lips. They also include consonants that singers may mistakenly believe to require jaw closing.

### Consonants requiring substantial jaw or lip closing—b, j, m, p, s, v, z

These consonants cause problems with preceding and subsequent vowels if they are formed too slowly. For [j], [s], [v], and [z] the jaw is closed to some extent to form the consonant. As the jaw closes the first formant is lowered, lowering the perceived pitch. As the jaw opens, the first formant is raised, raising the perceived pitch. To avoid these "scoops" in pitch, consonants must not be formed lazily.

As outlined below, the jaw should remain open to form [m], but the lips must be closed. The jaw should also remain open for [b] and [p] with the lips quickly closing and opening. If the lips are slowly closed and opened for the subsequent vowel, pitch scoops can occur with these consonants as well.

### Consonants requiring the tongue to seal the roof of the mouth—g, k, and ng ([ŋ])

These consonants are challenging because the obstruction of airflow makes it difficult to maintain resonance and keep a phrase moving, reducing the sense of legato.

"God" is a good example of a word involving the problematic [g], because it illustrates two additional problems that occur with this consonant:

- Pronouncing [g] too hard generates undesirable overtone frequencies (i.e., noise is created). It also distorts the meaning of the word ("cod" rather than "God").
- Slow production of [g] creates a diphthong. The mouth is fairly closed to create the consonant, but then the jaw must be opened to create the vowel [ɑ]. If the jaw is opened too slowly, a diphthong will be created.

### Consonant clusters

Consonant clusters typically require two distinct movements. With the aforementioned "bl" as in "blow," each consonant requires a distinct movement. The same is true of "pl" as in "plow." Singers should look for these and mark them in their repertoire for special attention.

## Think of [w] and "y" in terms of the vowels [u] and [i]

Although singers may think of [w] and "y" as consonants, they are actually vowels (technically, glides). By thinking of w and y as vowels, singers can improve tonal quality:

- [w] (as in "wonder") is formed similar to [u]—start by singing [u] with slightly more lip pucker and move quickly to the next vowel. In the transition to the next vowel [w] will be formed.
- "y" (as in "yet"—IPA [j]) is formed similar to [i]—start by singing [i] with the tongue closer to the hard palate and, from that position, quickly move the tongue to the position of the subsequent vowel. In the transition to the next vowel the [j] is formed.

## Keep the back of the jaw open when singing l, k, g, t, d, n, ng, m

Some singers close the jaw to produce these consonants, but jaw closing is actually unnecessary. Even though the lips must be closed to form [m], the jaw should remain open in the back to enhance resonance.

Singing these consonants with a closed jaw increases the likelihood of interference with surrounding vowels. Furthermore, closing the jaw leads to overusing the tongue to create the consonant, causing a loss of resonance because the tongue occupies too much of the resonating space.

*Try humming on [m] with the jaw somewhat closed. Then open the jaw at the back and notice the improvement in resonance.*

### Additional difficulties associated with [l]

Singers tend to form [l] with the tongue hitting the roof of the mouth, too far behind the front teeth, which forces the tongue back in the mouth (Vennard, 1967). In addition, too much of the tongue surface may contact the roof of the mouth. The *tip* of the tongue should be close to the teeth. (Vennard suggests putting the tongue on the teeth, but this is a bit extreme.)

- Richard Miller (1996, p. 92) concurs that English speakers tend to form [l] too far back which produces "a lazy, liquid consonant that encourages transitional sounds." Miller suggests executing [l] with a flick of the tongue and a quick return to the resting position against the lower bottom teeth.

*Try saying "tele" (as in telephone) over and over concentrating on forming both the "t" and the "l" in the same place (tongue just behind the front top teeth). Return the tongue quickly back to its resting place for the vowel. This is fairly easy because the tip of the tongue goes in the same place for both [t] and [ɛ]. Also try singing "blow," "clear," and "glory," combining the initial consonants into one efficient consonant cluster.*

## Voiced versus unvoiced consonants

Unvoiced consonants do not involve vocal fold vibration—they are produced by breath passing through the open glottis, with the sound shaped by the tongue, lips, teeth, and jaw. In contrast, voiced consonants carry pitch and some can be sustained.

An unvoiced consonant cluster that receives insufficient attention is "wh" (e.g., as in "where"). In speaking, "wear" and "where" are not differentiated, but it is necessary to do so in singing. Shape the mouth like a puckered [u] as for [w] and increase exhalation to get the breath to rush through the lips to make the [h] portion of the sound.

Some voiced and unvoiced consonants are produced using the articulators in the same way and can therefore be thought of in pairs. Consider [b] and [p]. Both are formed by closing the lips and quickly opening them. [p] is unvoiced and [b] is voiced but the lips are used in the same way. Table 6.1 lists example pairs of voiced and unvoiced consonants. A more comprehensive table is in Appendix A.

Both solo and ensemble singers can use knowledge of voiced and unvoiced pairs to great benefit. For example, when ending on the word "praise," an unvoiced [s] can make a choir sound like hissing snakes. By using [z] instead, the word would be completed on a sung pitch, pronouncing it more accurately and producing a more pleasing sound.

Sometimes a word clearly calls for a voiced consonant, but singers unwittingly use an unvoiced consonant because they lack good breath control.

## When to use an unvoiced consonant even though a voiced consonant is indicated

Even when the lyrics indicate a voiced consonant, using the unvoiced version can sometimes be helpful. For example, when singing "joy," the unvoiced consonant "ch" can be used to add emphasis and make the word sound more joyful!

Unvoiced consonants can also be helpful when entering on a high pitch. It is very difficult to coordinate glottal closure and airflow simultaneously on a high pitch. If airflow is started on the unvoiced version, the breath is already moving when the pitch needs to be sung.

| Voiced | Unvoiced |
|---|---|
| [v] | [f] |
| [g] | [k] |
| [d] | [t] |
| [z] | [s] |
| [b] | [p] |
| "j" (juice) | "ch" (choice) |

**Table 6.1 Examples of voiced and unvoiced consonants**

## Additional considerations for the voiced consonants l, m, n, ng ([ŋ])

Voiced consonants [l], [m], [n], and "ng" ([ŋ]) can be sung with long duration. The same is true of "r" (addressed separately, below).

Some singers, particularly amateur choral singers, close too quickly from the preceding vowel to these sustainable consonants. For example, when singing "moon," singers may give insufficient length to the [u] vowel by shifting too quickly to [n].

Nonetheless, for effect, a conductor or solo singer may want to give additional duration to one of these consonants, particularly when they end a phrase. (Singers should not, however, reduce the vowel length to accomplish this.) For example, extending [n] in "amen" will make the ending seem less abrupt. The key is to be conscious about circumstances and reasons for giving additional duration to these consonants. The danger is in extending them all the time.

- The use of additional duration also depends upon the musical genre. "Popular" music is more likely to involve extended duration voiced consonants than is "classical" music.

## "r"—a particularly problematic voiced consonant for singers

"r" has many IPA symbols depending on its pronunciation. To avoid unnecessary complexity, we use "r" when referring to a variety of pronunciations, but are specific in labeling the method of production (see Appendix A for specific IPA symbols). The major forms of "r" are:

- **Prevocal retroflex "r."** To sing "red" with a pre-vocal "r," start with the jaw closed and the tip of the tongue curled back (the retroflex position). Move quickly to the subsequent vowel.
- **Ending retroflex "r."** This is commonly used by English speakers at the end of words such as "river," and is often referred to as the "American r." The jaw is closed but not as much as for the prevocal "r." Again, the tongue curls backward.
- **Flipped "r."** Flipping is almost like singing "vedy" in place of "very." The difference is that the tongue touches the alveolar ridge (the raised area on the roof of the mouth behind the top front teeth) more quickly and with less firm contact than when singing "d." Only one contact with the ridge is made.
- **Rolled (trilled) "r."** The tongue is placed on the alveolar ridge and a fairly high breath pressure causes the tongue to flutter.

*Singers who have trouble with a rolled "r"' should try to form a "d" repeatedly with the tip of the tongue against the hard palate (just behind the alveolar ridge). Next, preface the "d" with a quick "h" or an accelerated breath exhalation. The rolled "r" requires higher than normal airflow to sustain it, but when singing, the duration of the roll is very short and should not have much impact on breath management.*

### *Singing "r" in North American English*

A flipped "r" can be used at the beginning of a word (e.g., "praise" and "raise"). In popular music, a prevocal retroflex "r" is more appropriate.

A rolled "r" can be used for dramatic emphasis on an initial "r" (e.g., "ring") and is appropriate in art song and oratorio literature. Singers who cannot form a rolled "r" can use a flipped "r" instead.

At or near the end of words (e.g., "river" and "word") the commonly used retroflex "r" creates a large cavity just behind the lower incisors due to the tongue tip curling back. Using the retroflex "r" dramatically lowers the frequency of the third formant, creating a dull sound. (Some people also form this by placing the back of the tongue on the roof of the mouth, creating a rather guttural "r"). Use of the retroflex "r" should be avoided, except, again, in some popular music.

- Vennard (1967) has good advice about handling this issue: concentrate on making the "r" at the end of a word silent. You will still sound it very slightly, but not create the unpleasant retroflex "r" (e.g., not "riverrr" but rather something in between "rivuh" and "rivah").

### *Singing "r" in Italian*

Here are useful rules for forming "r" when singing Italian:

- An "r" between two vowels is flipped.
- An "r" next to a consonant is rolled.
- A final "r" should be rolled.
- Never use a retroflex "r."

In Latin, "r" is never retroflex. A flipped or slightly rolled "r" is appropriate.

### *Singing "r" in German*

In German, the use of a flipped or *slightly* rolled "r" at the beginning of a word (e.g., reitet) is appropriate. When "r" occurs at the end of a German word (e.g., sicher) leave it nearly silent as in English.

Some English-speaking singers get carried away with the rolled [r] when singing German, rendering their sound unnatural. The German and French guttural "r" is not used in singing except in popular or folk music because resonance is reduced.

## Consonant exercises

### Nasal consonants with an open jaw

*Hang-gun-num-ee: On one pitch, move through the vowels quickly to sustain each nasal consonant ([ŋ], [n], [m]), finishing on the [i] vowel. Sustain the consonants shown in blue. Singing "hang" initially will help to open the jaw. Be sure to maintain that open jaw space as you sing the remainder of the exercise.*

## Singing consonants quickly

*Hold your dominant arm in front of you and imagine you are holding a wide paintbrush in your hand with a wall in front of you. Paint a horizontal brush stroke on the "wall," moving from left to right and then changing direction quickly. Do this several times. Now sing [ta] while "painting,"' with the consonant pronounced quickly on the change of direction and the vowel sustained during the "painting." Vary the consonant and vowel.*

This exercise also assists singing a legato line.

## For kids and everyone! Echo consonants

*Choose a group of either voiced or unvoiced consonants, e.g., [p], [t], [k]. Speak the consonants with a variety of rhythms and have singers echo these back. Increase and decrease the speed.*

## For kids and everyone! Efficient consonants

Make up nursery rhyme style phrases. Begin by speaking, then move to a variety of melodic patterns. Here are some examples:

*Efficient [m]—"Many mumbling mice, making merry music in the moonlight, mighty nice!"*

*Efficient [b]—"Baby bee, baby bee, beautiful baby bumble bee."*

*Efficient [t] and [l]— Try saying "tele" (as in telephone) over and over concentrating on forming both the "t" and the "l" in the same place (tongue just behind the front top teeth). Return the tongue quickly back to its resting place for the vowel. This is fairly easy because the tip of the tongue goes in the same place for both [t] and [ɛ]. Also try singing "blow," "clear," and "glory," combining the initial consonants into one efficient consonant cluster.*

## Singing "y" (IPA [j]) correctly

*Sing the German word "ja" on a descending triad (major or minor—ja, ja, ja). Imagine the initial consonant to be [i] and move quickly to [a].*

## Emphasizing initial voiced and unvoiced consonants for effect

*Choose a voiced consonant and vary how long you sing it. Try singing "mother" by varying the length of [m] from a very quick enunciation to up to four beats.*

*Try a more challenging variation by changing the length of unvoiced consonants such as [s] as in "soft" and [k] in "cool."*

### Ending retroflex (American) "r"

*Sing "far" with an "American r" (farrrr). Note how the jaw is somewhat closed and the tongue curls back slightly to form the "American r." Then sing "far" keeping the jaw open. First sing "fa, fa, fa," and then sing "far, far, far" imagining a very subtle, short "r" at the end. Concentrate on keeping the tip of the tongue at the base of the lower incisors. Do not close the jaw or let the tongue curl backward to help avoid singing an "American r."*

# Section II: Enhancements of Vocal Technique

# Chapter 7: Vibrato

Vibrato is an oscillation in pitch, usually involving variation of about a half step (a quarter step on either side of the pitch). Vibrato also involves some variation in amplitude (Vennard, 1967; Sundberg, 1994). Vibrato is an important aspect of mature sound because it contributes to perceived richness of tone. Good vibrato is consistent and controlled.

Seashore conducted the first comprehensive studies on the perception of vibrato in the early part of the 20th century. He concluded, "Much of the most beautiful vibrato is below the threshold for vibrato hearing and is perceived merely as tone quality" (Seashore, 1938, p. 46). Vennard (1967) concurs, noting that the listener hears only the mean pitch, and the variations in pitch are interpreted by the audience in terms of timbre—enhancing perceived tonal quality. More recent studies confirm these findings (Sundberg, 1995).

## Vibrato is a natural phenomenon

Vibrato is a natural consequence of a singer developing proper breath support and learning to relax the vocal apparatus. Richard Miller (1994) observes that vibrato also requires proper contact between the vocal folds—with a breathy method of production making vibrato unlikely. By the same token, a pressed method of production will not facilitate vibrato. Thus, lack of vibrato can indicate poor vocal technique.

- McKinney (2005) has a similar perspective, noting that vibrato is absent in breathy, strained, or harsh voices. This provides further evidence that lack of vibrato is indicative of less than optimal vocal technique.

Vibrato is a function of nerve impulses in the larynx that have a normal frequency of 5–8 per second. If the laryngeal area is appropriately relaxed, the laryngeal muscles will naturally pulsate in time with this frequency. Early studies showed that the cricothyroid muscles are most involved with pulsations in pitch and amplitude (Mason & Zemlin, 1966), though Titze et al. (2002b) make a convincing case for involvement of the thyroarytenoids as well.

## Vibrato is appropriate for most music

We believe that vibrant singing in most solo and choral music is best for both audiences and singers. Exceptions might be made for artistic reasons for certain types of music (see below), but "straight tone" should be the exception rather than the rule.

- Vibrato is best for audiences because of the aforementioned improvement in tonal quality.
- Vibrato is best for audiences because it improves intonation. Titze (2008a) says that muscles controlling pitch experience irregular tremors that make it impossible to control pitch well with "straight tone" production. Vibrato creates a more regular pulsation in pitch allowing for a more stable perceived fundamental frequency.
- Vibrato creates improved perceived choral intonation as outlined below.
- Vibrato is best for singers because they use optimal methods of vocal production. Singers who are asked to sing "straight tone" typically use a more pressed or more breathy form of production to eliminate their natural vibrato.
- Suppressing vibrato is tiring. Large and Iwata (1976) state that vibrato involves an alternating contraction and relaxation of the laryngeal muscles. Vibrato thus helps to prevent vocal fatigue.

Nonetheless, considerable controversy exists about the use of vibrato, particularly in choral music, but also in solo music of certain periods. This controversy is addressed later in the chapter.

## Desirable vibrato rate and range

Different sources recommend different "ideal" vibrato rates (number of fluctuations per second), but the vast majority fall within the range of 5–8 fluctuations per second, varying in extent from a quarter step to a half step above and below the sung pitch.

- Richard Miller (1996) argues that a pleasing vibrato rate is in the range of 6–8 fluctuations per second. Above eight, the voice sounds tremulous. Below six, it begins to approach a wobble because pitch variations are discernible as separate notes, creating an unpleasant distraction. Usually, slow vibrato rates accompany wider pitch excursions, which are also disagreeable to the listener. Miller also says that pitch variation should not exceed a semi-tone (a quarter step above and a quarter step below the sung pitch).

- Seashore (1938) found that great artists of his day had a rate between 5.9 and 7.8 pulsations per second, with most in the range of 6.3–6.9 per second.
- Vennard (1967) says 6–7 per second is most common, with total variation of up to a half step. Nonetheless, rates as low as 5 (Vennard's own rate), and as high as 8–10, are not necessarily objectionable. But rates of 8–10 per second in singers with normal vibrato are typically associated with short-duration, high intensity passages. Singers who are consistently in the 8–10 range would likely be perceived to have an unpleasant tremolo.

In recent years the acceptable vibrato rate appears to have decreased. Titze (2008a) argues that contemporary audiences prefer a vibrato rate in the range of 4.5–6.5 oscillations per second with an extent not exceeding a quarter step above and below the desired pitch. Corroborating this is a recent study of audience perception, which found that the highest rated singers had a consistent, moderate vibrato averaging 5.4 oscillations per second. Consistency was evidenced by minimal variation in oscillations per second and in pitch deviation (Robison, Bounous, & Bailey, 1994).

Note that if the vibrato rate is in the range of 4.5 to 5.0 oscillations per second, the variation in pitch should be even smaller than a quarter step. Otherwise the pitch deviations become noticeable, eliminating the psychological fusion of the pitch variation into the mean pitch. Sundberg's (1999) review of research on audience perception suggests, for example, that extent of variation should be on the order of plus or minus one-tenth of a step for optimal fused perception to occur at a rate of 5 oscillations per second.

## Vibrato problems

### Singers without vibrato

A person who has only begun to sing regularly may not have vibrato initially but should develop it over time. A person who sings regularly and lacks vibrato usually has one or more of the following problems:

- Imitation of a poor tonal model
- Breathy or glottal onset
- Incorrect breath pressure
- Tension in the vocal mechanism
- High larynx position

Sometimes singers lack vibrato because they are imitating the sound of a popular recording artist who sings without vibrato. In such cases, it may be helpful to give singers a sense of what vibrato feels like. For example, one might try moaning like a ghost or mimicking an opera singer. For the reasons outlined above, young singers should be encouraged to develop consistent vibrato even though some popular genres do not feature it.

That said, vibrato is most often inhibited by breathy or glottal onset and/or tension in the vocal mechanism. Coordinated onset is critical to create the optimal amount of closure in the vocal folds necessary for vibrato.

Another difficulty is hypo or hyper breath pressure—either too much or too little breath energy. Many singers need time to learn how much breath energy is required for their voice to resonate fully and vibrantly, and it can be especially difficult to ascertain from within a choir. Singers with insufficient breath support, for example, are unable to hear themselves clearly in a choral context. Steady reminders and exercises will help such singers to build their understanding and ability to sing with correct breath pressure and resonance, often resulting in the development of vibrato in the tone.

Freedom from tension throughout the entire vocal tract is also critical. With tension, the laryngeal muscles cannot relax sufficiently for natural pulsation to occur. A high larynx position is also associated with lack of vibrato (Shipp, Doherty, & Haglund, 1990). This is likely due to the fact that a high larynx is associated with a more pressed style of phonation, creating tension that is not conducive to vibrato.

Singers must take care to avoid forcing vibrato through artificial methods like breath pulsation or throat manipulation. These methods create a vibrato that varies excessively in pitch and is inconsistent. Furthermore, artificially induced vibrato involves high levels of tension and energy expenditure.

Vibrato is thus something that develops over time as singers learn to use coordinated onset and eliminate tension in vocal production.

### Singers with inconsistent vibrato

Some singers exhibit vibrato only at the end of a phrase or on sustained pitches. Inconsistent vibrato occurs for two major reasons:

- Some singers may use a glottal onset and/or may carry too much laryngeal tension during the phrase, relaxing only at the end or on longer pitches. Such singers are capable of producing vibrato, but they need to attend to the tension-producing factors that are inhibiting it during most of the vocal phrase.

- Other singers may have excessive breath flow during the passage, slowing down the vibrato rate as they relax on longer pitches or toward the end of the phrase.

In choruses blending is affected if some singers have vibrato only at the ends of phrases or on longer pitches. A related problem is a more wide-ranging vibrato at the end of a phrase. This is particularly important to avoid in, for example, Baroque music where a narrow vibrato may be desirable toward the end of a section to make chord tuning apparent.

Some singers may have a normal vibrato that becomes problematic with higher and/or louder portions of a phrase. This situation often results from a lack of breath support for those who exhibit wobble. For those with a tremolo, it is likely due to excess laryngeal tension and airflow.

Vibrato can also be inconsistent due to delayed onset of pitch variation. Onset of vibrato is faster with an open pharynx, raised soft palate, and comfortably low larynx. There is also some evidence that vibrato rate is more consistent when this technique is employed (Mitchell & Kenny, 2004).

Finally, as noted in Chapter 2 on breathing, use of abdominal muscles to control expiration is important for consistent vibrato.

### Curing the wobble

Undoubtedly problematic, both in choral and solo singing, wobble is characterized by a slow vibrato rate that may also vary dramatically in pitch. Wobble can result from:

- Lack of proper breath support, stemming from improper breathing technique, aging, and/or general physical inactivity that affect the abdominal and rib musculature. Weak abdominal muscles may be the prime problem. In a study of trained singers' ability to control vibrato rate, participants stated that they could increase the vibrato rate with more breath support and decrease it with less support (Dromey, Carter, & Hopkin, 2003).
- Slackness in the vocal folds that provides insufficient resistance to the flow of air (R. Miller, 1996). This slackness can be a consequence of aging, or lack of attention to how tightly the vocal folds are brought together.
- A heavy style of production. Such tactics include artificially depressing the larynx to create a darker sound and carrying lower register production (chest voice) too high with a pressed mode of vocal fold vibration.
- Poor condition of the laryngeal muscles due to lack of use (e.g., those who sing only once or twice a week). Lack of use is particularly prob-

lematic for older singers who also experience loss of muscle tone due to aging. Titze et al. (2002b) note that poor tone in the laryngeal muscles increases the time a muscle takes to contract, which could account for a reduction in rate of 1–2 pulsations per second. Such individuals can reduce their wobble by performing vocal exercises and by singing at lower dynamic levels when at the extremes of their range—less mass of the thyroarytenoid muscle is involved when singing softly.

- McKinney (2005) concurs that wobble in many amateur choral singers is due to a lack of vocal and physical exercise; they may only sing at choir practice and at performances. Singers should vocalize daily, even if only for 10 minutes a day, to keep their support and laryngeal muscles in good shape.

#### *Additional causes of and cures for the wobble*

Some additional thoughts about causes and cures for the wobble include:

- The cricothyroid muscles of the larynx and certain jaw muscles interconnect (Mason and Zemlin, 1966). If the jaw is somewhat tensed, it can tremble in time with pulsations in the cricothyroid muscles. Since the jaw muscles have substantial mass, this interconnection will inevitably slow the vibrato rate, producing a wobble.
- In a master class, Renée Fleming noted that a slow vibrato (in this case not involving wide pitch excursions) may occur when a singer involves the tongue and portions of the pharynx in vibrato.

### *Basic exercises to combat the wobble*

*Exercises to combat wobble include onset exercises to ensure a coordinated onset. Slides extending to a fifth can be employed to make sure abdominal support is consistent throughout phonation. Physical exercise of the abdominal muscles (as outlined in Chapter 2 on breathing) is also important. The sibilant exercise for breathing from Chapter 2 will help as well. These exercises are exceptionally important as singers age (see Chapter 13 on changing voices).*

The old saying "use it or lose it" definitely applies to singing! Keeping the muscles supple and singing more than just a couple of times a week will go a long way toward fending off the wobble.

### Dealing with tremolo

A tremolo involves vibrato in the range of 8–10 fluctuations in pitch per second. Many singers who exhibit tremolo have a strident, harsh sound usually caused by excessive breath pressure and laryngeal tension.

Tremolo is more common in younger singers and may be related to artificial attempts to create vibrato. For many singers with tremolo, the jaw and tongue exhibit a corresponding rapid shake (R. Miller, 1996).

General muscular tension may also cause tremolo (Titze et al., 2002b). Tense muscles respond rapidly in so-called "twitch mode."

*Exercises to free a voice from tremolo can include breathing exercises with a special focus on relaxing the airways during inhalation. We also recommend onset exercises to eliminate glottal attacks from Chapter 3 on initiation, creation, and release of sound, and the tension reduction methods from Chapter 14.*

Singers with vibrato problems (whether they be wobble or tremolo) can also benefit from voice training. Longitudinal studies have shown that voice training results in a lowering of vibrato rates for those whose vibrato rate is initially high, and raises vibrato rates for those whose rate is initially low. In addition, there is an increase in vibrato consistency (Mürbe, Zahnert, Kuhlisch, & Sundberg, 2007).

The bottom line is that the best sounding vibrato results from good vocal technique. Singers with poor technique will have inconsistent, wobbly, or tremulous vibrato. When singers are encouraged to attend carefully to proper technique, there should be no need to eliminate vibrato from their sound.

## The vibrato controversy

Controversy about vibrato in choral singing (and in solo singing of music from certain musical periods) has a long history. Conductors who consistently ask singers to eliminate vibrato tend to fall into two camps.

- One group thinks that vibrato is generally undesirable. Such conductors are sensitive to and take particular notice of the pitch excursion in vibrato and therefore seek to eliminate it. Or, they may have singers with a wobble or tremolo who stand out and threaten choral blend.
- The other camp thinks that vibrato should be eliminated in certain types of music. Some conductors aim to eliminate vibrato in performances of Renaissance and Baroque music because they believe that singers during those periods did not sing with vibrato. For some modern music (e.g., barbershop and some 20th century music such as Pärt) they seek to eliminate vibrato so as to achieve a particular vocal color.

### Perception of vibrato as generally undesirable

Conductors who consider vibrato undesirable in all choral singing often attend subconsciously to upper and lower excursions in pitch and are unaware that their audience members do not. As discussed above, the audience perceives vibrato within the normal range to create a rich tone and hear the pitch as the average of the high and low extent of variation.

It is also possible that such conductors may have had experiences with singers with a wobble or tremolo. The solution should not be to suppress vibrato in all members of the ensemble. Rather, wobble/tremolo should be addressed with those problematic singers, as outlined in the section above on solutions to vibrato problems.

Finally, some theorize that because the vibratos of singers in a group will not be in perfect phase with one another, good intonation is unobtainable. This assertion is misguided because the ear perceives the pitch to be the average of the high and low values, regardless of whether vibrato rates are synchronized.

- Vennard (1967) notes that in opera choruses composed of superb singers, all sing with vibrato and there is no question of intonation problems caused by vibrato.
- Furthermore, Alderson (1979) states that precisely because individual singers have different vibrato rates (and hence are not in phase with each other), they will tend to balance each other out and thus contribute to the perception of vibrato as richness of tone.
- In any case, Jers and Ternström (2004) observe that the choral singers in their study (singing with vibrato) were able to synchronize somewhat the pitch modulation of their vibrato.

If vibrato is minimal, it is easier to tell if a choral group is in tune because the smoothing aspect of vibrato makes it harder to hear dissonant "beats." Thus, in some cases a group may wish to use minimal vibrato to show the audience that they are in tune on a final chord (e.g., in barbershop music or Baroque music). Nonetheless, demonstrating good intonation to the audience isn't the primary goal of choral singing. Instead, the key is that the audience *perceives* a choral group to be in tune.

Note that regardless of a choral director's terminology, scientific studies confirm that there is no such thing as a truly "straight" tone because there is always some variation in pitch and/or amplitude. "Straight tone" is only the listener's perception and is not physiologically attainable (see Titze, 2008a; Walker, 2006).

### *Endorsements of vibrato in choral singing*

Numerous vocal authorities are consistent in their endorsement of vibrato in most choral singing:

- Robert Shaw (Blocker, 2004) argues that while a wobbling vibrato is destructive of blend, "... vibrato is as present in beautiful singing as it is in beautiful string playing" (p. 87).
- Vennard (1967) says, "When I hear concerts of choirs whose conductors have worked to eliminate [vibrato], I miss this vibrancy. It is true that they blend like one voice, and they make beautiful pianissimos. But this 'one' voice is breathy to my ears, and their fortissimos never thrill me... When there is an assignment for a solo voice in the group, it is usually disappointing, for this weak production is inadequate" (p. 205).
- McKinney (2005) argues vigorously for use of vibrato in a choral setting: "Vibrato is a natural concomitant of beautiful and expressive tone... There have been various movements, especially in the choral field, that have decried the use of vibrato in any form and have advocated the straight tone. Fortunately ... it has been classified not only as necessary for beauty of tone but also for physiological reasons" (p. 197).

### Perception of vibrato as inappropriate in certain types of music

Repertoire can be a guide as to how much vibrato is desirable, and some solo singers and ensembles sing with more vibrancy than others. That said, a well-focused, in-tune sound with a moderate vibrato is often fully acceptable, even in repertoire that might traditionally be thought to need a "straighter" sound. Certainly, singers should learn to access and utilize a variety of colors and techniques within their own voices. But all singers should sing in a healthy, vibrant manner most of the time, reserving less vibrant singing for special effect.

A more detailed discussion of vibrato in the Baroque (1600–1750) and Renaissance (1400/1450–1600) periods is presented below. Our conclusion from analyzing the historical literature is that vibrato was likely prevalent, but that wide-ranging vibrato was avoided, just as we prefer today.

## Vibrato in early music

The extent to which vibrato was used in Renaissance and Baroque music is unclear because no recordings exist from that time. We do, however, have historical commentary about vibrato as well as intriguing information about organ stops designed to imitate the human voice during these periods.

Music historians who contend vibrato was absent in early music make one or more of the following arguments:

- Musicians writing about vibrato described it as objectionable; from this they infer that vibrato was generally unused. When used, it was only as an occasional ornament.
- Boys sang the high parts and did not have vibrato.
- Singing took place in small venues or resonant spaces such as churches and did not require vibrato.

## Evidence from Renaissance and Baroque writers concerning vibrato

Writers in the 16th to 18th centuries used inconsistent terms for vocal ornaments and for vibrato. (The mere fact that there was commentary about vibrato suggests that it was present in singers' voices.) Some vocal authorities have misinterpreted criticism about trills or successive, rapid re-articulations of the same pitch (now called a "trillo") to be about vibrato. See Stark (2003) for a particularly detailed analysis of these and other vibrato issues.

A number of writers recommended that singers have vibrato, suggesting that vibrato was employed and viewed as desirable in early music:

- In 1598 Quitschreiber wrote, ". . . one sings best with a quivering voice . . ." (cited in Moens-Haenen, 1988, p. 158).
- In 1614 Friderici said, "The students should, from the beginning, become accustomed to singing with a refined naturalness, and, where possible, with the voice trembling . . . or pulsating . . ." (cited in Stark, 2003, p. 129).
- Michael Praetorius, a famous Baroque composer and musician, listed the desirable characteristics of singers in 1619. He wrote, ". . . first, a singer must have a nice, pleasant vibrato . . ." (Praetorius, 2004, p. 215).
- Benigne de Bacilly (1625–1690) called vibrato a "gift of nature" (cited in Sell, 2005, p. 12).

At the same time there were objections to the trillo (e.g., Vicentino as well as Finck in the mid-16th century; see Stark, 2003). Finck was particularly dismissive of the trillo, ". . . several who make the coloratura of the throat not dissimilar to the bleating of a she-goat, make a serious mistake; for no pleasure, nor distinction, nor suitability of embellishment is heard, but only rumbling and a confused and ugly racket is heard" (cited in MacClintock, 1979, p. 64). Clearly, this is not an objection to vibrato.

The following recommendations for instrumentalists provide further evidence of vocal vibrato in early music. The recommendations urge both string and woodwind instruments to imitate the human voice by using vibrato:

- In 1636 Mersenne (1957) wrote, "of all the artifices one esteems most, that which best represents the natural, it seems that one must not refuse the prize to the viol, which imitates the voice in all its modulations . . ." (p. 254).
- In 1535 Ganassi (1959) urged wind players to imitate the human voice by producing vibrato through variation of breath pressure.
- Rousseau (1687), who wrote books on both singing and the viol, stated that vibrato is natural to the voice and that viol players should endeavor to imitate the human voice by swinging one finger on the fret.

Moderate vibrato was distinctly preferred by some authors.

- Sanford (1979, p. 9) quotes Herbst (1642): "That he have a beautiful, lovely, trembling and shaking voice (. . . but with particular moderation)."
- In 1592 Zacconi commended singers who have vibrant voices but said that "it should be slight and pleasing; for if it is exaggerated and forced, it tires and annoys" (cited in R. Miller, 2006, p. 93).
- Mozart detested excessive variation in pitch but prized a more natural vibrato: "The human voice vibrates naturally—but in such a way—to such a degree that it all sounds beautiful—it is the nature of the voice. We imitate such effects not only on wind instruments, but also with violins—even on the clavier—but as soon as you go beyond the natural limits, it no longer sounds beautiful—because it is contrary to nature" (cited in Spaethling, 2000, p. 157).
- In the mid-17th century Bernhard complained about "tremulo," which he compared to the singing of the elderly (Bernhard, 1973). Today we could call this a wobble; it is not normal vibrato.

To summarize, many singers of early music apparently sang with vibrato—it is after all, a natural phenomenon that is imitated by instrumentalists precisely because of the beauty that it imparts to sound. Like today, a wide-ranging vibrato was viewed as undesirable.

## Evidence concerning the Vox Humana and Voce Umana organ stops

As implied by their names, the Vox Humana and Voce Umana organ stops are designed to imitate the human voice (Bush & Kassel, 2006). The Vox Humana stop in most older organs uses reed pipes that resonate at slightly different frequencies, creating an undulating, vibrato-like effect. In Italy the Voce Umana (or Piffaro) stop usually involves a set of flute pipes that are mistuned from the principal flute pipes to obtain a similar vibrato effect. The vibrato effect is improved by use of an accessory stop known as the Tremulant, which causes the wind pressure to vary. (This improvement is particularly true for the Vox Humana.) Variation in wind pressure induces both frequency and amplitude variations, as in the human voice.

- The value of the Tremulant in improving the vibrato quality of the Vox Humana is illustrated by the comments of a Baroque organ builder who installed a Tremulant to be used with the existing Vox Humana on an organ in Dublin, Ireland, in 1696–99. Of his installation, John Baptiste Cuvillie wrote, "... and to make it appear like a human voice I added a Tremblen [Tremulant] stop to it, and to make it the more natural ..." (see Boydell, 1992, p.20, and Bicknell, 1996, p. 189).

If singers in the Renaissance and Baroque periods did not sing with vibrato, we would expect the Vox Humana and Voce Umana stops to be included only in organs built after 1750–60. The above quote from 1696–97 and our review of the organ literature indicates that both the Vox Humana and the Tremulant can be traced at least as far back as 1537 when the builders of an organ at the Church of Notre Dame in Alençon, France installed both a Vox Humana stop (*Voix Humane* in French and an accessory Tremulant (*Tremblent*)—see Owen (1999). Audsley (1905) even states that the Voce Umana was incorporated into three Italian organs between 1470 and 1480 in Bologna and Lucca.

Sources as diverse as Burney (1775), Gregoir (1865), Bicknell (1996), May and Stauffer (2000), Owen (1999), Boeringer (1989), Heustis (2010) and Yearsly (1998) list numerous organs that were constructed with Vox Humana or Voce Umana stops (and Tremulants) between 1548 and 1750 in Germany, the Netherlands, England, Ireland, Spain, France, Italy, and the United States. Among these is an organ built at Naumberg, Germany in 1743–1746, whose stop list was influenced by Bach (May & Stauffer, 2000).

To summarize, the existence of the Vox Humana/Voce Umana on many organs in the Renaissance and Baroque periods provides important evidence that vibrato was used and admired in these periods.

### Did the boys who sang high parts have no vibrato?

Boys and men sang all parts in early church choirs and in some cases in secular performances. Some opposed to using vibrato in performances of early music assume that boys would not have sung with vibrato, and thus, early music should be performed without it (at least in the alto and soprano parts). Many countries on the continent of Europe with long choral traditions continue to utilize this tonal model. Some North American choral conductors have been heavily influenced by this tradition.

We would argue that the idea that boys cannot sing with vibrato is a misconception. Boys who received training and sang regularly likely developed vibrato over time. Henderson (1979) argues that in fact, beautiful boy soprano voices have a *natural* (her italics) vibrato. This vibrato will not sound exactly like adult vibrato, but it is vibrato nonetheless. Henderson therefore believes that adults should not be asked to produce a straight tone for Baroque music and argues forcefully that this can be disastrous for their voices.

- Phillips (1996) concurs that children who sing with proper vocal technique will naturally develop vibrato, just as do adults who sing with proper technique. He says, "Vibrato is not taught to the students, but rather is the outcome of vocal training that frees the voice, allowing it to pulse naturally" (p. 266).

### Did small or resonant spaces of the Renaissance and Baroque periods mean that vibrato was not present in early music?

It is important to distinguish between vibrato and resonance in early music. Some object to vibrato on the basis that early venues were typically resonant churches or more intimate chamber spaces that would not require a resonant voice. Thus, projection of sound was not so critical. But vibrato and resonance are separate issues. Performance space in the Renaissance and Baroque eras has nothing to do with vibrato, only with the need for resonance. A singer can easily lack vibrato (e.g., through use of pressed phonation) but produce high sound levels and vice versa. It is worth noting, however, that modern performance spaces in which early music is performed are often large—singers lacking resonance will be at a disadvantage when performing early music in such spaces.

Sopranos who do not use vibrato will be at a particular disadvantage in larger spaces since they will often use a somewhat pressed form of production to eliminate the vibrato. As outlined previously, pressed forms of production dramatically reduce the amplitude of the fundamental frequency. But sopranos depend upon a strong fundamental frequency at the upper end of their range to be heard well—they cannot depend upon the singer's formant in this region of their voices. Singing with vibrato is essential for sopranos in larger spaces (particularly those that are not resonant), unless electronic amplification is used.

## Singing with less vibrato in the choral setting

Most choral singers will be asked to sing with less vibrato at some point, whether with a conductor who prefers a "straight" sound at all times or just for certain repertoire.

Conductors should consider the way they talk about and refer to vibrato with their choirs. Words that are used can have a huge impact on the sound the choir achieves and the way they go about achieving it. Conductors use a variety of terms to refer to a desired amount of vibrancy. Christopher Jackson (2007) identifies three that are most relevant: "straight tone," "*senza* vibrato," and "stylistically appropriate vibrato" (p. 31). As we have noted above, the term "straight tone" can have negative connotations for singers as they imagine producing a sound completely devoid of vibrato, despite the fact that this is physiologically impossible! Instead, we suggest asking for a "narrow vibrato" (rather than Jackson's *senza vibrato* term, which communicates "no vibrato") or "stylistically appropriate vibrato," depending upon what is desired. Obviously most choirs will require a more detailed explanation of the conductor's view of stylistically appropriate vibrato.

Scott McCoy (2011) has found through EGG (electroglottograph) measurements in his voice science classes that when asked to sing without vibrato, singers achieve this in three ways:

- Pressing the vocal folds together more firmly
- Increasing airflow through the glottis by decreasing vocal fold pressure
- Making no apparent change in laryngeal adjustments. These singers seem to sing with or without vibrato without noticeably changing their mode of production. Perhaps the changes are so subtle that EGG measurements cannot detect them.

No single technique will allow singers to sing easily without vibrato, but pressing the vocal folds together more firmly or increasing airflow are methods that singers should explore. In addition, all of the elements of excellent vocal technique need to be involved and therefore monitored and supported by conductors and voice teachers. Singers should be encouraged to experiment with their own voices to discover how they can most easily achieve a sound with reduced vibrato.

### Vibrato in barbershop music

Barbershop music is often cited as a style where no vibrato is desirable, in part because barbershop groups may want to impress the audience with their tuning. As noted in this chapter, correct intonation is more apparent when vibrato is not used because it is easier to hear the dissonant "beats" when a group of singers is out of tune.

Nonetheless, even in barbershop quartets, vibrato creates a desirable vocal color. There is, however, a preference for a moderate vibrato that does not vary excessively in rate or pitch, a perspective that applies to all types of music.

The following observation about vibrato is from the youth chorus festival judging system of the Barbershop Harmony Society: "Vibrato is a normal phenomenon of proper breath management. In barbershop quartet singing, some vibrato in the voice, especially the lead voice, can be very effective in enhancing the emotional content of the music. However, too high a vibrato rate (especially in choruses) or excessive pitch or volume variation will erode ensemble sound" (Barbershop.org, 2010).

## Concluding thoughts about vibrato

We strongly suggest allowing voices to do what they do naturally—to sing with vibrato. The problem usually facing teachers and conductors is malfunctioning vibrato, rather than vibrato itself. For singers with vibrato problems, consult the information about causes and solutions in this chapter. Teachers can, of course, work with singers individually to resolve their vibrato problems; conductors should work with them in small group sessions. If necessary, conductors should refer them to a voice teacher for vocal rehabilitation. Asking everyone to sing without vibrato all the time is not the solution.

Even aside from the evidence concerning vibrato in early music, singers should sing in a way that is best for their voices and for the pleasure of the audience. If choral conductors consistently ask singers to eliminate vibrato, most will have to use either pressed or breathy phonation, neither of which is good for long-term vocal health and development. Moreover, expressive, beautiful sound is lost.

Of course conductors can choose the tonal color that they desire for their ensemble and for specific repertoire choices. But singers will be more receptive to requests for reduced vibrato if conductors demonstrate an understanding of how the voice works and acknowledge the vocal demands they are placing on chorus members:

- Avoid just saying, "sing with straight tone." Rather, suggest a tonal color with an explanation of specific ways to achieve it.
- If requesting reduced vibrato on high notes, rehearse those passages less frequently or an octave lower when learning the notes to avoid fatigue.
- Vowels such as [i] and [u] are particularly difficult to sing on high notes without vibrato, so be sure to modify the vowels appropriately, as outlined in Chapter 5 on vowels.
- Encourage more stagger breathing to provide vocal rest.

Singers should experiment with their own voices to find a tone color that is less vibrant for those special applications where reduced vibrato is desired. See the exercises below.

## Vibrato Exercises

### Experiencing vibrato

*Singers who lack vibrato can try singing a vowel such as [i] alternating between two pitches that are a half step apart, gradually changing pitch faster and faster until the sound dissolves into "vibrato." While this is not the same as natural vibrato, it encourages relaxed laryngeal muscles and allows singers to get a sense of what vibrato feels like.* Two starting pitches are illustrated below. You might also find it useful to start using a higher pitch such as $E_5$ for women and $E_4$ for men.

Other exercises such as moaning like a ghost or mimicking an opera singer (see above) can be used, but, in general, none of these exercises, including the one above, bring about natural vibrato. Vibrato will typically develop as singers release tension and use proper vocal technique over time. Thus, we do not recommend extensive use of these exercises.

### Singing without noticeable vibrato using good vocal technique

*Encourage singers to have good breath support, particularly abdominal muscle support. Compress the vocal folds together somewhat more tightly than is required for flow phonation but avoid fully pressed phonation. Also, vary the airflow—generally a faster flow rate will create a straighter sound.*

### *Messa di voce* exercise with and without vibrato

*Sing a messa di voce exercise (i.e., start on a vowel at a piano dynamic level; increase gradually to forte and then gradually reduce to piano). Sing first with vibrato and then without vibrato to play with the sound.* Teachers and conductors should ask singers to think about how they produced the two different tonal colors.

### Combating the wobble

The following exercises are useful for combating the wobble:

- *Onset exercises, to make sure there is a coordinated onset (Chapter 3)*
- *Slides extending to a fifth, to make sure abdominal support is consistent throughout phonation*
- *Physical exercise of the abdominal muscles as outlined in Chapter 2 on breathing*
- *The sibilant exercise for breathing in Chapter 2*

### Reducing tremolo

Exercises to free a voice from tremolo include:

- *Breathing exercises from Chapter 2 with a special focus on relaxing the airways during inhalation*

- *Onset exercises to eliminate glottal onset; see Chapter 3 on initiation, creation, and release of sound*
- *Relaxed vocal fry, which is outlined in Chapter 8 on vocal registers*
- *Tension reduction methods from Chapter 14*

# Chapter 8: Negotiation of the Vocal Registers

Abrupt changes in tonal quality may occur as singers move from one part of their range to another. While this may be desirable in certain musical genres, most soloists and choral singers dream of singing smoothly from the bottom of their range to the top. This is difficult because our vocal mechanism has distinct registers and does not operate in the same fashion at all pitches. The term "registers" parallels the use of this word with the organ, an instrument that produces different pitches and tonal qualities with different sets of pipes.

Most singers have some register transition problems, but a technically proficient singer should exhibit no register transitions—or at least none that the audience can detect! A working knowledge of vocal registers will enable singers to manage register transition issues and achieve a smoother sound. More specifically, this knowledge will help conductors, singers and teachers to:

- Understand specific pitch areas that might pose difficulties for singers depending on voice type
- Assist singers to pass through transitions smoothly by blending modes of vocal fold vibration
- Understand how vocal tract resonance adjustment can help with register transitions

Working on register transition issues during warm-ups is an essential step in enhancing singers' voices.

## What are vocal registers?

Until recently, most vocal authorities agreed that the term "vocal register" refers solely to the way in which vocal folds vibrate to produce sound. Registers cover certain portions of a singer's range, and pitches within a given register have the same general tonal quality.

This fundamental conception of registers has a long history, dating back to the famous 19th century singing teacher, Manuel P. Garcia (Henrich, 2006). Garcia, the first to observe the vocal folds using a laryngoscope, noticed that the vocal folds vibrated differently at low versus high pitches. This led him to develop the concept of vocal registers, which in turn led to an emphasis on skillful adjustments in use of laryngeal muscles to achieve register transitions.

- Contemporary studies using the electroglottograph (noninvasive electrical sensors measuring changes in vocal fold activity) provide convincing evidence of differences in vibration at different points in a singer's range (e.g., Henrich, Roubeau, & Castellengo, 2003).

Recent research has shown, however, that adjustments in the vocal tract above the glottis also contribute to successful register transition (e.g., D. Miller, 2008; Titze & Worley, 2009). Such adjustments are strongly connected to the issue of vowel modification, which prevents destabilizing crossovers of formant frequencies by important harmonics (typically, $H_1$, $H_2$, and $H_3$ are most significant). See Chapter 4 on resonance and Chapter 5 on vowels for more about such destabilizing crossovers.

## Two main registers

Vocal experts disagree about the number of registers and names for specific registers. For pedagogical purposes, though, it is possible to come to a fairly straightforward understanding of vocal registers and the differences between them. There are two registers used in most singing: the lower register (often called chest voice) and the upper register (often called head voice). There has been disagreement about whether there is a middle register, but as we will see, recent research supports the concept of mixing the lower and upper registers into what is often called middle or mixed voice (French: *voix mixte*).

### Lower register (chest voice)

At lower pitches, the vocal folds are thicker and come together firmly along a wide area (Bunch, 1995). The folds are thicker because the thyroarytenoid muscles, which largely govern pitch in this register, underlay the folds and bulge out the bottom part of the fold edge (Titze, 2000). The lower register has a higher closed quotient than does the upper register, contributing to the generally greater resonance associated with chest voice.

The term "chest voice" is often used because conductive resonance is felt most strongly in the chest at lower pitches. This term is familiar to many singers, but, as noted in Chapter 4 on resonance, the chest is not a resonating cavity that affects what is heard by the audience. Nor is the head a resonating cavity—except for the mouth, pharynx, and in the case of nasal vowels and consonants, the nasal cavities.

## Upper register (head voice)

At higher pitches sung in the upper register, the vocal folds are thinned and touch each other less firmly and over less area because the thyroarytenoids are not as involved and do not push the lower edge of the fold outward. The amplitude of the vibration (amount of vertical movement in the folds) is also less than in the lower register. In this register the cricothyroid muscles are more involved in controlling pitch.

Pitches sung in the upper register tend to have slightly lower dynamic levels and fewer high frequency harmonics. Thus, at the same pitch, the lower register sounds louder and richer to listeners than the upper register voice. This likely underlies the temptation for some singers to carry the lower register too high.

Figure 8.1 illustrates the vocal folds under conditions where thyroarytenoid control dominates versus conditions where cricothyroid control dominates.

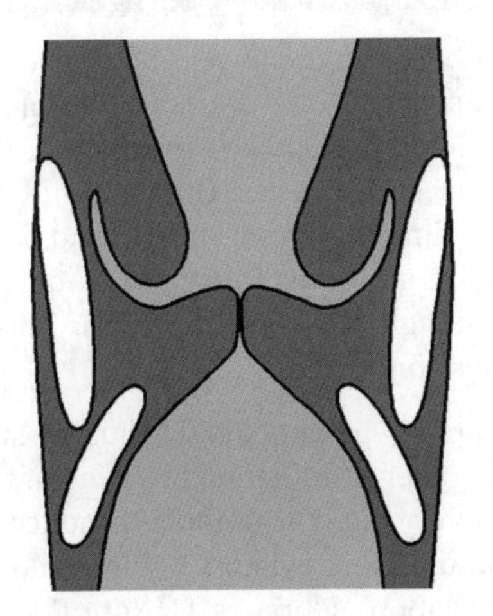

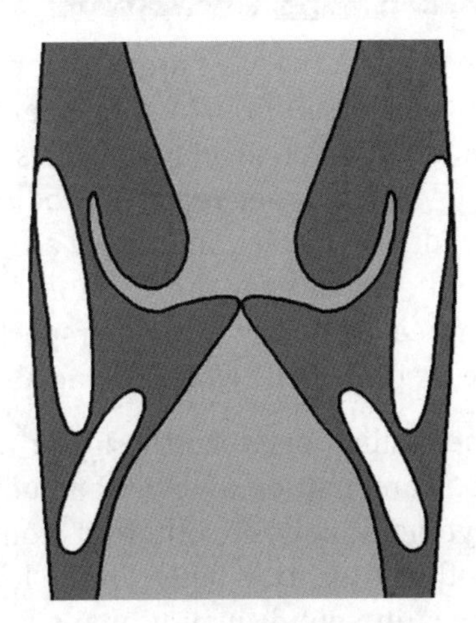

**Figure 8.1 Illustration of dominant thyroarytenoid control over vocal folds (left) versus dominant cricothyroid control over vocal folds (right)**

### *Upper register mechanism differs between men and women*

Recent research indicates that the upper register is produced somewhat differently in men than in women. Electroglottograph studies show that vocal fold vibration in men is surprisingly similar for both the lower and upper registers, whereas for women it is distinctly different (Henrich et al., 2003). In women the cricothyroids truly take control in the upper register as outlined above. In men the upper register involves shared control of the cricothyroid and thyroarytenoid muscles—the thyroarytenoid muscle continues to provide some degree of tensioning or bracing of the vocal folds even in this register (Georg, 2005). Consistent with this, Titze and Worley (2009) describe the upper register in men as a mixture of chest and falsetto registers. As such, some vocal experts view the male upper register as merely an extension of the lower register (e.g., D. Miller, 2008), rather than as a wholly separate register. Nonetheless, we still consider the male upper register to be distinct from the lower register on the basis of differences in timbre.

This difference between men and women does not negate the point made previously: the cricothyroids must be allowed to take more control (even in men to some extent) to stretch and thin the vocal folds to gain access to upper pitches with ease and good tone (Hirano, Vennard, & Ohala, 1970).

## Is there a middle register (mixed voice)?

Some vocal authorities argue that pitches between the lower and upper registers do not lie in a "middle register" because there are only two modal methods of voice production. This view holds that singers must choose either lower or upper register production for such pitches. Others argue that the middle register can involve a true blending of thyroarytenoid and cricothyroid control over the vocal folds, resulting in a distinctive tonal quality. We agree with this latter perspective, though we think the term, "mixed voice" is preferable when talking about this concept.

Pitches falling between the lower and upper registers should thus be sung with a combination of lower and upper register production. Blending of thyroarytenoid and cricothyroid control over the vocal folds produces a smoother transition between the lower and upper registers without sudden changes in sound quality or pitch perturbations ("breaks"). (Note that for men, there is already a blend of thyroarytenoid and cricothyroid control in the upper register, thus we are speaking of a bit more thyroarytenoid control in the narrow range of mixed voice available to men—see below for more about how this range is greater for women than for men.)

Recent research supports the existence of mixed voice at the laryngeal level:

- Lamesch, Expert, Castellengo, Henrich, and Chuberre (2007) have shown that mixed voice can be divided into two types, which they call Mx1 and Mx2. Mx1 is produced more in the lower register mechanism and Mx2 is produced more in the higher register mechanism. Mx1 allows for higher dynamic levels whereas Mx2 allows for softer dynamic levels.

- Kochis-Jennings, Finnegan, Hoffman, and Jaiswal (2011) have shown that there are distinct differences in thyroarytenoid and cricothyroid activity for registers they term "chest," "chestmix," "headmix," and "head." The two mixed voices correspond to Mx1 and Mx2 of Lamesch et al. (2007).

It is conceivable that mixed voice, most notably in women, may be more of a continuum from dominant thyroarytenoid control to a 50/50 split to dominant cricothyroid control. At this point, however, there have been no scientific studies providing evidence to support this idea.

## Modern singers have most difficulty with the upper register

In the past it was thought that men tend to speak in their lower register and women tend to speak in their upper register. Since singing is easier in the register used for speaking, it was widely believed that men have greater trouble singing in the upper register while women struggle with the lower register. Numerous contemporary vocal pedagogy books still suggest this to be the case.

We believe this view is antiquated. In the last fifty years, women in Western cultures have pitched their speaking voices lower and thus, like men, may have greater difficulty accessing head voice. Nonetheless, because some women do speak in their higher register (as do some men), we include exercises in this chapter to aid in the acquisition of the lower register.

## Transitions between registers (passaggi)

Transitions between registers are problematic for singers because the voice may abruptly change character when switching between one mode of production and another. In the worst case scenario phonation may stop, which is often referred to as a "break" or "cracking" of the voice. These transitional areas are technically referred to as "passaggi"—passages from one method of vocal production to another.

Surprisingly few vocal authorities explain the specific location of register transitions for each of the major voice types. Information about female voice types is particularly sparse. Most literature on the topic groups all voice types within a given gender together. While this allows for differences in individual areas of transition, conductors, teachers, and singers can benefit from more specific knowledge about where transitions are likely to occur, for example, in basses versus tenors.

Some (e.g., Vennard, 1967) argue that the major transition for both males and females is at or near $E_4$-flat based on research in the 1950s which purportedly showed that subglottal resonance interferes with phonation in this area. Titze (2000) debunked the $E_4$-flat sub-glottal resonance theory, noting that it was based on studies of cadavers. Subglottal resonance is in fact higher in live singers (around $B_4$).

Pitches at and around $E_4$-flat are significant, however, because of above-the-glottis resonance phenomena described in Chapter 5 on vowels. In this area there is the potential for the second harmonic frequency to cross over the first formant as pitch ascends, destabilizing vocal fold vibration. Nonetheless, formant frequencies are somewhat different among voice types and between men and women. And, men and women differ in the extent to which the thyroarytenoids are stressed in this area. Register transition issues must take into account both the degree of tensioning of the thyroarytenoids and above-the-glottis resonance. Based on this, we outline below approximate register transition areas that are different for men and women and different among voice classifications within the genders.

## Male register transitions

Table 8.1 shows approximate transitions between the lower register and mixed voice, as well as between mixed voice and the upper register for male voice types. The tenor transition range is a half step larger than for the other voice types to accommodate differences between Tenor I and Tenor II. We qualify these transitions as "approximate" because they vary slightly from singer to singer.

| Male Vocal Classification | Transition between Lower Register and Mixed Voice | Transition between Mixed Voice and Upper Register |
|---|---|---|
| Tenor | $C_4$–$D_4$ | $F_4$–$G_4$ |
| Baritone | $B_3$-flat–$B_3$ | $E_4$-flat–$E_4$ |
| Bass | $A_3$-flat–$A_3$ | $D_4$-flat–$D_4$ |

Adapted from Alderson (1979), R. Miller (1996), and Sell (2005)

**Table 8.1 Approximate vocal register transitions for male voice types**

For a majority of men, the most difficult transition is the second transition (passaggio) into the upper register. However, some men may also experience difficulties with the first transition if their voice is heavy for their vocal classification. Note that since mixed voice covers only a few pitches in males, some refer to the entire area between the first transition and second transition as the passaggio.

Male voices will have a strained quality in the passaggio if lower and upper register modes of production are not mixed. In addition, men who have not learned to sing in the upper register will experience a dramatic change in tonal quality as they approach the second transition. Such singers will have to resort to falsetto to produce notes around the upper transition and above. (We do not classify falsetto as a modal method of production and it is not the same as head voice—see the section on falsetto production below.) Nonetheless, by using appropriate exercises during individual practice and choral warm-ups, the upper register can be accessed if there is good breath support, engagement of the cricothyroid muscles, and appropriate vowel modification.

### *Male falsetto register*

While some modern authorities equate head voice with the falsetto register in males, we agree with Vennard (1967) that falsetto is distinctly different. Certainly the resonance characteristics of falsetto are quite different from head voice.

- Vennard (1967) described head voice as easily confused with falsetto but continuous with full voice.

The major difference between the male upper register and falsetto is the degree of vocal fold contact. In the male upper register, the vocal folds contact each other and vibrate along their full length. In falsetto, only a portion of the vocal folds make contact and airflow is higher (Large, 1984).

Men can sing higher in falsetto than they can in head voice. In head voice, even well-trained tenors can rarely exceed $C_5$, but almost any male voice can exceed this pitch in falsetto. At the same time, just as head voice can be used to produce pitches in the passaggio, falsetto can as well.

Falsetto is generally lower in volume and thinner (i.e., lacking in resonance) compared to head voice. It can also sound grainy or breathy. Nonetheless, with practice men can develop a stronger or reinforced falsetto with some degree of resonance and even with vibrato (e.g., countertenors). For most amateur choral singers, however, falsetto is used to sing high notes at a soft dynamic level that would be difficult in head voice. Men tend to use the falsetto register rarely, but they should be encouraged to practice in this register so that it is readily available when needed.

### Female Register Transitions

Women have a much broader range in their middle voice than men, but less range than men in their chest voice. (Contraltos have significant chest voice range, but true contraltos are rare.) This broad middle range means that the aforementioned Mx2 (headmix) method of production may be best at roughly $C_5$ and above (i.e., generally more emphasis on cricothyroid muscle control in the mix). Below $C_5$ more control by the thyroarytenoid muscles is typically needed (Georg, 2005). The extent to which the thyroarytenoid and cricothyroid muscles should control mixed voice also depends on the desired tonal color. Table 8.2 shows approximate vocal register transitions for the three major female voice types.

Individual singers' transitions can have substantial variability. For example, Echternach, Sundberg, Arndt, Markl, Schumacher, and Richter (2010) observed the transition from chest register to middle voice to occur anywhere from $D_4$–flat to $A_4$ for sopranos. The transition from middle voice to the upper register occurred anywhere between $D_5$–flat to $A_4$–flat. As these are professional singers, it is possible that their register transitions are, on average, higher than amateur singers.

| Female Vocal Classification | Transition between Lower Register and Mixed Voice | Transition between Mixed Voice and Upper Register |
|---|---|---|
| Soprano | $D_4$—$E_4$-flat | $E_5$—$G_5$-flat |
| Mezzo-Soprano | $C_4$—$D_4$-flat | $D_5$-flat—$E_5$-flat |
| Contralto | $B_3$-flat—$B_3$ | $C_5$—$D_5$ |

Note: Table 8.2 is based on our experience with voice classifications. However, Tarneaud and Borel-Maisonny (1961; cited by Large, 1973) list smaller differences in register transitions among female voice types than we show. They say the first passaggio for sopranos is the same as we have identified, but they include mezzo-sopranos at the same notes. They place contraltos only one step lower than the soprano voices. Similarly, while they agree with our placement of the soprano second passaggio, they list mezzo-sopranos and contraltos only a half step lower. Echternach et al. (2010) place the soprano transition to middle voice at an average of $F_4$. Miller and Schutte (2005) identified two professional mezzo-sopranos with a lower register to mixed voice transition which is similar to what we show.

**Table 8.2 Approximate vocal register transitions for female voice types**

## Vocal registers and resonance

As noted above, differences in resonance can also be used to characterize the registers (Schutte et al., 2005):

- In the lower register the nature of vocal fold vibration creates a prominent second harmonic (Titze, 2000; Miller & Schutte, 2005). For both men and women, vowels sung in the lower register generally have a first formant frequency that is higher than the second harmonic. Hence, the first formant typically reinforces the second harmonic in this register. (Exceptions are basses who sing at particularly low fundamental frequencies, where the third or fourth harmonic is reinforced by the first formant.)
- In middle voice for women and in middle voice and the upper register for men, $H_2$ will "outrun" the first formant frequency as pitch ascends. Thus, the resonance strategy should generally shift to the second formant in this register (as outlined in the section on vowel modification in Chapter 5 on vowels). This strategy requires a moderate jaw opening to drop the first formant well below the second harmonic to prevent an interaction between them. Otherwise vocal fold vibration will be destabilized as the second harmonic frequency crosses over the first formant frequency with ascending pitch.
- In women's upper register less vocal fold mass vibrates, reducing the amplitude of higher formant frequencies. In fact, this mode of vibration emphasizes the first harmonic—the fundamental frequency (Miller & Schutte, 2005). In the upper register women can reinforce the fundamental frequency with the first formant if they open the jaw as pitch ascends to keep the first formant always slightly above the fundamental frequency.

These relationships between important harmonic frequencies and the frequencies of the first two formants means that singers must alter their resonance strategies to transition between registers successfully.

## Negotiating the registers

The above discussion makes evident that singers must do two things as they make transitions to avoid experiencing register violations characterized by sudden changes in tonal quality and/or pitch disturbance:

- Modify vowels to prevent crossovers of harmonic frequencies with formant frequencies as outlined in Chapter 5 on vowels
- Change the mode of vocal fold vibration

Control over the mode of vocal vibration requires control of the vertical position of the larynx. Laryngeal stability is necessary to allow ascent into the upper register and to mix the lower and upper registers to achieve mixed voice. By monitoring laryngeal position and ensuring that it rises minimally, singers have an indirect method of letting the cricothyroids take over as pitch ascends. Moreover, maintaining the larynx in a comfortably low position allows the cricothyroids to contract through their whole range. This laryngeal position tilts the thyroid cartilage, allowing the cricothyroids maximal control over pitch (Sonninen, 1968). (When the cricothyroids contract, they stretch the vocal folds by tilting the cartilage forward, as shown in Chapter 3 on initiation and creation of sound.)

If the larynx is allowed to rise, as pitch ascends, the thyroarytenoid muscle approaches 100 percent contraction. At this point the cricothyroids can increase pitch only slightly more and with great effort. If the thyroarytenoid muscle is then relaxed suddenly to allow the cricothyroids to take over, the vocal folds must respond to sudden tensioning by the cricothyroids (Titze, 2000). Under this circumstance singers are unlikely to have any control over pitch, resulting in the sounds that accompany register breaks. This problem is particularly likely to happen beyond the second passaggio for both men and women.

## Additional factors to consider in register transitions

While women have substantial flexibility with vocal fold vibration strategies in the vicinity of the first passaggio, they must be careful to employ this flexibility wisely. For example, some women use upper register production almost exclusively in middle voice, leading to a weak sound in the lower middle voice and an inability to transition to the lower register (or at least an inability to transition without an obvious and sudden change in tonal quality). Firmer closure of the vocal folds in lower middle voice can also be helpful in creating a more resonant female voice in this area (Stark, 2003).

Similarly, if the shift up from the lower register to middle voice does not involve chestmix, women can have transitional problems. Men have the same problem if they carry lower register production too far into the passaggio (i.e., they need to lighten production as pitch ascends).

Men seem to have greater difficulty with register transitions. Titze, Riede, and Popolo (2008) state that because fundamental frequencies for men are lower relative to the formants than they are for women, men have less experience in dealing with crossovers of formant frequencies by the various harmonics. This suggests that special attention should be given to register and range exercises for male voices. In ensembles this can be done when rehearsing in sectionals.

Finally, it is worth mentioning that the degree of emphasis placed on lower versus upper register production in the area of mixed voice depends upon where the musical line is leading. In particular, if the direction is toward the upper register, be sure to use a lighter style of production (i.e., a mix favoring head voice), even on the lower notes.

### More on subglottal resonance and registers

As noted earlier, since the 1950s it has been thought that subglottal resonance in the area of $E_4$-flat interferes with phonation around this pitch by creating negative acoustic pressures that destabilize vocal fold vibration. Titze (2000) debunked this theory by pointing out that this frequency was based on cadavers and is in fact higher in live singers (around $B_4$). He has since proposed an alternative theory based on the first formant of the trachea and on formant frequencies above the glottis (Spencer & Titze, 2001; Titze, 2008a). This integrated theory is beyond the scope of this book; suffice it to say that resonance above the glottis appears to play a more significant role than resonance below the glottis. Nonetheless, subglottal resonance likely plays some role, and Titze is planning to continue study of subglottal phenomena (Titze & Worley, 2009). His future research in this area may provide additional ideas for coping with register transitions.

## Special registers in women and men

### Female whistle register

Women have a special high register known as the whistle register that is not available to men. The whistle register overlaps with their upper register but can exceed it by a large margin, ranging from roughly $A_5$ to $G_6$; potentially as high as $C_7$ (Georg, 2005). The whistle register is considered an extension of the upper register by some, the difference being that the vocal folds in the whistle register are fully stretched and thinned with only the front portion of the vocal folds vibrating (R. Miller, 2004). Others argue that there is in fact no contact between vocal folds in this register—that the breath simply whistles through the folds—hence the name "whistle register." When singers transition to this register, they may feel a sense of relaxation of their laryngeal muscles (Stark, 2003).

Whistle register pitches are used for "special effects" by popular music singers. They are unnecessary for "classical" soloists and for choral singing. Nonetheless, some believe that experimenting with the whistle register can help all women to achieve freedom of production at high pitches (Georg, 2005).

### Strohbass (pulse register)

Strohbass is German for "straw bass." It refers to the crackling sound of dry straw underfoot. Some singers refer to it as "vocal fry" because it mimics the sound of crackling meat cooking in a frying pan. A more technical term is the "pulse" register.

A relaxed vocal fry can be a useful device to help chronically tense singers (including those with hyperkinetic disorders) who press the vocal folds too firmly together. It is therapeutic for such singers because the vocal folds must be relaxed for this type of vocal fry, but the effort will be counterproductive if so-called "tense vocal fry" is used. Tense vocal fry is, however, helpful in treatment of some vocal fold disorders such as unilateral vocal fold paralysis (Cielo, Elias, Brum, & Ferreira, 2011). It may also be helpful as a therapeutic tool for breathy voices.

The role of vocal fry in normal singing is limited. Relaxed vocal fry is primarily useful for basses who need to sing the low notes required by some choral composers. It is characterized by a breathy quality due to minimal contact between the vocal folds. Vocal fry should not be used as a general method of vocal production.

## Exercises for smoothing out the registers

In addition to the exercises listed below, those in the next chapter on range extension may be helpful. Mastery of register transitions and range extension are closely related topics.

### Ghost/siren imitation

*Imitating a ghost or a siren is a relaxed and easy way to experiment with the vocal registers.*

This exercise involves quick slides into the upper register and corresponding quick slides down into the lower register. It frees singers from focusing on pitch control. In fact, singers may be pleasantly surprised at their ability to travel across the registers while doing this exercise. This will help them to gain confidence in negotiating the registers while singing, as well as a sense of how the various registers feel. Vowel modification strategies outlined in Chapter 5 are an essential part of this exercise.

## Octave slides

*A sequence of octave slides (extended portamenti) is a more controlled method of guiding singers through all of the register transitions. One approach is to start singing [a] on a pitch that is firmly in the lower register, moving the octave slides up by half steps until the top note reaches well into the upper register.*

While singing ascending octave slides, singers should monitor laryngeal position by placing a finger gently on the larynx to be certain that it rises minimally. Also, as pitch ascends, singers should further increase breath pressure and modify vowels appropriately. For example, men will need to modify from [ɑ] toward [ɔ] when moving into the upper register, including a fronting of the tongue as outlined in Chapter 5 on vowels.

## Extended arpeggios

*For a more advanced exercise, try an ascending arpeggio followed by a descending arpeggio with a dominant seventh, covering the range of a twelfth. As with octave slides, start in the lower register. With choral groups, start singing a vowel that can be used in the upper register by both men and women, such as [ɔ], though women will have to modify this to [a] at the highest pitches. Move the starting note up by half steps.*

When singing an extended ascending and descending arpeggio, imagine starting at the bottom of a Ferris wheel with the top note representing the top of the wheel. Think how the trip over the top seems effortless—strive for this same feeling when approaching the top note of an arpeggio by maintaining good breath support. Be sure to maintain support on the way down as well.

## For kids and everyone! Falsetto to lower register transition

*For developing male voices, start in falsetto and sing a descending arpeggio changing into the lower register (chest voice) for lower pitches. Sing "'hah" with an aspirated "h" to begin. Imagine beginning in a yawn, then sighing as singing. (Adapted from Cooksey, 1999)*

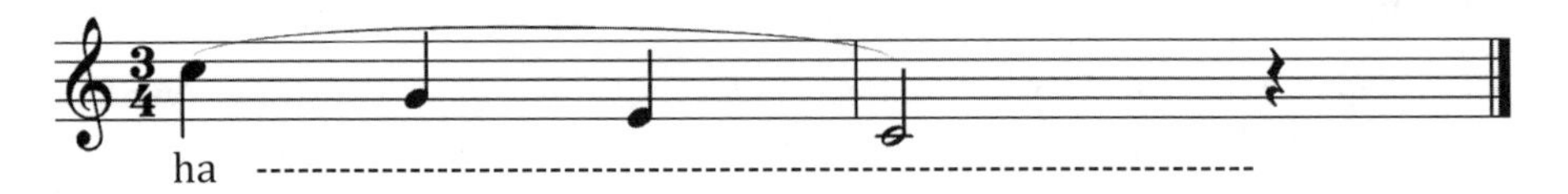


## For kids and everyone! Echoing

*The teacher/conductor sings simple pitches and rhythms in the various registers. Singers echo them back, modeling what is sung. Next, the teacher/conductor sings a pattern and then asks singers to sing the pattern in their heads with no humming or other sounds. After a short time, singers are directed to sing the pattern back. Try a variety of patterns and intervals. (Adapted from Phillips, 1996)*

# Chapter 9: Improving Range

Improving range is closely connected with the ability to negotiate vocal registers, so the preceding chapter should be read first. In this chapter we discuss:

- Ranges of various voice types
- Classification and misclassification of singers
- Detailed approaches to increasing range

Many developing and amateur singers may have limited ranges. Appropriate technique exercises will not only help them to increase their range, but will also give them the opportunity to see their own potential.

## Distribution of voice types

Vennard (1967) contends that most *amateur* singers are either mezzo-sopranos or baritones. True high voices (tenors and high sopranos) as well as true low voices (basses and contraltos) are rare in the amateur organization. Fishburn (1964) concurs. The proportion of mezzo-sopranos among women increases somewhat as women age (see Chapter 13 on changing voices).

We are unaware of any formal study that provides scientific evidence in support of Vennard's and Fishburn's arguments. Our experience is consistent with their observations as it relates to baritones, but as a proportion there are certainly more sopranos among premenopausal women than there are tenors among men. At the professional level there are in fact more sopranos than mezzo-sopranos (Vennard, 1967). We think this is due in part to the greater number of roles available for sopranos.

Most choral music is divided into low and high parts for both genders. The result in amateur choral groups is that the tenor section includes some high baritones who may use falsetto for high notes, while bass sections have baritones who struggle with the lower notes. Soprano and alto sections include many mezzos who face similar difficulties.

Choral conductors can do little about traditional choral composition (except to take advantage of eight-part arrangements!), but they can be cognizant of the problems faced by singers with middle voices forced to sing parts that are not in their optimal range.

Table 9.1 lists comfortable and maximum usable ranges for the standard choral four-part voice classification. The first two columns focus on the *average, amateur choir member*. Of course some amateurs can exceed these average usable maximums. For example choral repertoire will occasionally demand a $C_6$ from sopranos, and some in the soprano section can sing this. Fortunately, given audience sensitivity to pitches in this range, not many are needed. Similarly there are baritones in the bass section who can easily sing $E_4$ and mezzo-sopranos in the alto section who can comfortably sing $E_5$.

- The American Academy of Teachers of Singing (1997) is more conservative in its listings of range for average amateur choral singers. Their designated "safe range" is similar to our designation of the comfortable range for amateur singers. Our comfortable range for basses is higher than their recommended range, because the vast majority of amateur choral singers in the bass section are baritones—few true basses exist in these organizations.

As noted in the last column of Table 9.1, professionally trained singers have a somewhat greater range, particularly with respect to the upper register. In fact, a professional mezzo-soprano could have a higher range extending to $B_6$-flat or higher and a professional baritone's range could extend to $A_4$-flat or higher.

| Vocal Section | Comfortable | Maximum (Average Community Choral Singer) | Maximum (Professional Voice/Extensive Training) |
|---|---|---|---|
| Soprano | $D_4$–$G_5$ | $A_3$–$B_5$ | $G_3$–$D_6$ |
| Alto | $A_3$–$C_5$ | $G_3$–$F_5$ | $E_3$–$A_5$ |
| Tenor | $E_3$–$G_4$-flat | $C_3$–$A_4$ | $C_3$–$C_5$ |
| Bass | $A_2$–$D_4$ | $F_2$–$F_4$ | $E_2$–$F_4$ |

Note: maximum professional voice range based on Titze (2000).

**Table 9.1 Comfortable and maximum ranges for choral vocal classifications**

Conductors and teachers should be conservative about asking singers to venture outside of their classification's vocal range, particularly on the upper end. For example, true baritones should sing in the bass section of a choir. Singing tenor can damage their voices over time because they will have a tendency to use a pressed form of production. It is safer for them to sing the lower part, even though it is not a perfect match to their voice.

- Henderson (1979) also cautions choral directors against asking younger, true sopranos to sing alto simply because they can read music better or are more facile at singing harmony, because developing voices will rarely have the opportunity to improve upper register production if they always sing alto. Nonetheless, teachers of young sopranos who sing in choirs where directors are asking for a flute-like, straighter sound may want to advise their students to sing alto to assist development of a more focused tonal quality.
- The American Academy of Teachers of Singing (1997) warns of "the endless temptation of choral directors to encourage young people to sing certain parts not because their voices are ready for this particular tessitura but because the chorus needs more voices on that part."

Whenever possible, voices should not be sacrificed to balance sections—this can seriously limit vocal development. Instead, conductors should endeavor to choose appropriate repertoire or ask sections to alter their volume to produce balance.

## Tessitura versus range

Tessitura refers to the average pitch of a piece of music. It can also mean the range within which most pitches fall. A vocal composition with notes mostly close to the second passaggio and above has a high tessitura. These types of vocal compositions can be quite difficult for singers, because higher notes require greater breath pressure and involve more laryngeal tension.

Faced with a high tessitura, singers need more opportunities to take a breath, including for example, increasing the length of a rest where feasible. In addition, in choral groups, singers should stagger their breaths frequently. Conductors should avoid repetitive rehearsals of these types of passages to protect singers' vocal health.

The impact of high tessitura music on vocal health is a major concern, but an unusually low tessitura, although less frequently seen, can be problematic as well.

One reason that some voice teachers are reluctant to encourage their students to sing in choral organizations is the high tessitura of many choral works (American Academy of Teachers of Singing, 1997). Conductors should be sensitive to this issue, especially for younger, developing voices. The tessitura of a piece is just as important as range in selecting choral music.

## Classification and misclassification of voices in choral groups

In most choral organizations, some basses should actually be singing the tenor part and some altos should actually be singing soprano. These singers are misclassified because they have not learned to access their upper registers, a process that requires significant training and energy.

Often such singers have sizeable vocal instruments, which make gaining access to head voice difficult. They may be comfortable in a lower voice section, but they could have the potential to sing a higher part. Singers struggling to sing loudly on lower pitches in the bass or alto range may be candidates for a higher voice category. In addition, lighter baritones who can sing the second tenor line and altos who can sing the second soprano line on a four-part split may be better suited to a higher part.

The proper part for singers can also be gauged by how "heavy" or "light" they sound. That is, do they seem to have more low frequency resonance or more high frequency resonance?

Conductors should stay in touch with such singers to discuss opportunities for moving to another part that ultimately will be more comfortable and allow them to contribute more to the choral organization. It may also be helpful to refer them to a voice teacher to assist in making the transition to a different part.

## Accessing higher pitches

### Keep the larynx comfortably low

The previous chapter emphasized the importance of keeping the larynx comfortably low to transition to the upper register. A comfortably low laryngeal position allows the cricothyroid muscles to be more involved—the cricothyroids will stretch and thin the vocal folds to allow easier access to higher pitches. Here are some tips for accomplishing this:

- Singers can consciously prevent the larynx from rising as pitch ascends by touching it gently with a finger and being aware of its position. Preventing it from rising will reduce the involvement of the thyroarytenoid muscle in higher pitch production. This will take some work and practice to accomplish, but if singers allow only minimal ascension of the larynx, the cricothyroids will begin to take over as they sing higher notes. Singers should, however, avoid pushing the larynx down into an artificially low position, which will add tension and create a "woofy" sound.

- Recall from Chapter 2 on breathing that maintenance of appoggio helps to keep the larynx down, due to tracheal pull.
- Singers should consciously relax the muscles of the neck, jaw, and tongue. Remember that these muscles impinge on the larynx, and that relaxing them will help to allow the cricothyroid muscles to tilt the thyroid cartilage. The only tension that singers should experience is in the muscles of the ribs and abdomen that control and support the breath. (See Chapter 14 for methods of reducing tension in the neck, jaw, and tongue.)

Also, remember the other benefits of keeping the larynx comfortably low:

- When the larynx is low, total vocal tract volume is increased, lowering all formant frequencies, contributing to mellowness of tone.
- A low larynx, together with an open pharynx, contributes to the singer's formant.

Only singers who are belting for stylistic reasons should allow the larynx to rise and rely largely on the thyroarytenoid muscles on high pitches. Singers should use caution when singing in a heavy voice at the upper end of their range as this can cause vocal strain, fatigue, and even granulomas/nodules on the vocal folds (Bunch, 1995). Some popular performers who sing using "raw" belting have lost their voices (sometimes permanently). See the section on belting in Chapter 3 for methods of producing a belt sound that are less hazardous to vocal health.

### Increase breath pressure and pharyngeal space

As noted in the chapter on breathing, higher breath pressure is necessary to sing higher notes. McKinney (2005) goes further, saying that increased energy is required for higher pitches. Singing high pitches is hard work!

Women ascending to their upper register need more space as well. As pitch ascends they should lower the jaw to increase space, causing the pharynx to resonate at a higher frequency (i.e., the frequency of the first formant is raised). They should also strive to keep the soft palate lifted. This latter advice applies to men as well.

It may help to imagine biting into a large sandwich. As you do this, notice how your jaw is released, the tongue lies flat but is not pulled back in the mouth, the soft palate is lifted, there is a horizontal widening of the back of the mouth, the lip and cheek muscles are lifted, and the area above the upper lip is stretched horizontally.

## Titze's insights concerning access to the upper register

Titze (1999) has conducted a substantial amount of research on using nasal consonants to gain access to the upper register. (Recall that Chapter 3 on initiation and creation of sound discusses the benefits of partial vocal tract occlusion for assisting closure of the glottis.)

Research has shown that the upper portion of the vocal fold (involved in upper register production) is influenced mostly by air pressure above the glottis, while the lower portion of the fold is influenced by subglottic pressure. When air flow above the glottis is slowed by a partial occlusion such as a nasal consonant, the breath pressure required for phonation is reduced, making it easier for the upper portions of the folds to vibrate—precisely what is needed for head voice!

Recently, Titze (e.g., Titze et al. 2002a) has suggested singing through a straw to help the folds to vibrate at high pitches. Try different size straws, from stir-stick diameter through various sizes of drinking straws. Our experience is that a fairly small-diameter, standard-size drinking straw is a good starting point for most singers. However, Titze provides evidence that a stir-stick diameter may be better for some singers. Singers should experiment to see which works best for them.

- Singing through a straw has also been shown to have other benefits, including improved closure of the nasal port by the soft palate and improved vocal efficiency (Laukkanen, Horáčcek, Krupa, & Švec, 2011).

*Try singing five-note ascending scales on [m] or through a straw starting on A3 for males and A4 for females. Be sure to create space in the pharynx as you do this. Move up progressively.* You may find that afterward you can sing higher notes than you previously could. Even if you are not yet able to sing higher, your high notes will be less breathy and more focused after this exercise.

## Using falsetto to access head voice in males

Vocal technique authorities disagree about the value of falsetto as a device to help male singers access the upper register. Vennard (1967) is one of the strongest proponents of this method, and we agree with his perspective. This training device certainly has a long history in vocal pedagogy.

Falsetto can be helpful because the thyroarytenoid muscle is generally relaxed in this register (the cricothyroids are largely involved in pitch variation). By singing falsetto, male singers can gain some experience with lighter production even if they have not learned to sing in their modal upper register. Fortunately, the vast majority of males seem to know instinctually how to sing falsetto without instruction.

Males should use downward falsetto scales that move sequentially into the passaggio area. Tenors might start on $D_5$, singing five-note scales downward progressively on a variety of vowels, switching to modal voice at varying points in the middle voice range. This technique blends falsetto with the modal voice. Basses should start on $C_5$. Singers may find that [o] is a good vowel to start with. [ɑ] will likely sound most grainy—[ɔ] is a better choice than [ɑ] in this area of the male voice (as outlined in the discussion of vowel modification in Chapter 5).

Another benefit of practicing falsetto is that it will build a more focused (i.e., less breathy) falsetto sound. Tenors can use this focused falsetto to produce softer sounds at $A_4$-flat and above. Basses can use it to produce softer sounds at $F_4$ and above. Such use is generally restricted to the amateur choral setting; it is not an acceptable technique for well-trained singers, though it may be used with popular music for effect.

## Accessing lower pitches for female singers

Many sopranos do not use their lower register (chest voice), but it can be a valuable addition to their tonal palette and range. A soprano with access to chest voice has a greater range than any other voice type.

One method of learning chest voice is to sing descending passages that cross the boundary from middle voice to the lower register.

*Start on B4, using a downward sighing slide of a fifth. Low breath pressure may help. Try downward octave slides and even leaps for further development, starting no higher than $E_5$. A comfortably low larynx is important because it helps to lower all formant frequencies, giving chest voice a rich, mellow tone.*

- McKinney (2005) suggests a similar approach. He recommends singing descending five-note scales starting at $B_5$-flat.

*Once sopranos gain some facility with lower register production, try descending and then ascending arpeggios in this same range (8-5-3-1-3-5-8), lowering the starting note as you progress.* This will also help with developing Mx1 (middle voice with more chest content) in the range of $D_4$/$E_4$ to $B_4$. Firmer vocal fold closure is important in this context. This exercise can also be helpful for mezzo-sopranos and contraltos, but they should use a lower starting pitch. If progressing down to $C_4$ or lower, sopranos must transition into chest voice.

- As a more advanced exercise, McKinney (2005) suggests starting at A3, sliding up one octave and then singing a five-note descending scale. This can be varied using different starting notes at middle-C (C4) and below. McKinney recommends focusing on maintenance of a consistent vowel sound during this exercise.

## Handling leaps in pitch

A leap of a fourth or more can be a challenge for singers, particularly when that leap transitions a vocal register boundary.

Good breath support is critical for a successful leap. Often singers will take a breath just before the high note of an upward leap, but this actually makes it more difficult to sing due to the loss of space and calibration of breath pressure. Additionally, taking a breath at this point interrupts the legato line. Breath pressure must be prepared before arriving at the top note. The key is to mentally connect the lower and higher notes and physically connect them on the same breath.

- McKinney (2005) says that if a crescendo is indicated for an upward leap, crescendo on the lower note; otherwise the high note will seem too loud.

A slide (an extended portamento) from the lower to upper note can be helpful during rehearsal. Slides are a useful device to develop the muscle memory and breath pressure calibration necessary for negotiating a leap.

Another useful device to maintain support during individual practice is to use a thick physical therapy resistance band (or a large elastic such as a thick rubber balloon) that can be stretched with some difficulty. Grab the material with hands spaced about 4 inches apart and hold it vertically, close to your abdomen. When you start to sing the low note, stretch the material vertically, holding the stretch for the duration of the phrase. This device helps by assisting activation of the abdominal muscles. It also distracts singers from thinking about the larynx and from attempting to control laryngeal muscles directly to make the leap. The result is less laryngeal tension and a greater likelihood of an accurate leap.

Singers also might consider lowering the chin very slightly, which helps keep the larynx low and counteracts the tendency to physically reach for the high note.

While singers usually have more problems leaping upward as opposed to down, it is common on downward leaps for singers to relax breath support too much on the lower note, leading to a sound that is flat or lacking in resonance. Support should be maintained whether ascending or descending.

## Exercises to increase range

The following exercises are suggested for increasing range. Range exercises are particularly important to maintain access to both the lower and higher limits of our ranges as we age—use it or lose it!

### Image for creating space for higher pitches

*It may help to imagine biting into a large sandwich. As you do this, notice how your jaw is released, the tongue lies flat but is not pulled back in the mouth, the soft palate is lifted, there is a horizontal widening of the back of the mouth, the lip and cheek muscles are lifted and the area above the upper lip is stretched horizontally.*

### Slides

Sliding is an excellent approach to range extension because it helps maintain the correct breath pressure and weight of vocal production. In addition, it enables us to gradually create appropriate space and vowel modification for upper pitches. *Try sliding up and down the interval of a fifth. Start in middle voice and move into the upper register. Do the exercise in reverse to work the lower end of your range. Ascend/descend by half steps. Quick slides of an octave are also helpful—try not to hesitate on the top pitch; move through it rapidly. This prevents buildup of tension on very high and very low pitches.*

When doing these and other range exercises, singers should monitor their larynx as pitch ascends by touching it gently with a finger.

### Runs

Runs (scales sung in a fast tempo) are another good way to extend range as they too discourage tension in the extremes of the registers. *Try ascending and descending runs of a fifth and/or ninth. Increment the starting pitch by semi-tones (half steps). Be careful to initiate the sound with coordinated onset and appropriate pharyngeal and mouth space to ensure good resonance. Keep the abdominal muscles engaged to provide correct breath pressure and increase resonance space as pitch ascends.*

Tenors and sopranos can often vocalize on runs up to C; basses and altos can vocalize down to E. Singers should be encouraged to experiment with their range, but not at the cost of vocal health. They should be the guardians of their own voices and never strain themselves.

## Using falsetto to access head voice in males

*Males should use downward falsetto scales that move sequentially into the passaggio area. Tenors might start on D5, singing five-note scales downward progressively on a variety of vowels, switching to modal voice at varying points in the middle voice range. This technique blends falsetto with the modal voice. Basses should start on C5.* Singers may find that [o] is a good vowel to start with. [ɑ] will likely sound most grainy—[ɔ] is a better choice in this area of the male voice than [ɑ] (as outlined in the discussion of vowel modification in Chapter 5).

## Singing through straws/singing nasal consonants

*Try singing five-note ascending scales on [m] or through a standard straw starting on A3 for males and A4 for females. Be sure to create space in the pharynx as you do this. Move up progressively.* You may find that afterward you can sing higher notes than you previously could. Even if you are not yet able to sing higher, your high notes will be less breathy and more focused after this exercise.

## Extending the lower portion of the range

*To extend the lower portion of the range, try singing [siɑ]. Descend from the dominant to the tonic on [si] changing to [ɑ] on the lower pitch. This exercise can be done using a descending scale or slide. Both are illustrated. Continue descending by half steps while carefully monitoring tension. Never push the sound, but rather allow it to be released.*

*Low breath pressure may help. Try downward octave slides and even leaps for further development, starting no higher than $E_5$ for women. A comfortably low larynx lowers all formant frequencies, giving chest voice a rich, mellow tone.*

### For kids and everyone! Darts and Frisbees

*Sing [i], ascending run of a fifth, two times in quick succession. Then sing legato on [a]. Pretend to throw a dart during the first two runs. Then imagine tossing a Frisbee for the arpeggiated figure. (Adapted from S. Morrison, personal communication, August 8, 2008)*

# Chapter 10: Improving Intonation

Excellent intonation is one of the primary concerns of conductors, teachers, and singers. Wonderful repertoire can be sung with great conviction, but it will all be for naught if it is out of tune. No one wants to listen to out-of-tune singing! The good news is that attention to technique can cure many of the causes of poor intonation.

## Causes of poor intonation

Teachers and conductors sometimes assume that poor intonation is the result of singers not listening, or perceiving the pitch correctly. While this is true in some cases, the vast majority of singers try very hard to sing in tune. However, singers can find it difficult to recognize when they are out of tune because what they "hear" is not the sound that the audience hears due to bone conductance and directionality of sound (away from singers' ears). Telling singers that they are out of tune (either flat or sharp) is only part of the solution. Many singers will not know how to fix the problem.

The causes of poor intonation can be classified in two main categories:

- Individual intonation problems
- Ensemble intonation problems

Powell (1991) suggests two aspects of intonation for consideration: horizontal (melodic line) and vertical (harmony).

### Horizontal intonation (melodic line; relevant for both soloists and ensembles)

When singing their line, singers need to accurately perceive the spaces between pitches—the intervals. Even in the choral setting singers should think of their part as a melody and read the intervals accurately with attention to how the key signature affects spacing. In addition, they need to develop muscle memory for the correct distance between pitches. Pitches must be learned correctly the first time—if errors are not quickly corrected, they will become a part of muscle memory and will be difficult to correct later. Leaps are especially problematic because they can be a "shot in the dark" for many singers as they guess how far to move.

*Try utilizing slides to understand how much of a leap is required—a slide will allow for modifications in breath pressure and resonating space. Once both pitches are in tune, speed up the slide and eventually eliminate it altogether.*

Singers may find it particularly difficult to sing descending melodic lines in tune. Awareness of this tendency goes a long way toward fixing it. Singers should imagine that descending intervals are smaller than ascending intervals. They should keep support muscles engaged and preserve resonance space as they descend.

*Sing descending five-note major and minor scales on various vowels throughout the singers' ranges. Conductors and teachers should give singers immediate feedback on intonation.*

Horizontal intonation problems can be related to reading rather than recognizing music. Once singers are more familiar with their music, have developed muscle memory for the line, and are able to use the notation to recognize the music (rather than read it), many melodic intonation problems will disappear.

### *Solving individual intonation problems*

We mentioned many of the main causes of individual intonation issues in earlier chapters. They include:

- Tension in the neck, larynx or tongue
- Breath pressure (too much or too little)
- Insufficient or incorrect resonance space

It is also important for singers to think about the pitch of a vowel before singing it. Create the space for that particular vowel and sing any preceding consonant in that space as well.

Because singers perceive their sound differently than the actual sound they create, they must learn how it feels to sing in tune. For example, they must become used to the breath pressure and resonating space necessary to negotiate passaggi.

- Shaw advocates singing reasonably quietly at rehearsal (Blocker, 2004). He cites vocal excesses for many choral problems, including disturbances of intonation. He notes that every pitched musical instrument (except a few percussion instruments) can be "'forced' out of tune by too much pressure of air, bow, or fist" and that the voice is especially vulnerable to forcing (p. 87).

Immediate feedback from teachers and conductors during the warm-up helps build muscle memory for in-tune singing.

### Vertical intonation (harmony in ensembles)

As Powell (1991) states, a major difference between professional and amateur musicians is that professional musicians always listen and adjust to the sounds of those around them. Choral directors encourage their singers to listen, but providing guidance about accomplishing this is crucial.

In warm-ups directors can employ numerous harmonic progressions to assist with the tuning of chords and encourage active listening to self and others. A simple Bach Chorale can be very useful.

*Try sustaining a four-part major chord of your choice. Change the pitches systematically, part by part, to form new, sometimes dissonant chords. (See the exercises section of this chapter for an example.) Singers should be encouraged to notice the shifts in intervals between parts.*

Powell (1991) suggests exposing and tuning octaves between parts first, then moving to fifths, etc. Singers will find it helpful if their conductor points out the scale degree that they are singing or the function of their pitch (the leading tone, the third of a major triad, a four-three suspension, etc.). Whatever approach you adopt, assist the singers in correcting the problem, as opposed to just telling them they are sharp or flat.

The following corrective steps are helpful:

- Isolate the problematic interval (e.g., a fifth between the basses and tenors).
- Tune the interval—use slides or adjust the vowel as necessary. For example, if a section is flat, try an adjacent brighter vowel with a higher second formant.
- Add in the other voice parts one by one.
- Have all parts sing the chord together.
- Finally, sing the chord in its context.

## Repertoire-specific intonation issues

Singing in tune in the warm-up is an important step toward consistently excellent intonation. However, repertoire offers many additional challenges. If your choir sings in tune in general but experiences occasional poor intonation, consider the following:

## Text/lyrics

Sometimes singers can successfully learn a passage of music on a single, basic Italian vowel (cardinal vowel); however, once lyrics are added, or if lyrics have been used since the beginning, intonation may suffer.

*Sing a problematic passage of music on only a single cardinal vowel. If pure vowels have been established in the warm-up, singers should have a reference for how to produce these sounds.*

*If the intonation problems disappear, sing the same passage with the written vowels, but without consonants. In choral groups, listen carefully for places where the vowels disagree—i.e., singers do not have the same reference point for the vowel (are singing different vowels) or are not producing the vowel in the same way. Point out the correct vowel to sing and monitor how it is being produced.*

Shaw advocates singing on the vowels with a single preceding consonant to learn rhythm as well (Noble, 2005).

*Finally, add the consonants. Chapter 6 discussed how consonants can distort or pollute vowels, altering pitch. Singers should be reminded to use articulators quickly and efficiently, always returning the tip of the tongue to the base of the lower front teeth.*

This process may take some time, and other factors may contribute to intonation problems (e.g., breath pressure, tessitura, fatigue, etc.).

## Tessitura

As noted in Chapter 9 on improving range, tessitura is the range where most of the pitches lie for a passage or piece. In our discussion of registers, we noted that the some of the most challenging areas for inexperienced singers are the transition areas or passaggi. If a piece of music stays in or near a passaggio, intonation can suffer unless there is careful attention to breath support and relaxation techniques. Simply reminding singers about the technical demands of singing in a passaggio will help. Singers can also try more frequent stagger breathing in ensembles, or inhalations of slightly longer duration than usual to give the vocal mechanism more time for recovery. The following exercise is helpful for both choral and solo singers:

Practice the recovery portion of the breath cycle by elongating it. *Sing the passage in question. Singers should release the abdominal and rib muscles so that the subsequent inhalation can be complete and relaxed. For soloists and for ensemble group-breaths, the breath should be significantly longer (e.g., a quarter rest becomes a half rest by reducing the duration of the preceding note). If stagger breathing is necessary for an ensemble, singers should take at least three seconds to inhale before singing again. Then continue to sing the passage. Repeat the exercise with slightly shorter breaks for the breath cycle (dotted quarter/two seconds etc.). Finally, sing in time.*

This exercise will build stamina and encourage awareness of the breath cycle.

### Key of the piece being sung

Some keys are more difficult than others, likely because of their tessitura, but also because of the unique relationship of intervals in the singing voice. The voice is not a fixed pitch, equal-tempered instrument. For example, conductors can create intonation problems for their choirs by programming a cappella music that moves from flat keys to sharp keys. If the choir is singing in tune with itself, but the entire piece consistently sinks in pitch by a half step (or goes sharp), conductors should consider lowering (or raising) the key of the piece by a half step. In early music, spirituals, folk songs, show tunes and some other genres, small variations in key can go a long way toward allowing an ensemble to "settle" their intonation. However, in "classical" music notated since the mid-18th century this solution is not appropriate, as composers wrote in certain keys for particular reasons.

### Dynamic level

Recall that Shaw cautions against oversinging (Blocker, 2004). This is usually caused by high levels of breath pressure and/or pressed phonation as pitch ascends. Under such circumstances pitch control is more difficult.

Undersinging also poses problems for intonation as the tone may be somewhat breathy, due to less than optimal vocal fold vibration and a lack of resonance. Additionally, in the choral setting good intonation requires singers to be able to hear both themselves and others (see the section below). Those who undersing likely are unable to hear themselves. Since they aren't conspicuous in the choral texture, they are harder for conductors to identify than those who oversing. Conductors should watch singers carefully to make sure they are inhaling properly and engaging support muscles. If not, it is quite possible that they are undersinging.

### Vowel differences within and between ensemble sections

Conductors can eliminate many intonation problems by ensuring that singers are producing the same vowel sound in the same way. This is an example of where careful attention to uniform production of vowels in the warm-up pays off. If conductors suspect that vowels are not in agreement, they can try the following:

*Isolate the word. Ask the choir/section which vowel sound(s) they should be singing. Correct them if necessary. Remember that diphthongs can be especially confusing. Have the singers sing only the vowel(s). If necessary, isolate sections (tenors, sopranos, etc.). Now ask the choir to sing the word as written (with consonants). Finally, put it back into the context of the passage.*

Remember that singers will not look exactly the same, even when singing the same vowel. They should, however, create the sound in the same way inside.

## Extraneous factors affecting intonation

Solving intonation problems can involve other "nonmusical" considerations. These apply particularly to ensembles, but they also apply to solo singers.

### Energy level

A tired singer will struggle to sing in tune. A singer who is pumped full of adrenaline will also have intonation problems. Conductors should anticipate where the choir might be in terms of energy, and plan rehearsals accordingly. For example, planning slow, sustained a cappella repertoire for long periods of rehearsal time may result in the choir learning to sing a piece out of tune because of fatigue. Whenever possible, assist the choir to learn a piece in tune so that muscle memory will help rather than hinder at performance time.

### Acoustics of the room

Ternström and Sundberg (1988) ascertained that acoustical feedback received from the singing space can affect intonation. Some spaces offer helpful information to singers by way of reverberation. Others offer too much or too little information. Thus, the space that a soloist or ensemble rehearses in can greatly influence intonation and overall sound. The acoustics of some rooms permit singers to hear themselves and others, encouraging singing with a full sound. Other environments may be so reverberant or dry acoustically as to discourage comfortable, full singing or to prevent accurate hearing of other singers.

Of course acoustics of the rehearsal space may differ from the acoustics of the performance space. Teachers and conductors should help singers build muscle memory in rehearsal. Singers should trust that memory (and teacher/conductor feedback) when singing in different spaces.

### Standing position of the singers in ensembles

Ternström and Sundberg (1988) also found that ability to hear both oneself and other singers has an impact on intonation. If singers cannot perceive their own sound, it is obviously difficult for them to know when they are singing in tune. Singers may not be able to hear themselves if they are not signing loudly enough or if someone is oversinging next to them. Additionally, intonation problems can result if a singer cannot hear the person next to them. Whenever possible, try to seat singers according to voice quality and according to height (singers cannot hear someone who is substantially taller or shorter than they are).

One useful formation that encourages good intonation has sopranos and altos in the front, from left to right, and basses and tenors in the back, from left to right. This formation allows the outer parts to tune to each other.

- Lamb (1988) also advocates this formation from the perspective that it emphasizes the polarity of parts.

See Chapter 12 on blend for more about effects of standing position on choral sound.

## Concluding thoughts about intonation

Good vocal technique will always improve intonation. When individuals sing with resonance and excellent breath support, sound is more in tune. Ekholm's (2000) study of singing styles in the choral setting (solo, soloistic, and blended) found that the majority of listeners (who were voice teachers) reported problems with intonation when singers attempted to blend with those around them. Singing in a "trained mode," that is, with good technique is the most consistent defense against poor intonation. With careful monitoring, teachers and conductors can assist their singers in taking an active role in anticipating, avoiding, and fixing intonation issues.

## Exercises to improve intonation

Paying attention to the spacing of intervals for a given key, development of muscle memory for pitches, and good vocal technique go a long way toward improving intonation. A few intonation-specific exercises may be helpful as well.

### Slides to help with leaps in pitch

*Try utilizing slides to accurately perceive how far a leap really is—a slide will allow for modifications in breath pressure and resonating space. Once both pitches are in tune, speed up the slide and eventually eliminate it altogether. Experiment with different intervals. Also, practice downward leaps in pitch.*

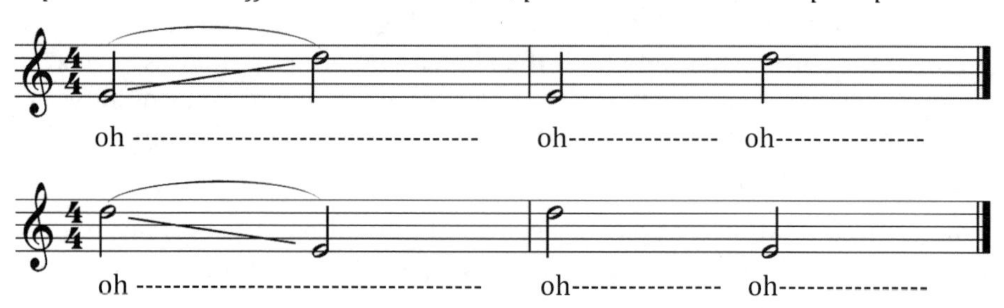


### Major and minor scales to learn intervals

*Sing descending five-note major and minor scales (fifth—tonic) on various vowels throughout singers' ranges. Vary the key. Give singers immediate feedback on intonation.*

### Horizontal and vertical intonation

The following exercise concentrates on vertical intonation but involves horizontal intonation as well. Notice that sopranos and basses must tune octaves at the start of each of the first two measures. Encourage the singers to notice the shifts in intervals between parts and to note which part of a chord they are singing (root, third, suspension, etc.). A chorale is another possible choice. These types of exercises should be sung in a variety of keys.

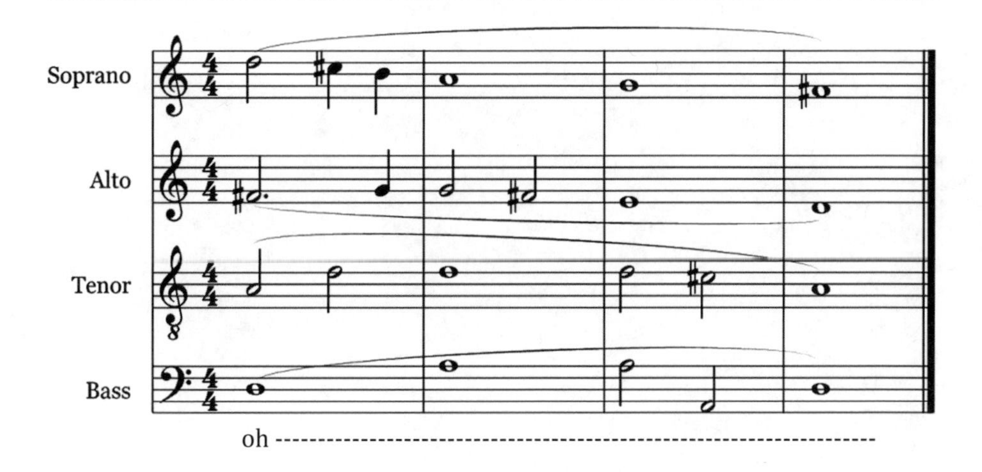
Soprano
Alto
Tenor
Bass
oh

# Chapter 11: Legato, Staccato, Accents, Melismas, and Dynamic Control

Several styles of vocal production are difficult for many singers:

- **Legato** creates continuous sound. This should be *the* fundamental method of vocal production, but many singers leave too much space between words and/or syllables in a musical phrase.
- **Staccato** is properly created by releasing a sound quickly. Unfortunately, many singers think that staccato involves a glottal onset to create a short, crisp sound.
- **Accents** are created by the nature of the onset or the way the sound begins. Numerous singers create accents with problematic tension.
- **Melismas** (runs), or passages of rapid pitch changes, are the bane of many singers. Agility is a difficult skill to acquire, particularly for heavier voices within a given vocal classification. Nonetheless, some helpful techniques can make these fast passages less of a trial.
- **Dynamic control** involves the ability to sing with a full range of sound level throughout one's publicly usable range. Singing softly on high pitches can be especially difficult.

This chapter is designed to help singers gain mastery over these advanced techniques.

## Legato involves vowel-to-vowel continuity

The term *legato* comes from the Italian verb *legare* which means "to join." In a legato musical line, the singer joins together all of the words in a phrase to produce a pleasing, continuous sound. For this reason legato is generally the most preferred method of production.

As outlined in Chapter 6 on consonants, if singers let them, consonants can easily intrude on the continuity of sound. Quick, efficient enunciation of consonants is essential to prevent this intrusion from happening and to ensure the resonating space for vowels is not compromised.

- Vennard (1967) has another perspective. He believes that most singers who have difficulty singing a legato line allow the vowel

> preceding a consonant to fade in preparation for creating that consonant. As an antidote to this Vennard suggests that singers think of a crescendo (we would say a small crescendo) from one syllable to the next.

Having a concept of where a phrase is going is also important for a legato line. For example, maintaining intensity of expression through the most important word or syllable in a phrase is helpful.

### Creating a legato line

Eliding consonants is particularly important for the creation of a legato line. This involves connecting the final consonant of the preceding word with the word that follows. For example, sing "mist on the moor" as "mi ston the moor." In this example there should be no stopping of the vowel sounds except to pronounce the consonants quickly.

Even complex consonant clusters should be elided. Consider for example this phrase from Haydn's *Creation*, "The wonder of his works displays the firmament." Singers should elide "works displays" as follows: "wor—ksdi—splays."

As noted in Chapter 6 on consonants, sometimes a slight pause or glottal stroke before a vowel may be desirable in preference to slavish adherence to legato. For example, singing "her eyes" as "he—reyes" would sound strange. Instead, sing "her {e}yes" where the brackets indicate a slight glottal separation.

Be sure to maintain or accelerate the breath pressure on consonants that consume a lot of air (unvoiced consonants) to keep the musical line going. For example, when singing "king," do not interrupt exhalation or close the glottis after the "k" is formed.

### Language requirements that necessarily interrupt the legato line

The language being sung may require an interruption of the legato line. For example, Chapter 6 on consonants discussed the use of a soft glottal for words beginning with a vowel within a German phrase. This will necessarily interrupt the legato line.

Italian may be the easiest language for legato production because it has fewer consonants than English and other Germanic languages. Nonetheless, a number of Italian words have double consonants, and it is important to stop very briefly on the first occurrence prior to forming the second consonant. For example, if *notte* is pronounced [no]-[te], it will mean "note," not "night."

### Images to help with creation of legato

Singers can imagine vowels of a vocal phrase as a flowing river. Consonants are dropped precisely and quickly into the river so that they do not interrupt the flow.

Singers can hold their dominant arm in front of them and imagine they are holding a wide paintbrush in their hand with a wall in front of them. *Paint a horizontal brush stroke on the "wall," moving from left to right and then changing direction quickly. Do this several times; it will provide a physical sensation of making fast, barely perceptible transitions that keep the sound going. Now, sing a phrase, quickly reversing the brush between the syllables of words in the phrase.*

## Staccato

### Stop the tone by ceasing exhalation to sing staccato properly

Staccato is a release gesture that should be accomplished by stopping the breath, rather than a hard, glottal onset followed by a tight glottal closure. While singers may think that staccato has to do with onset, it is all about a quick release after a coordinated onset.

- Sundberg (1993) adds that to produce a staccato sound, subglottic pressure must be reduced to zero in the spaces between notes and the vocal folds must be opened. The singer must then immediately create the correct subglottal pressure for the next note based on pitch and dynamic level. If the correct pressure is not created, intonation will suffer. His analysis illustrates why staccato singing is so difficult and again emphasizes the critical need for control over breath support. With, for example, an upward moving staccato line, singers must use one level of breath pressure for the starting note, go to zero, then suddenly increase pressure by just the right amount for the next note. This is technically very difficult.

An aid to learning staccato production is to breathe in very slightly after each note—this makes it easier to stop the sound and there is less likelihood of closing the vocal folds to accomplish the stoppage of sound.

Singers must take care to prevent the breathing mechanisms from collapsing during the singing of staccato notes. After inhalation, the intercostal and abdominal muscles should maintain the expanded position of the ribcage and abdomen for as long as possible.

### *Abdominal musculature and diaphragm should pulsate*

Henderson (1979) used a fluoroscope to observe the diaphragm of a trained singer. She found that during a staccato passage the diaphragm pulsated. This is accomplished by pulsing the abdominal muscles, a particularly important technique with a grouping of staccato notes. The image of bouncing on a trampoline may help.

## Accents

While staccato is all about release, an accented pitch is all about onset. The method of onset will depend upon the composer's markings and the context of the accented note. Depending upon circumstances, accented pitches sometimes require a glottal onset, but singers should usually try using higher breath pressure at the start of the note followed by a sudden reduction in pressure. This increase in breath pressure at the start of a note applies both to words that begin with vowels and to those that begin with consonants. Singers may feel this as a little bounce in the abdomen which creates the sudden increase and decrease in breath pressure. The result is a louder sound at the beginning of the note followed by a decay of intensity. This is one way of achieving a tenuto accent (–). Tenuto can also mean emphasis in duration—a slight elongation of the pitch (rubato). A commonly used musical notation for a marcato accent (>) illustrates rapid dynamic change very nicely. A martellato (hammered) accent (^) combines a glottal onset with a staccato release.

Choose any simple exercise and vary the articulation of the pitches for each repetition. Make conscious choices/suggestions about the way to achieve each type of accent. Include staccato, staccatissimo (very short staccato), tenuto, marcato, and martellato.

## Melismas

### Use the upper portion of middle abdominal muscles to support runs

The key to singing melismas is relaxation of all muscles that impinge on the larynx plus slight pulsation of the upper rectus abdominal muscles.

- Richard Miller (1996) has a helpful image. He says that the epigastric area of the abdominal wall (the upper middle portion of the abdomen just below the sternum) should move in a manner similar to what occurs during rapid, silent panting. Thus, melismas are like a quick staccato, but incorporated into a legato line.

If singers' larynxes are moving as they sing melismas, they are likely attempting too much direct control over laryngeal muscles to change pitch. They are also likely lacking sufficient breath support. Singers can gently touch the larynx to create the awareness necessary for stabilizing its height.

Richard Miller (2004) provides an extended discussion of an approach to learning melismas through initial staccato execution of passages. Here is a simplified summary of his recommendations:

- To gain a sense of bouncing the abdominal wall (pulsing the abdominal muscles), sing a rapid "hm, hm, hm, hm, hm" as though engaged in stifled laughing. Singers should be sure that the epigastric area of the abdominals is bouncing. Raise and lower the pitch while doing this, ending with a descending five-note scale.
- Use this same pattern of exercises, open the mouth and sing using [ɑ]. If singers have difficulty, *as a learning device*, they can sing "ha, ha, ha, ha, ha." As outlined below, this is not a good method for singing melismas, however, and this crutch should be discarded as quickly as possible.
- Using five-note ascending and descending scales, first sing a sequence using [ɑ] in staccato style; then sing the scales legato but retain a sense of the small abdominal pulsations of staccato. Certain literature requires more articulation of melismatic passages. In these cases the amount of movement in the epigastrium will be greater.

## Avoid continued use of the "ha-ha-ha-ha" crutch

Some conductors advocate singing runs with the assistance of [h] to differentiate the notes (e.g., "ha-ha-ha-ha"). Indeed, this can be a useful learning device if used with great moderation—a very small [h]—but in general it is a poor device that creates noise and reduces vowel resonance due to interruption of the legato line. (Recall that the vocal tract resonates best during the closed phase—if the glottis is deliberately opened, the period of time during the melisma that the glottis is closed is dramatically reduced.) This style of singing melismas has other problems as well:

- It creates tension and makes it difficult to sing the notes quickly.
- The constant opening and closing of the glottis associated with this method creates a series of collisions between the vocal folds that can be damaging (Sundberg, 1987).
- It is inefficient due to loss of breath associated with aspirated onset (R. Miller, 2004).

Using "ha, ha, ha" to sing melismas can be thought of as an aspirated type of glottal articulation. Sherman and Brown (1995) have suggested what appears to be a nonaspirated glottal articulation to sing melismas. That is, the glottis is rapidly opened and closed to sing the notes of a run. They argue that this creates cleaner separation of pitches than is attainable with abdominal pulsation. And, they find that choral groups can learn this method more easily than abdominal pulsation. While we agree that glottal articulation methods (whether aspirated or nonaspirated) can assist learning, they are undesirable endpoints—both have the problems of noise, reduced resonance, and excessive airflow (indeed Sherman and Brown acknowledge the higher airflow). This noise can be seen in the sound waveforms of the glottal articulation method (Sherman & Brown, 1995). In short, advocates of glottal articulation methods overlook the quality of sound that is produced. A staccato-like legato singing of melismatic passages using epigastric pulsation produces the most pleasing sound.

### An approach to learning melismas

Learn melismas by singing slowly to develop muscle memory for the pitch sequences. As soon as you know the patterns, sing short sections (e.g., one or two beats) at performance speed. Once each section has been learned they can be combined, again at performance speed.

## Dynamic control

Most singers who use flow phonation and have developed balanced resonance can sing relatively loudly. Singing softly with a supported sound can be more difficult, particularly at high pitches.

- Coleman (1994) found that a major factor in the greater dynamic range of trained versus untrained choral singers is the ability of trained singers to sing more softly.
- Cooksey (1999) suggests that singing *mf* and *f* dynamics at first is indicated for young voices, as these dynamic levels require less physical manipulation. Fine dynamic control (*pp* in particular) can be developed later as a more advanced skill.

*Messa di voce* is an excellent exercise for learning how to gain better dynamic control. Start in the middle of the range on a vowel such as [o], singing very softly. Crescendo to a forte sound, then back down to pianissimo. This exercise is most difficult at high pitches. In the exercises we include a standard *messa di voce*, but also a reverse *messa di voce* that may be easier to sing at high pitch levels.

- Vennard (1967) argues that *messa di voce* is also an excellent exercise to help with the development of breath control. In addition, it helps to develop proper onset because a glottal attack will be heard easily and a breathy onset will not produce a clear tone at soft dynamic levels. He notes that this exercise forces one to coordinate the vocal registers—to start with a light production incorporating head voice and to shift into more of a lower register (chest voice) type of production approaching the forte section of the exercise. (This assumes that the exercise is sung in the middle register [i.e., in mixed voice]). The most difficult aspect of the exercise is the decrescendo—shifting from lower- register production to upper-register production to soften the sound.

### Soft production at high pitches

Singing softly at high pitches is one of the most difficult tasks for singers. A major culprit is a tendency to relax breath support too much (and thus decrease breath pressure excessively). It is true that subglottal pressure needs to be reduced for a softer sound (and thus there should be less vigorous engagement of abdominal and intercostal muscles), but support needs to be maintained. Otherwise, singers have a tendency to tighten the larynx and strangle softly produced high pitches.

- As Henderson (1979) says: "Keep energy in your 'piano' dynamic so that it will be alive and intense and will be supported" (p. 179).

Some singers relax the arytenoids to open the glottal space slightly as a method of singing high pitches softly. Although this method reduces the amplitude of vibration of the vocal folds, it is a poor technique because it produces a breathy sound (unless desired as an effect).

## Exercises for legato, staccato, accents, melismas, and dynamics

### Legato—singing text using only the vowels

*One method to create a legato line is to sing a piece of music using only the vowels. (You may wish to start by singing on only one vowel to make this easier.)*

With no consonants to interrupt the flow of tone, the sound will be continuous. This is trickier than it seems for some singers because they may not be accustomed to thinking about vowels outside the context of the words themselves. Thus, until singers are comfortable with this approach, it is best to write in the IPA symbols for the vowels above the staff. In fact writing in the vowels will help with singing them correctly because it focuses attention on them. This is particularly important for diphthongs and for words with neutral vowels ([ʌ] and [ə]) that should be sung using [ɑ].

*After singing the music in this fashion, singers should sing the words with the consonants, concentrating on maintaining sound production with no stopping between words. Quick, efficient production of consonants will help greatly.*

### For kids and everyone! Legato image

*Think about the story from Winnie the Pooh where Pooh and Piglet are playing a game that later becomes known as "Pooh Sticks." They stand together on one side of the bridge and toss pinecones into the water, then race to the other side of the bridge to see whose pinecone has emerged first. Imagine the water as the vowel sounds and the pinecones as the consonants, dropped quickly into the ever-present, ever-moving water.*

### Staccato and tenuto

*Sing two notes staccato on the same pitch, then start a five-note ascending scale ending with staccato notes. Substitute other vowels.*

*Sing a legato arpeggio followed by a staccato arpeggio, followed by a tenuto arpeggio. Start with [e] and then substitute other vowels.*

### Contrasting accents

*Sing an ascending run of five notes. Sing the first note martellato (glottal onset and quick release) and the following four notes staccato.*

### Getting a sense of melisma

The following exercise makes it easy to gain a sense of what a melisma should feel like. Singers should execute the run as though they were giggling (T. Stalter & J. Brueck, personal communication, April 5, 2011).

### For kids and everyone! Melismas

*On a five-note ascending and descending scale, sing "bubble, bubble, bubble, bubble, bubble, bubble, bubble, bubble, bubble"—two eighth notes on each pitch. Add additional consonants such as, "bubble, trouble, bubble, trouble." (Adapted from Cooksey, 1999)*

### Complex melismas

This exercise breaks apart a melisma from Handel's "And He Shall Purify" into two components. Rehearse each component slowly until learned, moving as soon as possible to performance speed (quarter-note = 92–96). Then sing the entire melisma, slowly at first if necessary, again moving to performance speed once learned. (Parts should sing down octaves as appropriate.)

### *Messa di voce* exercises to learn dynamic control

*Sing a messa di voce exercise in the middle range (i.e., start on a vowel at a piano dynamic level; increase gradually to forte and then gradually reduce to piano). Try varying the beginning and ending dynamic levels (e.g., start pianissimo and crescendo to fortissimo). Less experienced and younger singers can try the exercise at first without specific start and end dynamics. For them, start at a comfortable, medium dynamic and crescendo a bit, then come back down gradually to the starting dynamic. Work to start more softly and crescendo more, little by little.*

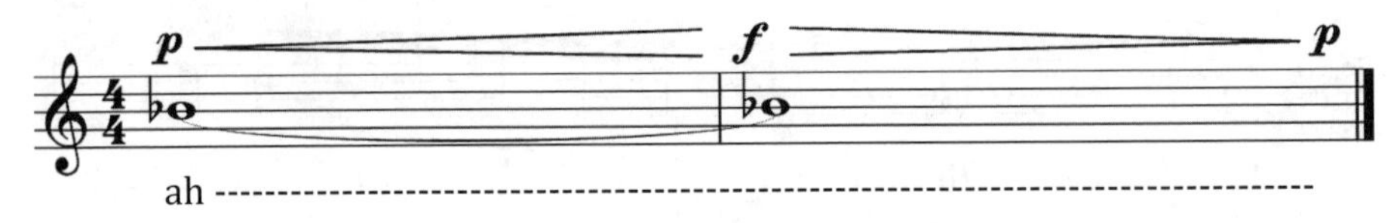


*Sing a reverse messa di voce in the upper register, followed by a standard messa di voce in the upper register. We recommend a reverse messa di voce to start in the upper register because it is more difficult to initiate a pitch at a low dynamic level in the upper register. (Upper note is for upper voices; lower note is for lower voices; tenor and bass are an octave lower than written.)*

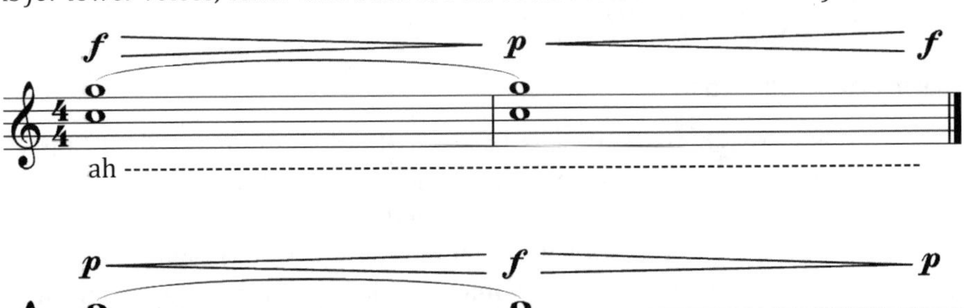

# Chapter 12: Improving Choral Blend

Blend in choral singing can be defined as perceived homogeneous sound—the combining of disparate voices into one uniform-sounding ensemble. Goodwin (1980) defines blend as "an ensemble sound in which individual voices cannot be separately discerned by a listener" (p. 25). Conductors and singers are always searching for ways to produce better choral blend. Vowel and consonant production, rhythm, desired choral sound, covering, use of falsetto, voice matching, and positioning are some of the strategies that can be considered to achieve blend.

## Blend philosophies

Numerous sources discuss how to select voices for a choral ensemble that will be flexible and easily blend with others (e.g., Bassinger, 2006; Eskelin, 2005; Noble, 2005). The presumption is that conductors should not include singers who do not fit their tonal model. The reality is that most conductors of amateur ensembles cannot pick and choose voices—and *should not* do this! All singers can and should benefit from the experience of ensemble singing.

The earliest, most fully articulate proponent of a blended choral sound was F. Melius Christiansen, director of the choir at St. Olaf College. His ideas about blend have influenced many conductors, including ideas about precise enunciation of consonants and consistent production of vowels. Nonetheless, his approach to choral blend tended to produce an artificial sound that was not always well received by audiences. Latimer and Daugherty (2006) describe a *New York Times* review of a 1927 concert of the St. Olaf Choir that characterized the sound of the female choir members as "so impersonal in character that it suggested the voices of boys" (Downes, 1927, p. 17).

Such a sound is often produced by asking women both to use covered vowel production (see Chapter 5 on vowels) and to eliminate vibrancy in their singing (i.e., use a "straight tone" method of production). Not only is this artificial and unreflective of the full tonal quality of women's voices, but it also causes vocal tension. Indeed even in Christiansen's day many vocal pedagogues argued that his approach to choral singing "caused unnecessary and unhealthy tension in the vocal mechanism" (Latimer & Daugherty, 2006, p. 19).

Many credit the Robert Shaw Chorale for "opening the door to a much wider range of possibilities for choral tone" (Basinger, 2006, p. 4). Nonetheless, some choral directors continue to attempt to achieve blend by altering the production of individual voices, which fuels the argument by some voice teachers that developing voices should not participate in choirs (Ekholm, 2000).

We maintain that blend can be achieved without sacrificing individual vocal integrity. Recent research supports the move away from the technique of requesting all singers to sound the same or sacrifice individual tone quality and individuality to achieve choral blend (Knutson, 1987). The techniques in this chapter are intended to assist all singers in moving toward a good ensemble sound without "neutralizing idiosyncrasies of individual singers" (Smith & Sataloff, 2006, p. 182).

## Choral sound

Conductors' concepts of desired choral sound can have a substantial effect on how they go about achieving blend. One school of thought strives for a homogeneous sound from the highest through the lowest voices. Another point of view is to work for blend largely within vocal sections but with distinctive colors for each section. A third perspective is to use both concepts, varying the blend of the ensemble based on the repertoire sung. A subscriber to this theory may seek to create a wall of even sound on an eight-part chord in, for example, an Eric Whitacre piece, while still capturing the distinctive warm, resonant quality inherent in the soloistic bass and alto voices in repertoire by Brahms and others. As noted in Chapter 4 on resonance, the quality of sound can be subtly influenced in a number of ways, allowing the voice parts to maximize or minimize their inherent differences.

## Keys to a blended sound

Smith and Sataloff (2006) suggest the following as essential elements of a blended sound:

- Color (no individual voices identifiable, distinctive color for each section, distinctive color for the ensemble as a whole)
- Balance (individual sections are balanced within the ensemble)

- Tuning
- Diction (vowels and consonants performed uniformly)

This is a helpful set of issues to keep in mind, but we think the ingredients for blend are more numerous and multifaceted. The following are our recommendations for improving and refining blend.

### Uniform vowel production within sections

Robert Shaw cites "distortion of voweling" as making sectional unison impossible to achieve (Blocker, 2004, p. 87). As noted in Chapter 5 on vowels, if singers within a section are producing vowels differently, the first and second formant frequencies can be excessively different, leading to a lack of uniformity in sound. Remember, however, it is not necessary for every singer to look exactly the same on the outside—it is the inside that counts. Singers can obtain a good tonal and physical reference when conductors take time in the warm-up to establish the desired vowel colors and the preferred method of achieving them. Providing singers with this reference will make uniformity of tone quality in the repertoire much simpler.

Uniformity of vowels is important for all singers in a choir, but we especially emphasize uniformity *within a choral section.* When sections are called upon to sing notes near the top of their range for instance, those sections will need to modify their vowels to produce an appropriate sound that is neither pressed nor bright and brassy. Singing a slightly modified vowel in these sections will not harm the sound—it will actually contribute to better blend, provided all singers have the same concept of the desired modification.

### Precise, quick consonants

Weston Noble (2005) describes what he calls "the 'original sin' of the amateur vocalist" (p. 57)—closing on the vowel by anticipating the consonant that follows, shortening the length of the beauty of the vowel. Also, if some choral group members are lazy in their production of consonants, a less than cohesive sound will result, with some singers appropriately moving quickly to the next vowel while others are creating consonant noise. Refer to Chapter 6 on consonants for strategies and exercises to improve individual and group production of consonants.

### Precise rhythms

Noble (2005) quotes Robert Shaw as saying "The bottom line of blend is rhythm! You directors work so hard at unifying the vowel and never arrive at the vowel together—how can you achieve blend?" (p. 57).

Often, the underlying problem is not the production of a consonant but rather the singer's perception of time or rhythm. Singers need constant encouragement to watch the conductor and to find ways of physically incorporating the pulse and subdivisions of that pulse. Long, sustained pitches are particularly difficult. It does not take long for singers to lose the sense of where they are rhythmically if they are not paying close attention.

*Try subdividing sustained pitches, either audibly or mentally. Sing a passage on a neutral syllable and rearticulate each subdivision (da-da-da-da on eighth notes, for example). Another technique is to tap the pulse (or a subdivision of it) with your toe or finger. Avoid tapping the foot as this can be distracting to others.*

Highly rhythmic passages can also cause difficulties. A lack of blend will occur if choral singers are moving at different times. In such cases rehearsing to the rhythm without the pitches can be helpful.

*Either chant the passage in a high pitched, sing-song tone quality (more easily linked to the singing voice than regular speaking) or sing it slowly on one constant note. After a couple of repetitions sing the correct pitches and increase the speed so that muscle memory does not occur at a slow tempo. This can be difficult to correct! Rather, practice shorter sections up to performance tempo and systematically add more notes as facility increases. Then sing the passage as written.*

### Precise cutoffs

All singers have experienced poor cutoffs, particularly when they involve noisy consonants like [s]. Sometimes singers fail to watch the conductor's indication of a cutoff and sometimes conductors fail to indicate clearly the cutoff. A singer's individual perception of the passage of time may be at fault as well. Regardless, conductors should endeavor to explain clearly where final consonants should be placed or where the sound should stop. They should show it with their gesture as clearly as possible, and singers should practice efficient releases to produce blend right through the ends of phrases.

### Attention to dynamics

Blend is improved when all singers within a section produce the same dynamic level. If some sing much louder than others, especially with a pressed or heavy style of production, those singers will stand out, resulting in a lack of blend.

- Robert Shaw emphasizes the perils of oversinging, noting that both "distortion of voweling" and "disturbances of vocal color" are results of singing too loudly (by some or all singers). He states that they "impede sectional unison—which is the *sine qua non* of good choral discipline" (Blocker, 2004, p. 87).
- Many blend problems related to dynamic level disappear if singers listen to each other. Indeed, when singers are in groups and listen to each other they will naturally adjust their dynamic level, as well as pitch and formant frequencies (Titze, 2008a).

Of course balancing of dynamic level across the entire choir is also important when the same dynamic level is indicated in the music for each section.

### *Sopranos and dynamics*

Remember that sopranos sing at pitch levels in a range where the human ear is keenly sensitive, thus chastising them for their louder perceived volume is unproductive. If sopranos are asked to reduce their volume, a reduction in sound quality, intonation, as well as blend may result. If this is the case, consider encouraging the other sections to sing out more.

### *Developing singers and soft dynamic levels in a choral setting*

Developing singers are encouraged by their voice teachers to sing with a full sound to facilitate the development of supported, resonant singing. Singing softly is, simply put, a more advanced skill. Offering helpful techniques and reminders about soft singing can be beneficial. Also, more often than not, allowing a comfortable level of production is important. Learn very soft passages at a slightly louder dynamic than you might ultimately perform them so that singers can have the mechanics of the rhythms, pitches, and words under control before attending to extreme dynamic levels. We also recommend more frequent stagger breathing.

## The role of covering to produce blending

Some conductors favor a slightly darker tone because darker voices are easier to blend—brighter voices tend to stick out. We favor a natural tone that includes a mix of darker and brighter resonance, but there is certainly a range of tonality that is acceptable to audiences.

Use of a covered method of production is one way to achieve blend when a specific part stands out too much. For example, if most parts are in the lower portion of their range during a piano section but one section is asked to ascend the scale, it may stand out too much. If this is the case, you can ask singers to use a covered approach to production, particularly if a bright vowel such as [i] is being sung (e.g., sing [i] with the mouth formed to sing [o] or [ɔ]).

A covered method of production is ultimately an unhealthy method of production if sustained and should be used sparingly because an improper alignment of the vocal tract relative to the vowel to be sung will produce undesirable tension.

## The role of falsetto to produce blending

Tenors are frequently asked in the choral literature to sing a high tessitura. Many untrained tenors (especially younger singers) will find it difficult to sing $A_4$-flat or even $G_4$ and above in modal voice without breaking or without a pressed mode of production. In such cases asking them to use falsetto may help to blend their sound with other sections. This is particularly true for quiet passages. For this to be effective, they need to practice falsetto periodically to improve its quality, otherwise it will be too grainy or inconsistent to employ as an effective blend device. (Professional singers should not need to use falsetto for this purpose because they should have developed the ability to sing reasonably softly at higher pitches in the modal upper register.)

The need for basses to use falsetto is rare, because they are more likely to be the anchor in the chord structure. Falsetto can be helpful, however, when basses must sing $E_4$ and above for an extended period or at a soft dynamic level.

## Voice positioning

Conductors know that the arrangement of singers within a chorus can definitely influence blend (Smith & Sataloff, 2006). Nonetheless, only recently has research been conducted to ascertain scientifically the benefits of various approaches to the positioning of singers.

There are two levels of consideration when arranging a choral ensemble:

1) placement of sections
2) placement of individual singers within sections

### Section placement

Chapter 10 on intonation discusses some of the benefits of placing basses and sopranos in near proximity. A common arrangement of singers puts basses behind sopranos and tenors behind altos, with the conductor immediately in front of the sopranos/altos.

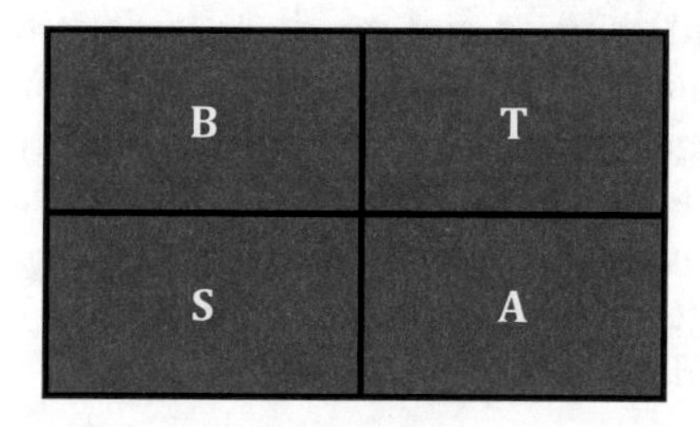


Another standard arrangement puts singers within their sections in columns that run from the back of the ensemble to the front. Soprano columns are placed on the left, followed by bass, tenor and alto columns. Conductors of choirs with fewer male singers favor this arrangement, which again allows good contact between the outermost parts (sopranos and basses):

| S | S | B | T | A | A |
|---|---|---|---|---|---|
| S | S | B | T | A | A |
| S | S | B | T | A | A |
| S | S | B | T | A | A |
| S | S | B | T | A | A |

Mixing singers in quartets (SBTA) throughout the choir is a popular arrangement in ensembles with strong, independent singers. This arrangement takes advantage of an improved self-to-other loudness ratio that allows singers to hear themselves and others better (Daugherty, 1999):

| S | B | T | A | S | B |
|---|---|---|---|---|---|
| T | A | S | B | T | A |
| S | B | T | A | S | B |
| T | A | S | B | T | A |
| S | B | T | A | S | B |

Daugherty's (1999) "circumambient formation" is another arrangement that allows an improved self-to-other loudness ratio. Singers are placed two feet apart (shoulder to shoulder) on risers with one riser row empty between rows. Both audience and singers prefer this formation to closer formations, and singers feel a greater freedom of production. However, this amount of spacing can be impractical with larger groups.

Interestingly, studies have identified few acoustical differences among these formations. That said, singers and conductors definitely perceive each of these formations differently and have preferences (Aspaas, McCrea, Morris, & Fowler, 2004). Singers sing more or less freely and confidently depending on where they stand, which has a potentially significant impact on choral blend. How often have ensembles gone from rehearsal to a performance venue that necessitates a different standing formation, only to find that their careful work on blend was all for naught!

Our conclusion is that conductors can use these formations as a guide to good possibilities, but each ensemble needs to find its preferred arrangement for positioning of sections and to practice being flexible as performance spaces may demand.

### Positioning singers within sections

Positioning singers within sections is another important way to achieve blend without altering healthy vocal production. Noble and others advocate elaborate voice-matching trials (Ekholm, 2000). One approach starts with an anchor, "ideal" voice (based on conductor preference) or with a pair of voices that have a natural blend. Singers then perform a simple vocal exercise together. One by one, other singers are added, removing those whose sound does not have a favorable effect on the whole and keeping those who do blend. Jordan (2007) uses the visual image of a comb to illustrate voice matching. Combs vary in their thickness and spacing of teeth. As such, some combs can interlock. Put another way, the formant amplitudes and frequencies of some singers fit together better than others. Singers whose formant amplitudes and frequencies do not mesh well can create a combined sound that is too loud, out of tune, strident, etc.

Eventually all singers are placed within a line or block. This should allow the section to sound blended and to give individual singers the freedom to sing naturally. See Noble (2005) and Jordan (2007) for more detailed descriptions of approaches to voice placement.

Although this method is impractical for large choruses because it is so time-consuming, it does take into account factors of blend between singers such as tone color, vibrato, pitch, physical height, size of tone, and individual perception/execution of rhythm. All of these factors can be perceived by the conductor when hearing voices together. Gardiniere's (1991) study of more than 100 choral conductors' perceptions of the blend produced by Noble's methods of voice matching led to the conclusion that matching has a perceptible benefit that "transcended individual taste or preference" (cited in Ekholm, 2000, p. 125). A recent study by Killian and Basinger (2007) further verifies the utility of voice matching.

## Concluding thoughts on blend

Conductors need to consider carefully their aesthetic goals for blend in their ensembles. Whenever possible, they should choose ways to achieve these goals that are founded on proper vocal technique. Indeed, many technique-related tools are available to achieve blend: efficient consonant production, uniform vowel production within sections (with appropriate vowel modification for higher pitches), precise rhythms, precise cutoffs, and balanced dynamic levels among sections. Placement of sections and voice matching/placement of singers within sections are also possibilities. All of these techniques allow for creation of a more natural, blended sound that eliminates the need to use more artificial methods such as extensive or "straight tone singing." Conductors can achieve blend goals without compromising individual voices and singers can use healthy methods of vocal production—a win-win!

# Chapter 13: Changing Voices

This chapter discusses why and how voices change during adolescence and as singers age. We also discuss vocal technique issues during these changes. Conductors, teachers, and singers will benefit from knowing what happens to voices during these stages of development and how to manage the changes that occur.

## Overview of voice change during childhood and puberty

Voice changes occur during adolescence because of increases in hormones associated with sexual maturation. A major effect of these hormones is an increase in vocal fold length for both girls and boys and an increase in vocal fold thickness for boys. The percentage of increase in vocal fold length is much greater for males than it is for females and is associated with the development of the "Adam's apple." These changes lead to a lowering of both speaking and singing pitches during childhood and adolescence.

Other important changes during adolescence include:

- Lengthening of the vocal tract, which is somewhat greater for males than females. Significant change occurs from about ages 9 to 14 with some further lengthening in females to about age 16 and in males to about age 18 (Fitch & Giedd, 1999). Recall from Chapter 4 on resonance that a longer vocal tract lowers all formant frequencies. This leads to a change in timbre during adolescence that might be characterized as "deeper" or "richer."
- The larynx, pharynx, and mouth increase in size, leading to the potential for improved resonance.
- Lung capacity increases, improving the ability to sustain notes for longer periods.

This list includes many positive aspects of adolescent development that will ultimately lead to a singer's adult voice. However, the process of change is often difficult. Young singers no longer have the childhood voice with which they have become comfortable. Instead, they have what have been called "cambiata" voices during this period of change.

### Difficulties with vocal change

When voice change occurs in boys, some will experience it more gradually than others. Certain boys have little difficulty with the lowering of their voices—many could ultimately be tenors as adults (Phillips, 1996). Others will experience a faster change from one stage of development to another and thus may have sudden instabilities in their voices. They may be more likely to sing the bass choral part as adults.

Since the amount of change in singable pitches is less for girls, until recently little attention was paid to their experience of voice maturation. Nonetheless, girls experience many of the same problems with changing voices. Briefly, some of the most difficult aspects of the vocal maturation process are:

- Loss of previously singable high notes, particularly for boys but also for girls
- Reduced range at certain stages of development
- Difficulties with pitch control and pitch matching
- Breathiness or "huskiness" related to an incomplete closure of the rear portion of the glottis during puberty and even late adolescence. (While breathiness is perhaps more common with girls, it occurs with boys as well.) The laryngeal muscles have not developed sufficiently to close the newly enlarged vocal folds.
- Difficulty with achieving coordinated onset, which is related to the glottis closure problem
- Abrupt register transitions, or "breaks in the voice" (Gackle, 2006)

We analyze these issues in detail for each gender in a later section of this chapter.

## Earlier voice change in recent years

Since the 1940s the average age at which vocal change begins has been decreasing in the United States. This trend has accelerated in the last 30 years and is associated with further decreases in age of onset of sexual maturation (Herman-Giddens et al., 1997; Herman-Giddens, Kaplowitz, & Wasserman, 2004). While earlier sexual maturation since the 1940s is in part due to improved nutrition, the causes of earlier sexual maturation are not fully understood. Indeed, nutrition may not explain the accelerated trend since 1980, given that other developed countries have not all seen further decreases in onset of sexual maturation. For example, a recent study comparing the United

States to Denmark showed no decrease in age of puberty commencement among Danish children from 1964 to the 1990s (Juul et al., 2006).

For an overview of the timing and rate of vocal change, see Figure 13.1, a chart of age and speaking fundamental frequency based on smoothed data from Lee, Potamianos, and Narayanan (1999). Speaking fundamental frequency (SFF) is the average frequency of the speaking voice. It is commonly used as an indicator of vocal change. The SFF is strongly related to the lowest singing pitch, which is typically 3–4 semitones (half steps) below the SFF after the initial voice change (Cooksey, 1999). We want to emphasize, however, that the pitches shown for the various age groups and genders are averages. There is substantial variability in age of vocal change onset and in the specific pitches associated with each age. At the individual level the observed *change* from childhood baseline provides the most useful clues about the stage of vocal development.

Figure 13.1 shows that boys and girls have the same SFF up to age 9 (between $C_4$ and $D_4$-flat). Between ages 9 and 10 and continuing to age 11, girls decrease a quarter step to $C_4$ and boys decrease to $B_3$. Further change continues to age 12 where both genders have decreased to $B_3$-flat and girls have reached a level close to their adult SFF (adult female average SFF is roughly $A_3$-flat). Boys then decline precipitously to $G_3$-flat at age 13, reaching close to their adult-mean SFF of $B_2$ at age 15. (They may decline a bit further after age 18.)

In sum, the maximum change for girls occurs between ages 11 and 12 and for boys between ages 12 and 13 and again between ages 14 and 15. Yet both genders experience initial changes between ages 9 and 10. Note also that the patterns of maturation mean that female voices at age 18 will have a degree of maturity that is far greater than that of males who have been undergoing more substantial change over a longer period of time. Tenor voices are the last to reach maturity and in fact will not be reasonably mature until the mid-twenties.

How does this timing of voice change compare with earlier studies? One point of comparison is a 1940 study which showed that boys' SFF was the same at ages 10 and 14 (Fairbanks, 1940). Clearly that is not the case today. Another point of comparison is Titze's (2000) composite summary of two studies published in 1976 and 1980. His chart shows females not reaching $B_3$-flat until about age 14 (compared to age 12 in this more recent study). Males did not reach $F_3$ until about age 16 (compared to age 14 in this more recent study). Vocal development appears to be about two years earlier in the late 1990s compared to the late 1970s.

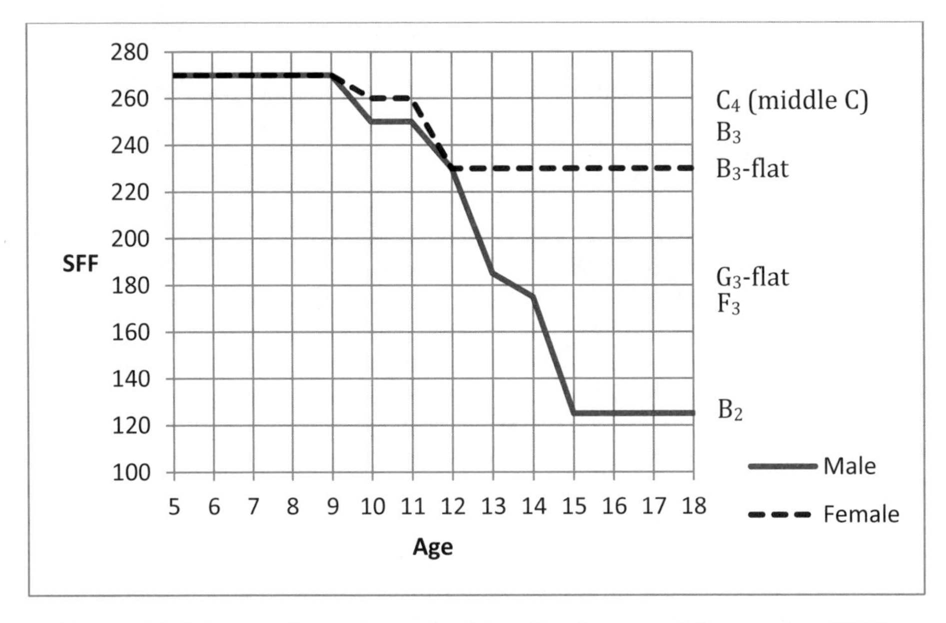


**Figure 13.1 Age and average speaking fundamental frequency (SFF)**

## Vocal development in adolescent boys

The most accepted and studied approach to categorization of the characteristics of changing boys' voices is that of John Cooksey. He wrote an influential series of articles in the *Choral Journal* (1977a, 1977b). His system of categorization has been studied and extensively validated both by him and others. Cooksey's book, *Working with Adolescent Voices*, summarizes his work on boys' voices and provides guidance concerning girls' voices as well (Cooksey, 1999). It also contains numerous suggestions for working with changing adolescent voices, including methods of determining changing voice categories, seating plans for changing voices, and repertoire. We highly recommend this book to anyone working with adolescents. (As shown in the SFF age chart, the term "adolescent" may apply now to some children as young as ages 9 and 10. Even in grades 3 and 4 music teachers may encounter some voices that are starting to change.)

Cooksey describes five maturational stages in boys, in addition to a pre-change stage (Cooksey, 1977a, 1999). These stages along with some comments about them are summarized below. Where adult choral parts are indicated, the voice is not the equivalent of the adult version, rather it is an indication of the part that might be sung during this stage, with recognition that range and resonance characteristics will often be limited.

- **Unchanged Voice (prechange).** This is the boy soprano, though some are altos. Just prior to puberty, boys reach their maximum childhood range. There is good dynamic range and voices are agile.
- **Mid-Voice I ("Alto").** Loss of high notes begins. Breathiness occurs, particularly on upper pitches. Range decreases by about four half steps to 16–17 half steps. Lowest singing pitch and speaking pitch are reduced only a half step. Height and weight begin to increase.
- **Mid-Voice II ("Tenor").** Adam's apple becomes apparent. The speaking voice lowers two half steps below the unchanged voice; however, our analysis of the data from Cooksey (1999), Killian (1999), and Killian and Wayman (2010) suggest that the decrease in lowest singing pitch is somewhat more noticeable, i.e., three half steps below the unchanged voice. Range is further reduced by a half step. Cooksey (1999) describes the voice as "husky" but "thicker" than Mid-Voice I. Height and weight increase further and there is increased lung capacity. Falsetto register starts to develop.
- **Mid-Voice IIA ("Tenor").** The lowest pitch lowers substantially (four half step reduction from Mid-Voice II). Range is similar to Mid-Voice II, but upper pitches are often strained and breathy; obvious register breaks occur. Additional weight gain and increase in height are noticeable. Cooksey cautions that boys in this stage may use an excessively heavy method of production as they experiment with their new lower notes (Cooksey, 1999). There is greater difficulty matching an intervallic fifth in this stage than in any other stage (Willis & Kenny, 2008).
- **New Voice (New "Baritone").** The lowest sung pitch lowers an additional four half steps. Range is similar to Mid-Voice II and IIA. Baritone quality is somewhat light. Notes may be missing between the modal and falsetto registers. We suggest downward scales starting in the falsetto register to help with bridging to the modal registers. This will also help with development/retention of head voice. Weight and height increase further as do chest and shoulder development. Agility is limited. As with Mid-Voice IIA there is a tendency toward heavy production. The suggested falsetto exercises can also help with this problem.
- **Emerging Adult Voice (Developing "Baritone").** This stage involves a further three half-step lowering of lowest sung pitch, but range increases 3–4 half steps. Sound quality improves, becoming more clear and focused. In his book, Cooksey (1999) uses the term "emerging adult voice" to recognize that not all individuals in this stage will become baritones; some will develop into tenors and basses as they continue to

> mature. Indeed, even at this point some may have ranges that better fit the tenor or bass classifications. However, those ranges will be restricted relative to the comparable adult voice. Physical development continues in this stage, with vocal tract cavities approaching final volumes, further increasing the opportunity for improved resonance.

As voices mature from junior into senior high school they take on more of the characteristics of adult voices, though with less range (Phillips, 1996).

An illustration of the vocal range associated with each stage is shown in Figure 13.2. The lower pitch is an average of Cooksey (1999) and studies by Killian (Killian, 1999; Killian & Wayman, 2010). These studies have similar findings for the low end of the range. Studies are more variable with respect to mean high pitch, which in part reflects how variable the highest singable pitches are during development. We have shown the result for Killian and Wayman's (2010) choir group, which generally had higher upper range limits than a group of band members who did not sing in choir. These choir members seem particularly accomplished, especially considering the upper mean pitch for the unchanged voice group ($C_6$). (Cooksey says that the upper pitch for unchanged voices is likely to be $G_5$, which is consistent with our experience.) As a result the choir members in Killian and Wayman's study exhibit more change in range across the stages than described by Cooksey.

The studies by Killian and a study by Fisher (2010) provide further evidence that vocal change is occurring earlier. For example, 46% of boys were exhibiting change in grade four (Fisher, 2010). In grade five 56% were showing change, and 74% were showing change in grade six (average of results from Killian, 1999, and Fisher, 2010).

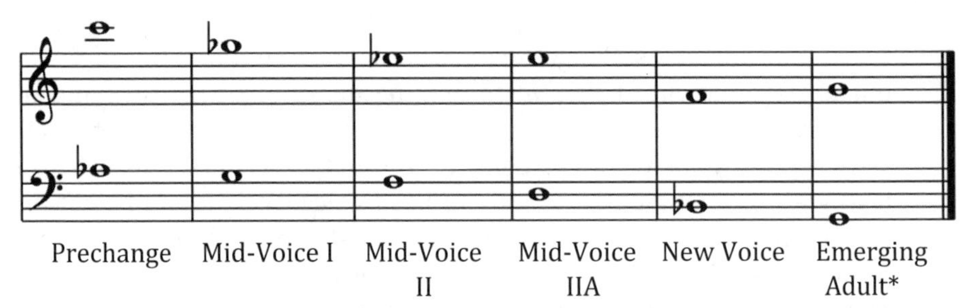


Note: Mean highest pitch is for the choir group in Killian and Wayman (2010). Mean lowest pitch averages over findings from Cooksey and Killian. *$E_5$ is actually the mean high pitch for emerging adult voice choir members in Killian and Wayman (2010). This was likely falsetto. We have estimated the high end of the modal voice for the emerging adult range based on other trends in their data.

**Figure 13.2 Mean lowest and highest pitches for Cooksey male stages of vocal development**

## Vocal development in adolescent girls

Gackle (1991; Huff-Gackle, 1985; Gackle, 2008) proposed four stages of development for adolescent females. She now refers to these as "phases" to emphasize the gradual nature of female adolescent voice development (Gackle, 2006).

Although Gackle's phases and their characteristics are based on her extensive experience working with female adolescent choirs, no systematic program of research has been published to date to validate these phases and their characteristics. Nonetheless, her ideas have been influential and may assist those working with young voices. Note that unlike males, there is little change in the average highest pitch that can be sung and only small changes in average speaking fundamental frequency (SFF) and in the lowest pitch that can be sung. Gackle says vocal development in females involves shades of change, like shades of colors. The voice is still treble but the color becomes richer, warmer, and has greater depth (i.e., resonance characteristics change over time). Listed below are summaries of Gackle's phases.

- **Phase I—Prepubertal (pre-change).** Phase I is a light, flexible soprano voice. Gackle describes the tonal quality as "flute-like." Similar qualities to the prechange male voice are present, but there is less potential to achieve high sound levels. There are no obvious register transitions. Comfortable range is $D_4$ to $D_5$. First soprano would be a common part assignment.
- **Phase IIA—Pubescence.** Average speaking and lowest singable pitch both lower a half step. Perhaps the most noticeable change is the development of breathiness, particularly when singing high notes. Some may experience register transitions in the vicinity of $F_4$ to $B_4$-flat and agility is reduced. Interestingly, Gackle shows an increase in range due to an expansion of the upper singable pitch by two half steps along with the aforementioned decrease in lowest singable pitch. (This is quite different from the initial stage of change for males, who experience a reduction in range.) Part assignment might be second soprano though some may still be able sing first soprano. Breast development begins and height starts to increase.
- **Phase IIB—Puberty/Post-menarche.** This is the most difficult and unstable phase of female voice development. Average speaking fundamental frequency may lower an additional semitone. Comfortable range lowers by three half steps at the lower end of the range and by two half steps at the upper end of the range (now $B_3$ to $C_5$), but the changes can be highly variable. Breathiness can occur throughout the range. Register transitions appear in the vicinity of both $F_4$ to $B_4$-flat

(lower register to middle voice) and $D_5$ to $G_5$-flat (middle voice to upper register). (The indicated areas of register transition seem quite large but may accurately reflect the highly variable nature of this stage.) Singing the alto part may be easiest during this phase, but girls should not be categorized arbitrarily and should have the opportunity for vocal exercises that extend into the upper parts of the range that are comfortable. Similar to boys in Cooksey's Stage IIA, some girls may want to sing only in their newfound chest voice, but this should be avoided. Part assignments may be second soprano or alto, but what is comfortable may vary over time. Girls should be encouraged to switch parts as they feel necessary.

- **Phase III—Young Adult.** Entering this phase, the voice begins to stabilize. Breathiness decreases, though in our experience some degree of breathiness may persist for a few more years. Timbre becomes richer due to increased vocal tract length and size of resonating cavities. The transition between middle voice and the upper register stabilizes at the adult level during this phase. Average speaking fundamental frequency lowers an additional half step. Range and comfortable range both increase substantially ($A_3$ to $A_5$ and $A_3$ to $G_5$, respectively). Agility improves. All part assignments are possible depending upon comfort and vocal character.

It is instructive to consider the age ranges proposed by Gackle for each phase in relation to the average speaking fundamental frequency observed in recent research (see Table 13.1). Remember that Gackle's age ranges are based on her experience with adolescent females in the 1980s. Comparing her age ranges to the approximate mean age for the average speaking fundamental frequency in a more recent study (Lee et al., 1999), provides further evidence that the phases of vocal development may be starting earlier. Note, however, that SFF is not a perfect indicator of vocal phase. For example, while young adult level SFF is now reached on average at age 12, it is unlikely that this is the average age of those in the young adult voice phase. Neither, however, is it likely that 15 (the midpoint of Gackle's range) is the average age today for this phase. The truth probably lies between, but the key point is to be alert for earlier maturation and encourage students to change voice parts as needed.

| | Phase I Pre-pubertal | Phase IIA Pubescence | Phase IIB Puberty | Phase III "Young Adult" |
|---|---|---|---|---|
| **Range** | $B_3$-flat to $F_5/G_5$ | $A_3$ to $G_5/A_5$-flat | $A_3$ to $E_5/F_5$ | $G_3/A_3$ to $A_5$ |
| **Comfortable Range** | $D_4$ to $D_5$ | $D_4$ to $D_5$ | $B_3$ to $C_5$ | $A_3$ to $G_5$ |
| **SFF** | $C_4$ to $D_4$-flat | $C_4$ | $B_3$ | $B_3$-flat |
| **Age range Gackle 1991** | 8–11 | 11–13 | 13–15 | 14–16 |
| **Mean age associated with SFF 1999** | 9.5 | 10.5 | 11.5 | 12 |

Notes: Range and tessitura (comfortable range) from Gackle (2008). SFF is the average speaking pitch based on the midpoint of the pitch range estimated by Gackle (1991) for each phase. Mean age associated with Gackle's SFF for each phase is estimated from Lee et al. (1999).

**Table 13.1 Selected characteristics of adolescent girls during the phases of the Gackle classification system**

## Vocal technique issues in child and adolescent voices

### Registers in unchanged voices

Although Gackle describes unchanged female voices as not having registers (or at least not noticeable register transitions), Phillips argues that children do have lower and upper registers (and mixed voice). In general, singing below $C_4$ requires use of lower register production (Phillips, 1996). Similar to adults, children can extend chest register into middle voice, but it is too often carried to higher pitches that are more appropriate for head voice. This can be just as harmful for children as it can be for adults. Phillips contends that many children in the United States have not been taught to access head voice, largely because vocal exercises disappeared from the general music curriculum by the mid-1950s. As a consequence children use chest production exclusively and consequently have a more limited vocal range than they are capable of. If, however, they are introduced to head voice, they can have a range of $A_3$-flat to $F_5$ by fifth grade and a two-octave range from $G_3$ to $G_5$ by the sixth grade. However, this range assumes they have not already started to experience the voice transitions of adolescence by these grade levels.

### Teaching children and adolescents about vocal technique

We think that virtually all of the vocal technique issues addressed in this book should be taught to children and adolescents over time. This is not to say that they should be taught with the same depth or with as much technical information as might be communicated to adults, but the range of technical issues is as relevant to children and adolescents as it is to adults.

- Both Phillips (1996) and Sell (2005) believe children and adolescents should be taught about vocal technique. Sell argues that they should also learn the proper terminology. If they can learn musical concepts such as pitch, rhythm, and notation, they can also absorb the language of vocal technique.
- Sell (2005) argues further that singing should not be a mystery for children. Teaching children almost *exclusively* by means of imagery, as is often done, does them a disservice. We agree.
- Cooksey (1999) supports teaching vocal technique through a variety of exercises outlined in his book. These cover many of the topics included in this book. He outlines exercises for posture, breath control, vowel consistency, resonance, articulation, development of agility, register transitions, and dynamic control, among others. Adaptations of some of these exercises appear in this book.

### Inform and support adolescents undergoing vocal change

Sell (2005) argues that the process of voice change must be explained to adolescents and that they find periodic testing of where they are in the process of change to be interesting. Cooksey (1977a) concurs and we agree.

Discussing with adolescents about what is happening to both genders' voices and the paths they may take to vocal maturity can be helpful. Unless boys and girls are supported and encouraged to sing during this period, and to be patient with their voices, they may stop singing. They need to understand that they are experiencing a normal part of maturation that is connected to the other physical changes they are experiencing. Adolescents are impatient by their very nature—a year seems like a lifetime for teenagers. Knowing what will be happening can encourage them to keep singing through this difficult period.

### Vocal models and adolescent girls

Adolescent girls (and boys) often model their tonal quality on popular artists. Popular female performers can have a breathy quality or may sing in a low range. Others have a Broadway belting style which some adolescents may be tempted to imitate to sound more mature. Both breathy singing and raw belting can have serious consequences for the young voice—young voices are particularly prone to damage from use of inappropriate technique. Conductors and teachers need to be aware of these issues as they work with young voices.

It is particularly important to help adolescent girls develop a more focused tone with better resonance. In mixed-gender middle school and high school choral groups it is often difficult to achieve dynamic balance between sections because girls have excessively breathy voices and boys are trying out their emerging chest voice.

## Part assignment during vocal change

Choral conductors should be sensitive to the need to move adolescents whose voices are changing to lower parts as necessary. Singers should also feel free to move to a higher part on days that their voice feels more comfortable at that level. Girls should be encouraged to rotate parts as comfortable to enable continued access to head voice and to gain more experience with chest voice at lower pitch levels.

Cooksey (1999) outlines a time-saving group audition method that conductors and teachers can use for part assignment. We outline this below for each gender, with some simplification. Given the embarrassment that both genders may feel during his period, it is best, if possible, to do this separately for each gender. For both genders, choose a song with limited range in the key of C such as "America" or "Kum-ba-yah" ("Come By Here").

### *Boys*

1) Identify boys singing an octave lower than the treble singers.
    a. These are "baritones" (bass part in SATB arrangements). Listen to this group again to check for any who can actually sing in the treble octave—these are "tenors" (at least in this stage of their development). Be sure, however, that they are not lower voices singing up the octave in falsetto.
2) Move the key up to F and ask the remaining boys to sing again. (You can push the key up to G, if necessary.)
    a. Assign to the soprano part boys who sing easily in the upper octave. But see below about labeling and seating issues to avoid embarrassment.

b. Those who sing the highest notes less easily can be placed in the alto section, or perhaps the tenor section for repertoire that does not require low tenor pitches.
c. Those who cannot sing the highest notes in this key should be assigned to the tenor part.
d. Listen carefully to be sure some baritones singing in falsetto register have not slipped through to the tenor group.

Boys whose voices have not changed may need to be assigned to the alto or even tenor parts for social reasons, particularly in junior high school (Cooksey, 1977b). Phillips (1996) suggests referring to boys whose voices have not changed as "first tenors." Seat them near the alto section and have them sing the alto part. Alderson (1979) suggests seating boys who still sing soprano or alto between female sopranos/altos and male tenors/basses so that they are not segregated from those male singers whose voices have changed.

### *Girls*

1) Ask girls to sing the song in the keys of both C and F. (Again, G can be used for the higher key if necessary to assist in discernment.) Identify girls who sing clearly and easily in each of these keys.
    a. Girls who sing clearly and easily in both keys can be divided evenly between soprano and alto parts (and should alternate those parts periodically).
    b. Girls who can sing clearly and easily in only the lower or higher keys should be assigned accordingly to alto or soprano.
    c. Girls who do not sing clearly in either key can be divided between the two parts depending upon which is most comfortable.

Given the short periods of time over which young voices can change, repeat this procedure at eight-week intervals to ensure that no one has fallen through the cracks in the interim.

Finally, conductors and teachers should always be alert to facial and bodily signs of tension that may indicate a need for a possible move to a different vocal section (e.g., chin rising in an attempt to sing high notes that were previously comfortable).

## Keep boys singing during the period of change

Some vocal authorities argue that boys who are going through dramatic vocal changes should wait until their voices have stabilized before singing. Indeed, this has been the historic practice in the Church of England choir program. This approach has several problems:

- When boys do sing again, most will have only lower register capability with little access to the upper register. Continuing to sing through the period of vocal change can help ensure that boys have a fuller range when their voices stabilize.
- When they are singing, boys are continuing to learn about music. Removing them from choral groups means that they are no longer progressing in their musical abilities. Even if they are having difficulty with pitch control and register breaks, they can still improve breathing, resonance, articulation, language skills, music literacy skills, repertoire, etc.
- This approach contributes to the phenomenon of decreasing male participation in choral groups. Indeed, Cooksey (1993) argues that if boys are encouraged to sing through the period of vocal change, more will continue to sing as adults.

For both genders one of the joys and benefits of choral singing is that changing voices can be socially and vocally supported by those around them. While social support may seem obvious for girls, the social component of a singing ensemble can be very encouraging and reassuring for boys and young men as well as their voices change. Solo singing can be frustrating and embarrassing while going through these vocal changes, but choral singing allows adolescents to continue to sing at a high level and develop their voices without focusing on the flaws or limitations of their current instruments.

Adolescence is a difficult time, full of raw emotion and self-doubt. Singing in a choral group can give adolescents a sense of peace and happiness as exemplified by this comment from an anonymous seventh grade student:

> "All of the ugliness binding me disappears . . . suddenly I feel beauty all around as I open my lips . . . and my heart . . . and my mind . . . simultaneously to a song!" (Williams, 2006).

## Vocal exercise issues specific to adolescents

While virtually all of the exercises in this book can be useful for adolescents, certain exercises need special attention during this period:

- Onset exercises can reduce breathiness and the related difficulty of starting sound. They are not, however, a panacea for these problems, as muscles controlling glottal closure will be weak for a period of time.

- Legato exercises can help with creating sustained sound throughout a musical phrase.
- Staccato exercises can provide further assistance with coordinating glottal closure and opening.
- Register bridging. Register transitions are particularly difficult during the period of vocal development.
- For males, falsetto exercises can help to develop a lighter approach to higher pitches to avoid carrying chest voice too high.

Cooksey (1999) suggests confining most vocalises for a mixed choir during the years of vocal change to what he calls the "Composite Union Range." Girls in all developmental phases and boys in the Mid-Voice IIA stage or earlier can sing together between roughly $B_3$-flat and $A_4$, though this range may need to be lowered to $B_3$ to $G_4$. Boys in the New Voice and Emerging Voice categories can sing in the same range an octave lower. This does not apply, however, to register bridging and falsetto exercises, which need to go beyond these boundaries.

## Aging voices

As we age, so do our voices. A number of physiological changes affect the larynx:

- Women's ovaries secrete less estrogen, particularly after menopause. While the ovaries continue to produce some estrogen (estrone) after menopause, they also secrete testosterone (Fogle, Stanczyk, Zhang, & Paulson, 2007). These changes in hormonal balance are associated with increases in the density of vocal fold tissues, resulting in lowered speaking pitch (Gilbert & Weismer, 1974). This generally translates into a lowering of the singing range.
- In men there is a decline in testosterone level that is associated with a slight increase in speaking pitch, raising the lowest singable pitch by a small amount but not appreciably increasing the highest singable pitch.
- Over time, portions of the laryngeal cartilages may calcify and even transform into bone (ossify). This can limit range and may affect high pitches the most.
- Muscles atrophy, and laryngeal muscles are not exempt. For example, in some older individuals the thyroarytenoid muscles atrophy, with the vocal folds exhibiting a characteristic bowed appearance. The result is incomplete closure of the glottis, producing a breathy or hoarse sound that is often heard in elderly singers. This problem can also be caused by degradation in neuromuscular control.

- Mucus and other secretions that help to lubricate laryngeal tissues decrease in quality and quantity (Ramig et al., 2001). Perhaps related to this is a reduction in hydration of the mucosal tissue at the edges of the vocal folds (Abitbol, Abitbol, & Abitbol, 1999). Older singers need to be particularly vigilant about staying hydrated. See Chapter 15 on vocal health for more on this subject.
- Accumulation of fluid in the tissues (edema) is a common problem associated with aging, particularly in women (Ramig et al., 2001). Vocal folds are affected like any other tissue and puffiness created by edema will produce a hoarse sound.

While the effects of aging on the larynx are important, vocal scientists are now also paying attention to its effects on breath control. A recent study has shown an association among aging, diminished respiratory capacity, and reduced vocal quality (Awan, 2006). It certainly stands to reason that aging would also affect muscles controlling breathing such as the intercostal and abdominal muscles. Given the importance of breath support for singing quality, maintenance of muscles controlling breathing is essential for preserving vocal function as we age. Breathing exercises and physical exercises for the abdominals outlined in Chapter 2 on breathing are critical for maintaining the ability to create good breath support.

Finally, loss of hearing can affect a singer's ability to control the voice, with respect to both pitch and amplitude. Older singers who seem to be having such problems may need to be referred to an audiologist.

## What characterizes the aging voice?

One way to answer this question is to ask middle-age and older singers about their experience with their voices as they aged. Boulet and Oddens (1996) asked male and female professional singers ages 40–70 about their views and experiences, because of professional singers' natural attention to these issues. Roughly 75% stated that the voice changes around age 50, but only 29% of women and 28% of men thought the changes were negative. Most frequently mentioned negative changes included:

- Loss of high notes—both genders but particularly women
- "Less supple vocal cords"—both genders but mostly women
- Change in timbre
- Voice less steady
- Breathiness/huskiness—reported mostly by women

The change in timbre described by both genders is notable. In the past this has been reported only for women because the changes in vocal fold tissues related to menopause have been connected with some loss of higher-frequency harmonics. These findings suggest that a general process of aging alters vocal tissue composition in at least some singers of both genders.

Another approach is to compare younger and older singers on various physiological and acoustical measures. This research suggests the following are characteristics of aging voices (Luchsinger & Arnold, 1965; Biever & Bless, 1989; Ramig & Ringel, 1983; Ferrand, 2002; Awan, 2006):

- Incomplete closure of the glottis and associated breathiness
- Acoustical noise and shimmer (indicates vocal roughness)
- Reduced amplitude of vibration of the vocal folds (lower sound level)
- Less control over pitch
- Less range
- Wobble

## Vocal aging can be delayed

Until now we have been painting a grim picture of vocal aging. Nonetheless, aging of the voice can be delayed by adopting healthy practices. Foremost is to keep physically fit. Many studies have demonstrated that vocal quality and sound level can be preserved into the seventies and even into the eighties for those whose physiological age ("real age") is younger. Regular exercise, both aerobic and strength training, along with a well-balanced diet and weight control contribute to the continued ability to sing well into old age. Taken together, these behaviors help to prevent cardiovascular disease, which is critically important for singers given that reduced blood flow is thought to be a major cause of laryngeal dysfunction associated with aging.

- For example, Ramig and Ringel (1983) examined measures of vocal quality and range in three age groupings of men—25–35, 45–55 and 65–75. They also measured their physical condition and divided them into poor and good groups. Men in good physical condition had better vocal quality and greater range than those in poor physical condition. This difference was more pronounced in the older age group.

Other actions that singers can take to prevent premature aging of their voices include (adapted in part from Heman-Ackah, Sataloff, Hawkshaw, & Divi, 2008):

- Use good breath support. Exercises such as the sibilant exercise can also help individuals who may be experiencing atrophy of breathing muscles.

- Avoid excessively pressed phonation that can damage the vocal folds over time. At the same time avoid breathy phonation. Onset exercises may help older singers who have excessively breathy voices.
- Always warm up prior to singing.
- Use techniques to enhance resonance, thereby increasing the efficiency of singing.
- Use good vocal technique, not only in singing, but also in everyday speech.
- Stay well-hydrated and take preventive measures to avoid gastric reflux (see Chapter 15 on vocal health).
- Do not smoke.

Finally, frequent singing can delay atrophy of laryngeal and breathing muscles. As we noted earlier, singing at one rehearsal per week and one performance per week is insufficient. Singers should strive to sing at least 10–15 minutes per day to stave off the atrophy of muscles important for singing.

# Chapter 14: Reducing Tension

Muscle tension is necessary to accomplish many of the tasks of singing. For example, muscles controlling the vocal folds must be contracted to enable closure of the glottis; abdominal muscles must be contracted to maintain breath pressure. But excessive and extraneous tensions are the enemies of good tonal quality. The most problematic tensions involve the:

- Neck/larynx/pharynx
- Jaw
- Tongue
- Lips
- Shoulders
- Legs

In this chapter we discuss various manifestations of tension in these areas and provide exercises to assist relaxation.

## Larynx and neck/pharynx tension produce a strident sound

As noted in Chapter 3 on initiation and creation of sound, muscles that control the vocal folds are not under direct, conscious control, with the exception of the cricoarytenoids and interarytenoids (which control opening and closing of the glottis). However, there are other muscles in and near the vocal tract over which we do have some degree of control. Any extraneous tension affecting these muscles will have a deleterious effect upon sound because of the way such tension impinges on the vocal tract.

All singers are guilty at one time or another of trying to directly control the muscles of the larynx affecting pitch. This can easily lead to excess pressure on the vocal folds.

- McKinney (2005) states that a pressed, edgy, strained sound results from tension in the vocal folds and in other muscles of the larynx and neck. If breath support is excessive, the combination can be particularly disastrous. He describes the resulting sound as harsh, strident, and grating.

Some singers also have a tendency to rely on neck and/or constrictor muscles of the pharynx to help control sound. This is virtually guaranteed to impair vocal function and produce poor tonal quality (Bunch, 1995).

When the constrictor muscles of the pharynx are tense, the diameter of the pharynx decreases. The potential for this can readily be seen in Figure 14.1 which illustrates the upper, middle, and lower constrictors. The upper constrictor is attached to a ligament at the sides of the rear portion of the jaw, forming a muscular wall on the sides and back of the throat. The middle constrictor is attached to the hyoid bone. Since the larynx is suspended from this bone, constriction of this muscle will obviously affect the larynx as well as the pharynx. The lower constrictor muscle is attached to the oblique ridge of the thyroid cartilage and thus can have a direct effect upon the larynx.

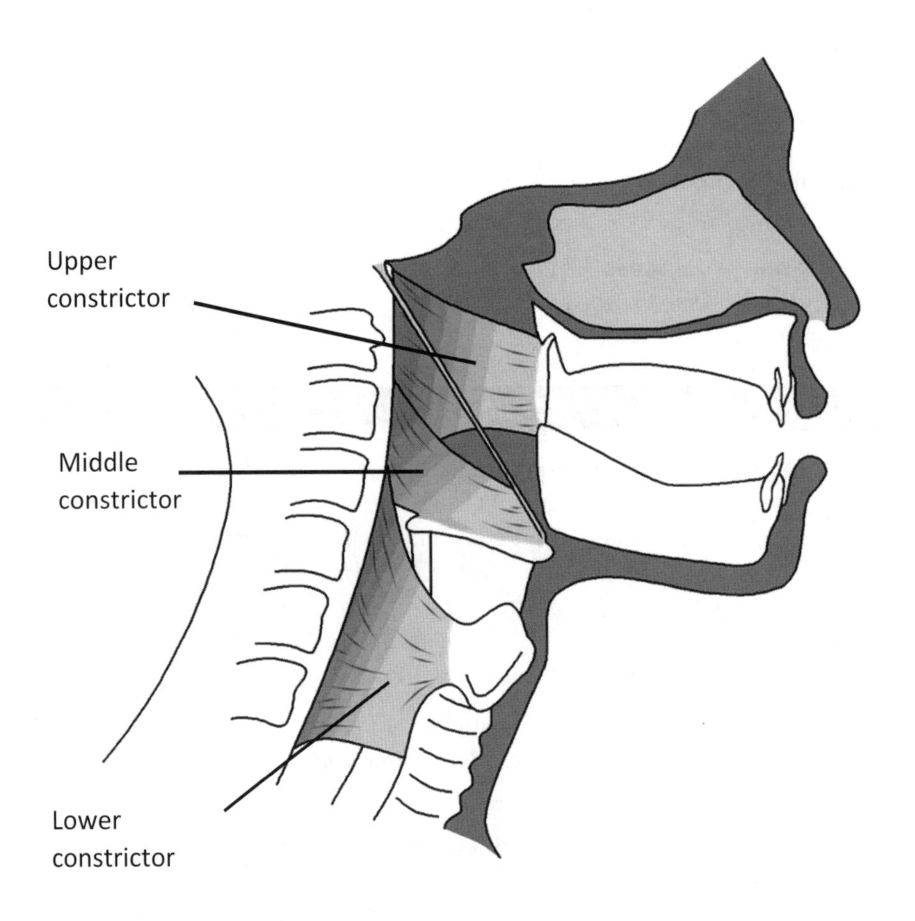


**Figure 14.1 Illustration of oropharynx and laryngeal-pharynx constrictor muscles**

Tension in these muscles also increases the density of the pharynx walls, exaggerating resonance of higher frequencies. In addition, tension in them can raise the larynx, which shortens the length of the vocal tract and increases all formant frequencies. In short, tension in the neck and pharynx can result in an excessive prominence of higher frequency harmonics (Fisher, 1966).

- Marafioti (1922) states that excess tension contracts the larynx and pharynx and stiffens the tongue and soft palate. He argues that this tension can also bend the epiglottis over the laryngeal opening. To see an illustration of the connection between the epiglottis and the tongue, see Figure 14.2 (also shown in Chapter 4).

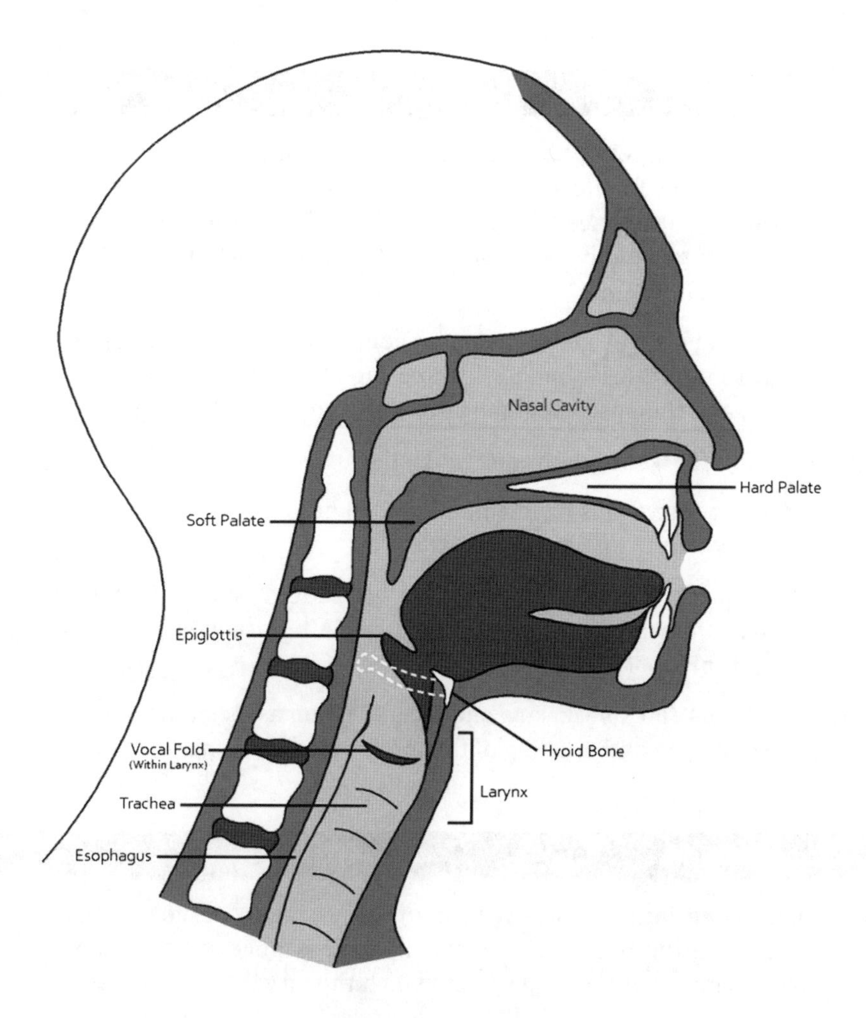


**Figure 14.2 Illustration of the vocal tract**

### Neck/pharynx tension can be a carryover from speech production that lacks good breath support

Some singers have a poor approach to speech production that they may carry over to singing. Speaking without proper breath support is fairly easy, and many of us do this. We may, for example, engage in upper chest breathing and tightening of the pharynx when we lack enough breath at the end of a spoken sentence. This method forces out enough breath to complete what we want to say—but with poor production. When we carry this method of production over to singing, the results are even worse. Conductors and teachers need to model proper speech production by being mindful of breath support when speaking.

## Jaw tension

Jaw tension is very common among singers due in part to an incorrect understanding of how to effectively release the jaw to create space in the pharynx. Hearing about the need for an "open throat," some singers drop the jaw excessively and tense the jaw muscles to keep the throat open. This can also induce laryngeal tension.

Jaw tension may also be generated from holding the jaw in a fixed position in an attempt to improve resonance by creating pharyngeal space. Tension can accumulate, and the position of the jaw may become rigid and tight.

*Try sustaining [ɑ] while gently massaging the jaw joints with a finger.*

Jutting the jaw forward is problematic as well because it creates tension and forces the larynx into an elevated position.

- Vennard (1967) believes that jaw freedom is very important and that it affects pharyngeal resonance: "A tight jaw is a symptom of a tight throat" (p. 117–118).

Figure 14.3 illustrates neck, jaw, and facial tension associated with excessive lowering of the jaw and opening of the mouth when singing [ɑ].

## Tongue tension

The tongue is a large muscle with many connections to vocal tract structures, including the pharynx. Of particular importance is the connection of the tongue with the hyoid bone, from which the larynx is suspended (Figure

14.2). Tongue tension can easily change the resonance characteristics of the vocal tract.

**Figure 14.3 Illustration of neck, jaw, and facial tension when singing [ɑ] incorrectly**

### Holding the tongue back/excessive tongue flattening creates a throaty sound

When the tongue is too far back in the mouth, it lowers the larynx excessively and constricts the pharynx. Excessive flattening of the tongue will have a similar effect. Lower frequency harmonics can bypass this constriction, but high frequency harmonics cannot. In addition, tongue tissue crowding the pharynx can absorb high frequency harmonics. Depression of the larynx also lowers all formant frequencies.

*Place your finger gently on the larynx. Move the tongue backward from its normal resting position and feel how this pushes the larynx down.*

Fisher (1966) and Tetrazzini (Caruso & Tetrazzini, 1975) both describe the resulting sound as "throaty." Fisher also says that even a slight change in the amount of constriction in the pharynx caused by tongue position can have a substantial effect on tonal quality. Recall from Chapter 4 on resonance that this may also cause the pitch to sound flat because of diminished high frequency harmonics. Even high fundamental frequencies can be affected.

- Fleming (2005) notes that even during her years in a master's degree program at Julliard, she still struggled with her tongue falling back, strangling her high notes, and sometimes cutting them off. One of her teachers placed a honey drop on the center indentation near the tip of the tongue. Reflexively, the tongue rises somewhat and remains in a forward position. Only exercises using [ɑ] can be performed when doing this, but this is the vowel for which this type of tongue problem is most likely.
- Fisher (1966) adds that allowing the tongue to fall back creates vowels that sound too dark.

It is worth noting in this context that singers should not deliberately flatten the tongue as a way of creating pharyngeal space.

- Bunch (1995) says that this creates a shortened and narrowed resonance chamber, resulting in a strident tone.

*Sing [a] in the middle of the range with a relaxed tongue and then depress it or force it back. You will hear a dramatic change in tone.*

### Tetrazzini's test for tongue tension

One of Tetrazzini's talks on singing addressed the "Mastery of the Tongue" (Caruso & Tetrazzini, 1975). She views the tongue as a major problem for most singers because it is such a large muscle whose roots, even with slight movement, can affect the larynx unfavorably.

Singers who have any tendency toward tongue tension (and most singers do at one time or another), can use a technique advocated by Tetrazzini to check for its presence: *Feel the underside of your jaw behind the chin—if your tongue is tense (and particularly if it is depressed) you will feel a lump or hardness in that area.*

## Tongue groove—is it a sign of tension?

A groove in the tongue is most obviously seen when someone sings [ɑ] on a note in the upper register. Some vocal experts believe the creation of a subtle groove is a natural development, while others claim that it is a sign of muscular tension. For example, Henderson (1979, p.125) believes that a grooved tongue is "caused by extreme muscular action" and that it "blocks the air flow through the mouth and changes the shape of the oral resonating cavity." We suspect, however, that Henderson refers to an extreme example of a tongue groove brought about by a conscious effort to shape the tongue. In fact, her illustration of this problem with a photograph of a singer shows the deepest groove we have ever seen, with the sides of the tongue markedly elevated.

In contrast, Vennard (1967) asserts that a modest tongue groove develops naturally over time. Our experience is in accord with his perspective. Much like vibrato, proper vocal production will often naturally result in a small groove. The key is to avoid trying to create a groove, as attempts to do so will likely result in tension and alter resonance.

A modest groove likely enhances space in the mouth for higher pitches.

- Tetrazzini argues that there should indeed be a slight furrow in the tongue, which naturally increases in depth as pitch ascends (Caruso & Tetrazzini, 1975).
- Marafioti (1922) also believes that a groove in the tongue is helpful because it increases oral space. He stipulates that the proper groove is created through complete relaxation of the tongue on the floor of the mouth. He warns explicitly against a stiff, contracted tongue.

## Lip tension

McKinney (2005) cites a number of indicators of lip tension:

- Holding the lips rigidly in one position
- Pulling the lips back into a continuous, forced smile. Usually too many teeth will be exposed, creating an excessively bright sound.
- Holding the lips against the teeth, creating a dark, muffled sound

Some singers also make the mistake of pushing the lips too far forward. Even when singing [u] the lips should never be puckered excessively.

We do, however, recommend raising the upper lips and cheek muscles slightly to create a pleasant smile. If only four upper teeth show, the lips have not been raised excessively (Vennard, 1967).

Figure 14.4 illustrates a forced smile with an excessive number of teeth exposed. Note the associated lip and facial tension.

## Shoulders

Shoulder tension invariably affects the neck and thus the larynx. Raised shoulders are a common problem. Some singers keep their shoulders in a fixed, raised position while others unconsciously lift the shoulders when they inhale, particularly if they are engaging in upper chest breathing. Instead, shoulders should be comfortably relaxed in their sockets. Shoulder tension can also occur from holding a music folder; conductors and teachers need to remind singers to relax their shoulders and maintain excellent posture—the shoulders do not hold music!

**Figure 14.4 Illustration of a forced smile**

Hunched shoulders (shoulders pushed forward) are another common source of muscular tension. Hunched shoulders lower the sternum and rib cage, reducing the area available for the lungs to expand during inhalation. Singers who concentrate on expanding the back of the ribs should be careful to avoid inadvertently hunching their shoulders to increase back expansion.

## Legs

Leg tension can be a serious problem for some singers. Leg muscles that are tensed for too long will cause the legs to tremble and even shake. Locked knees are a common indication of tensed leg muscles, as both the lower and upper leg muscles must be tensed to accomplish this posture. Knee locking limits the return flow of blood to the heart and thus to the brain. This is a major cause of fainting, usually when choir members are standing on risers (McKinney, 2005). As noted in Chapter 2 on posture, a *slight* tuck of the pelvis will position the knees slightly forward to prevent locking.

## Concluding thoughts on tension

Tension often compensates for something that is missing in vocal technique. It can also be a way that our bodies attempt to support or energize sound. Often focusing on the desired sound can allow us to wean ourselves from the sensation of energy or support that we get from nonproductive tension. Concentrate on what *does* need to happen and much of the extraneous tension will disappear.

## Exercises to reduce tension

### Neck relaxation

**Head tilt and rotation.** This exercise is one that we recommended in Chapter 2 as part of a set of exercises to release tension and assume good posture. *Tilt the head from side to side; then tilt the head forward and move it move it slowly in a half-circle to the back and to the front again; repeat to the right.*

**Backward neck stretch** (Fisher, 1966). *Place a chair near a wall such that when you tilt your head back it just touches the wall.* This stretching of the neck muscles can help to relax them, just as a runner relaxes calf and hamstring muscles by stretching them.

**Side neck stretch.** *Lean your head to the left. Place your left hand on the top right side of your head. Gently pull the head to the left. It should require very little movement of the head before you feel the muscles on the right side of your neck stretching. Do the same with your head tilted to the right with the right hand gently pulling on the top left side of your head.*

### Jaw freedom exercises

**Jaw wiggle** (Vennard, 1967). *Vennard suggests wiggling the jaw from side to side while vocalizing. Singers can also look at themselves in a mirror at home and move the jaw slowly up and down within a limited range. Remember to release the jaw in the back when opening it to get a sense of what it feels like to move the jaw without tension. Then increase the range of movement until you feel tension. Now sing an ascending and descending octave scale, lowering the jaw when ascending and closing it somewhat when descending. (Men should reduce jaw opening as they ascend into the first passaggio but can increase jaw opening past the second passaggio as discussed in the vowel modification section of Chapter 5.) Monitor to be sure there is no tension when you do this.*

**Sing and chew.** *Sing an easy exercise such as a slide of a third. Sing [a] and* *chew at the same time, moving the jaw gently in circular motions in all directions. Imagine a cow chewing grass while singing!*

### Tongue relaxation

**Lax vowels** (Fisher, 1966). A number of vowels are considered "lax" because they require minimal tongue tension. *Sing lax vowels such as [ɛ], [ae], and [U] to experience less tension. Then sing neighboring vowels in the Vowel Spectrum and see if you can keep the same relaxed sensation.*

*Tetrazzini (Caruso & Tetrazzini, 1975) suggests pushing the tongue forward out of the mouth (without stiffening it) and withdrawing it slowly.*

### Vowel exercises to bring the tongue forward

**Springboard exercise.** Fisher (1966) lists a variety of words which use front vowels. Each word starts with a consonant that requires the tongue to contact the area near the alveolar ridge on the roof of the mouth. *Sing the consonant quickly, using the contact with the ridge area as a springboard to keep the tongue forward on the subsequent vowel. Sample words include:*

- tea, deep
- tick, tin
- tail, day
- den, net

### Shoulder relaxation

*Raise the arms over the head and stretch toward the ceiling. Then shrug the shoulders several times. Finally, roll the shoulders in a circle to the back and then to the front, letting them relax into their sockets.*

**Scapular retraction** is an exercise to help reduce hunching. *In a standing or sitting position, attempt to pull your shoulder blades together in the back. Hold the position for ten seconds. Repeat several times.* This of course is an extreme backward shoulder position, which is helpful in counteracting forward hunching, but it is not the position you want for singing.

### Leg muscle relaxation

**Calf muscle stretch.** *If your calf muscles are tense, a variation on the runner's stretch is an excellent exercise. Stand facing a wall with your feet about one foot from it. Place your hands on the wall at head height to brace yourself. Move one foot back about two feet. Straighten that leg until you feel your calf muscle stretch. Hold for 30 seconds and repeat with the other leg.*

**Quadriceps stretch.** *If your front upper leg muscles are tight, stand sideways next to a chair or wall. Brace yourself with the hand closest to the wall. Lift the foot of your leg farthest from the wall behind you. Grasp it with your free hand and pull it as close as is comfortable to your buttock. You should feel a stretch in your quadriceps but do not overdo the stretch. Hold for 30 seconds and repeat on the opposite side.*

# Chapter 15: Guarding Singers' Vocal Health

As noted in Chapter 3 on initiation and creation of sound, the human vocal instrument is composed of small structures but is capable of producing amazing sound. It goes without saying that keeping our instruments in good health requires keeping our bodies in good health through a well-balanced diet, regular exercise, avoidance of harmful substances, and good sleep habits. This chapter focuses on issues specific to the vocal instrument:

- Vocal fold hydration and factors affecting hydration
- Safe amount of daily singing
- Meal consumption prior to singing
- Gastric reflux
- The common cold; coughing
- Medications that may cause vocal fold hemorrhage
- Hormonal factors affecting the voice
- Surgical considerations
- Choral conductor's role in vocal health

Please note that this chapter is intended to provide general information about health issues of particular relevance to singers. It is not meant to provide diagnosis or treatment information for specific individuals. Singers should consult their health care providers for such advice.

## Hydration

We noted in Chapter 3 that when our bodies are not properly hydrated, the mucus coating of the vocal folds is more viscous, making it challenging to get the folds vibrating. Higher pitches are exceptionally difficult to sing without sufficient hydration.

Singers need to be consistently hydrated. Drink plenty of fluids throughout the day, well prior to singing. Fluids consumed just before or during rehearsal will not immediately assist hydration but may be helpful for washing away irritants.

After waking, the body tends to be very dehydrated, so drink a couple of glasses of water soon after rising, particularly if singing in the morning. Singing a few vocalises while showering also helps because of the inhalation of warm, moist air. We suggest waking at least two hours before singing to allow time for the sinuses to drain (a source of excess mucus) and mucus on the vocal folds to thin. Some singers find that guaifenesin (Mucinex), an over-the-counter product, can be helpful in thinning excess mucus.

Singers who live in a dry climate (including winter in a normally temperate climate) should have a humidifier in their homes. Dry air passing over the vocal folds contributes to their dehydration. If you do not have central air humidification, use a portable humidifier, preferably in the room where you sleep.

Another benefit of well-hydrated vocal folds is that they are less prone to injury from voice use and recover more quickly if injured (Verdolini-Marston, Sandage, & Titze, 1994).

### Are caffeinated beverages and alcohol dehydrating?

Coffee and other beverages containing caffeine were once thought to be dehydrating. However, recent research has shown that caffeinated beverages have a diuretic effect that is similar to that of water itself at moderate levels of consumption (Armstrong, 2002; Armstrong et al. 2005). People who are regular coffee drinkers will experience less of a diuretic effect than those who drink coffee less frequently. Some people, however, are more sensitive to caffeine and more susceptible to dehydration. If you are sensitive to caffeine and plan to drink coffee before singing, drink some water as well.

Alcohol is definitely dehydrating. If you consume alcoholic beverages, be sure to compensate with additional amounts of water.

### Antihistamines and dehydration

Allergies lead to sneezing, coughing, swollen tissues, and excess mucus. All of these phenomena interfere with singing. Many singers with allergies find that taking an antihistamine is helpful and can make the difference between singing clearly and having great difficulty singing.

Singers are commonly advised to avoid antihistamines because of their dehydrating effects. Yet, scientific evidence on the dehydrating effect of these medications on the voice is scarce. There is, however, a controlled, experimental study (Verdolini et al., 2002) of diphenhydramine hydrochloride (Benadryl), an over-the-counter medication that has been in use for many years. The study showed that a 50 mg dose (a standard adult dose) did not affect secretory hydration or the phonation pressure threshold (i.e., amount of breath pressure required to sing a specific note). In sum, while many published sources advise against diphenhydramine hydrochloride because of its supposed dehydration effect, there is no scientific evidence to support this.

Singers with allergies should nonetheless be alert to the potential for antihistamines to affect vocal function as each individual can react differently to the same medication. Also, be wary of medications that combine antihistamines with decongestants, which can thicken mucus (Sataloff & Hawkshaw, 2006). Some singers find that loratadine (Claritin) causes few problems with dehydration, but no formal studies have been conducted.

### Diuretics and dehydration

Diuretics cause the body to excrete water and are thus dehydrating. Singers may be taking diuretics as a part of therapy for high blood pressure or to relieve premenstrual fluid retention. The above-cited study by Verdolini et al. (2002) confirmed that a diuretic did in fact cause dehydration and increased the amount of breath pressure required for phonation.

Singers who take diuretics for high blood pressure may wish to consult with their physicians regarding alternative medications. Female singers who use diuretics because of fluid retention in the vocal folds during the premenstrual period should be aware that this fluid is bound and cannot be excreted with use of a diuretic (Sataloff & Hawkshaw, 2006).

## Safe amount of daily singing to prevent vocal fatigue

The safe amount of daily singing depends in part on the style of production that a singer uses. A singer who carries a lot of tension in areas affecting the larynx and sings using a pressed form of production will be able to sing only for short periods without risk of developing hoarseness. Hoarseness occurs as a result of excessive friction between vocal folds and consequent swelling. An overblown style of production can similarly cause problems.

Even singers who use good vocal technique should limit continuous rehearsal to two hours. A three-hour rehearsal will require a break to allow singers to recover.

- You might think that skilled and experienced singers can sing for longer periods of time. But even Renée Fleming sings no more than 2–3 hours per day (Fleming, 2005). Fleming also notes that singing high tessitura passages (those with high average pitch) is very tiring and should not be done continuously for long periods of time.
- Henderson (1979) relates the sad story of a 17-year-old tenor whose vocal folds became bowed and thus incapable of producing consistent tones. He had sung in an all-state chorus with rehearsal

periods lasting 4–5 hours per day. In addition, the songs chosen by the conductor involved too high a range for a young tenor voice.

## Meal consumption prior to singing

### Timing of meals before singing

Eating before singing is important because of the energy required in what is truly an athletic endeavor. Nonetheless, eating too close to a performance is problematic because unfinished digestion can result in burping and other hindrances to singing. A full stomach also interferes with breathing because the diaphragm must descend to fill the lungs. Most authorities recommend eating an hour and a half to three hours before singing (e.g., Henderson [1979] recommends two to three hours, and Fleming [2005] recommends an hour and a half [and a moderate meal]).

- Caruso would have only a sandwich and a glass of Chianti for dinner prior to a performance. He said, "... when the large space required by the diaphragm in expanding to take in breath is partly occupied by one's dinner, the result is that one cannot take as deep a breath as one would like and consequently the tone suffers and the all-important ease of breathing is interfered with" (Caruso & Tetrazzini, 1975, p. 46).

A small amount of alcohol may relax a nervous singer, but too much alcohol is dehydrating and detrimental to cognitive functioning.

## Gastric reflux

Gastric reflux can damage the larynx and is a well-known cause of what is commonly referred to as "heartburn." However, gastric reflux can also damage the larynx without associated heartburn symptoms. In fact, this is now considered a different condition that is called laryngopharyngeal reflux—LPR (Selby, Gilbert, & Lerman, 2003).

LPR can cause subtle changes in the voice, inability to sing for extended periods, hoarseness, coughing, and in some cases laryngitis. Additional possible symptoms include bad breath, extended warm-up time (especially in the morning), the sensation of a lump in the throat, and chronic sore throat (Sataloff & Hawkshaw, 2006; Koufman, 1991).

The effect of reflux on the voice is more prevalent than previously thought

(Koufman, 1991). Therefore, every singer should take preventive measures including the avoidance of food and alcohol consumption within three hours of sleeping (alcohol tends to relax the sphincter in the esophagus that prevents reflux). Weight control has also been shown to be an important preventive measure.

Singers who experience LPR should adhere to the above recommendations, and should elevate the head of the bed using blocks (i.e., multiple pillows are insufficient). They should also avoid acidic beverages such as coffee and soft drinks, citrus fruits, chocolate, fatty foods, onions, spicy foods, and tomato-based foods (National Digestive Diseases Information Clearinghouse, 2010). Treatment with antacids, H2 histamine blockers (which reduce acid secretion) and proton pump inhibitors (which reduce acid secretion even more effectively and for a longer period of time) may also be useful. Examples of H2 histamine blockers include ranitidine (Zantec) and famotidine (Pepcid). Examples of proton pump inhibitors include lansoprazole (Prevacid) and omeprazole (Prilosec).

- Treatment with proton pump inhibitors for eight weeks with adherence to dietary restrictions has been shown to reduce a measure of hoarseness associated with laryngopharyngeal reflux (Selby, Gilbert, & Lerman, 2003).

While all of these examples of H2 histamine blockers and proton pump inhibitors are available over the counter, singers should consult a physician if symptoms last for more than a short period of time.

## Singing and the common cold

While preschool children (and the people around them) are most at risk for contracting colds, even healthy adults will suffer a few colds each year (Mayo Clinic, 2010). A cold is a viral infection (rhinovirus) of the upper respiratory tract (nose and throat) that generally resolves within one to two weeks. Colds typically do not involve fever and are therefore distinct from the flu and other infections of the respiratory tract.

Because both the nose and throat are affected by a cold, singers can experience some distress. If singing is not necessary, a week of vocal rest (not singing and very little speaking) will usually get most people through the worst of a cold. That said, many people are able to sing through most colds, depending on symptoms. Sinus congestion can be uncomfortable, but as previously noted, the sinuses are not resonance chambers so congestion will likely not affect the sound of the voice to listeners, despite the altered perception of the singer! Swelling in the throat and tonsils can be problematic, however, because pharyngeal resonance will be compromised. Imagine the change in sound in a resonant room if you added shag carpet—soft, swollen surfaces absorb sound and make the space smaller.

A cold is also the likeliest cause of a cough (Pratter, 2006). When the upper airway structures become irritated, the body responds by coughing in an effort to clear the airways of the irritants. A cough is physically created when the vocal folds are quickly pushed together and then blown apart by an expulsion of breath, much like glottal onset but more extreme. Therefore, extended coughing and even clearing of the throat can irritate the vocal folds. To avoid harm, try swallowing instead of attempting to clear the throat. Alternatively, keep the glottis open and use a forceful contraction of the abdominals to expel mucus. If possible, singers should avoid singing when suffering from a cough.

If postnasal drip and drainage are extreme, the vocal folds may become inflamed and will cease to close fully. Postnasal drip can cause a chronic cough, which is usually much worse in the morning. Coughing can be especially problematic as the friction created between the folds can cause swelling and dysfunction. Hoarseness and/or difficulty in phonating can develop. If this is the case, vocal rest is best. If there is no difficulty phonating, a singer should be able to continue to sing safely.

Singers who suspect that their vocal folds are swollen/retaining fluids, must rest their voices. Singing with inflamed vocal folds risks laryngitis, and possibly vocal fold polyps (Sundberg, 1987). Indications of swelling in the folds include an inability to phonate in one area of the voice (typically, loss of upper register production), breathiness in the sound (folds not coming fully together), and difficulty with onset—often a delayed onset. Physical fatigue can be another red flag as a body fighting illness will need to generate much more energy to support and produce sound.

A good test of the ability to phonate is to sing "Happy Birthday," staccato, in the upper register or falsetto (for males). If this is easily accomplished, the singer can safely continue singing. If not, some vocal rest is indicated.

If a singer has a bacterial infection, antibiotics are generally prescribed. If at all possible, it is best to suspend singing until the entire dose of antibiotics is finished. Rest and plenty of fluids will assist the antibiotics in doing their job.

The most treacherous time for singers' vocal health may be as they are recovering from a cold or other illness. The vocal folds and surrounding tissues often heal much more slowly, and since we cannot see them, it is tempting to resume full singing before everything is mended. Not only can singers develop compensatory bad habits, they can also do permanent damage to their vocal folds (granulomas, nodules, etc.).

### Treatment of colds and coughs

Recommended treatments for a cold are rest and plenty of fluids. Gargling with salt mixed with warm water can be effective in relieving and shortening the period of irritation in the throat. High-volume, low-pressure nasal irrigation is safe and usually remarkably effective (neti pot and other commercially available nasal irrigation systems). This is essentially a saltwater gargle for the nasopharynx that can shrink mucosal swelling, promote sinus decompression, and even remove irritants (Playe, 2010). Reduction of irritants by consuming soothing beverages such as warm tea can also be helpful. Use of a cool-mist humidifier is recommended as well.

Medications for coughs include cough suppressants such as dextromethorphan and expectorants such as guaifenesin (Mucinex). Expectorants are used to aid productive coughs in removing phlegm from the lungs. If a cough is productive, it is wise to avoid suppressing it so that problematic excretions can be ejected from the body. But rather than coughing, use the technique involving an open glottis and forceful contraction of the abdominals to expel mucus.

Some coughs caused by postnasal drip associated with colds are not productive. If not treated, coughing can continue for some time after the cold is over. First-generation antihistamines such as brompheniramine maleate (Dimetane, Dimetapp) and chlorpheniramine maleate (Chlor-Trimeton), taken with naproxen (Aleve) as an antiswelling agent and pseudoephedrine as a decongestant, are an effective treatment for such unproductive coughs (Pratter, 2006). More recently developed nondrowsy antihistamines, commonly taken as a treatment for allergies (e.g., loratadine), are not effective in treating coughs caused by the common cold (Pratter, 2006).

Many people advocate the use of zinc lozenges or throat sprays at the onset of a cold. While there have been conflicting findings from the various studies (Jackson, Lesho, & Peterson, 2000; Caruso, Prober, & Gwaltney, 2007), a systematic review of thirteen clinical trials finds support for zinc lozenge efficacy (Singh & Das, 2011). The review authors conclude that if zinc is used within 24 hours of experiencing symptoms, both the duration and severity of symptoms is reduced. Avoid using zinc lozenges on an empty stomach to avoid stomach upset.

Because zinc ions may prevent the cold virus from attaching to and infecting cells in the nasal cavity, direct application of zinc to the entrance to the nose within the first 24 hours of the onset of cold may also be effective (Hirt, Nobel, & Barron, 2000). However, persistent anosmia (complete loss of the sense of smell) has been reported as a possible side effect. While this may be caused by introduction of zinc gel or sprays further than just inside the entrance to the nose, the potential for this to occur may represent an unacceptable risk (Augusto, 2006).

Finally, prevention of colds and other respiratory disease is most important. Zinc supplements, taken for at least five months, have been shown in two clinical trials to reduce the frequency of colds (Singh & Das, 2011). Studies have also shown that frequent hand washing with soap and water or hand sanitizers with 60–95% alcohol is an effective defense against infection, including gastrointestinal illnesses (Bloomfield, Aiello, Cookson, O'Boyle, & Larson, 2007). It is also helpful to clean devices used by many people, such as television remote controls and telephone handsets in hotel rooms. In addition, when singers have colds, they should cough or sneeze into a tissue or the crook of their elbow rather than into the air or their hands.

## Medications with the potential to cause vocal fold hemorrhage

Singers are frequently warned about using nonsteroidal anti-inflammatory medications (NSAIDS) such as aspirin, ibuprofen, naproxen, and celecoxib (Celebrex), which have the potential to lead to vocal fold hemorrhage. While this danger might be overstated for a product like ibuprofen, it is a real possibility, particularly if a singer is also taking Vitamin E or another supplement or medication that has blood thinning properties. It is particularly important to be cautious if taking NSAIDS at high dosage levels or taking multiple NSAIDS. Also, singers should use great caution if drinking alcohol when using NSAIDS, as alcohol dilates the blood vessels. For a safer alternative, use acetaminophen (Klein & Johns, 2007).

Increasingly, middle-age and older singers diagnosed with cardiovascular disease are receiving antiplatelet therapy. This therapy is designed to reduce the chance of a clot forming in a blood vessel, which could result in a heart attack or stroke. Warfarin (Coumadin) is the classic therapy, but it has a remarkably high risk of hemorrhage (Shehab, Sperling, Kegler, & Budnitz, 2010). In fact, there is a recent case study of a singer who experienced vocal fold hemorrhage while on warfarin therapy (Neely & Rosen, 2000). Although warfarin is still prescribed, in recent years a different antiplatelet therapy has become more common. This is called dual antiplatelet therapy and involves use of aspirin and clopidogrel (Plavix). The risk of hemorrhage with this therapy is substantially less than with warfarin, but the risk is still quite high (Shehab et al., 2010). Singers who are on such therapies should be careful to avoid pressed phonation, extended periods of singing, and high tessituras.

Singers should consult their physicians concerning the potential for vocal fold hemorrhage as a consequence of taking other prescribed medications. Sometimes medications that they might not associate with the potential for hemorrhage have significant risks. An example is erectile dysfunction medications, which have seen a meteoric rise in use among men and even among some women (Korkes, Costa-Matos, Gasperini, Reginato, & Perez, 2008). These medications cause dilation of the blood vessels, which has the potential to lead to bleeding. The risk is exemplified by a recently published case study of a 31-year-old male singer who lost his voice after he experienced a vocal hemorrhage after using vardenafil (Levitra) (Singh et al., 2010).

## Hormonal factors affecting the voice

Women's menstrual cycles can cause variation in voice quality. The premenstrual phase, as noted above, may be associated with fluid retention in the vocal folds. This may also occur during ovulation (Sataloff and Hawkshaw, 2006). Fluid retention in the folds alters vibration characteristics which can be detrimental to range, resonance, and sound amplitude. It may affect up to one-third of female singers (Abitbol et al, 1999).

Modern oral contraceptives with a lower progesterone percentage are less likely to affect the voice compared to older formulations. Thompson (1995) states that oral contraceptives do not have a significant effect on the voice. In fact a recent small-scale study suggests that low-dose, monophasic oral contraceptives actually increase premenopausal women's vocal quality (Amir et al., 2003). Specifically, less variation in amplitude and in fundamental frequency occurred among women using oral contraceptives in comparison with a control group. (Monophasic oral contraceptives involve a fixed daily hormonal dose for 21 days followed by 7 days of a nonactive pill.)

Nonetheless, individual responses to such medications can vary. Women who notice a deleterious effect may wish to consult with a health care provider about alternative formulations or an alternative contraceptive method.

Aging is also associated with hormonal changes, especially in women. Hormone replacement therapy (HRT) has been used to help maintain laryngeal function and reduce mucus thickening. Estrogen therapy, a type of HRT, also prevents the lowering of pitch range associated with menopause (Murry, McRoy, & Parhizkar, 2007). In recent years some controversy has erupted about the safety of HRT both in estrogen-only and combined estrogen-progestin formulations. Currently HRT is not recommended for long-term use, and individual risk factors must be carefully considered even in short-term use for abatement of menopausal symptoms.

Women over the age of fifty are more susceptible to hypothyroidism (low thyroid hormone levels) than are men. Prevalence increases further with each decade. Hypothyroidism can lead to a thickening of the vocal folds and, consequently, a lowering of vocal range. The symptoms of hypothyroidism are often very subtle and diverse, making it difficult to diagnose on the basis of symptoms alone. Symptoms may include fatigue, unexplained weight gain, hair loss, swelling in the hands and/or feet, hoarseness, and cognitive effects such as difficulty concentrating and/or memory lapses. Fortunately, the TSH (thyroid stimulating hormone) blood test can readily detect this condition, and if diagnosed, levothyroxine therapy is an effective treatment.

## If surgery is contemplated

Individuals who need general anesthesia for surgery typically require intubation, which involves passing a tube through the glottis into the trachea to assist breathing. If the tube is too large, singers may be at risk for vocal fold trauma. Indeed, singers often complain of hoarseness after surgery involving general anesthesia. Be sure to consult with your surgeon and anesthesiologist prior to surgery to discuss the possibility of using a small-diameter tube (e.g., pediatric-size tube). You may also wish to discuss alternatives such as conscious sedation combined with local anesthesia.

Singers who must undergo vocal fold surgery will be happy to know that more modern operative techniques are associated with reduced tissue trauma. Newer techniques ensure the removal of damaged/diseased tissue with minimal effect upon healthy tissue. Nonetheless, submucosal scarring that can affect voice quality might occur (Sataloff & Hawkshaw, 2006).

Singers who have contact granulomas, contact ulcers, or vocal nodules that are affecting their singing should avoid surgery until a course of vocal therapy has been pursued first. A major reason for doing this is that these vocal fold abnormalities are strongly connected with unhealthy vocal practices. Recurrence is highly likely when treatment only involves surgery (Bloch, Gould, & Hirano, 1981).

- Ylitalo and Lindestad (1999) found that the recurrence rate for contact granuloma after surgery was 92%. The cure rate for vocal therapy alone was 51% but was less (35%) for those who received therapy after failed surgery. Individuals who previously had surgery required twice as much vocal therapy as those who did not have surgery, and they took twice as long to recover. While this was only a retrospective study, it provides further support for a conservative approach to granulomas prior to surgery. Surgical intervention prior to voice therapy is likely to be unsuccessful in the long run and prolongs the time to recovery once vocal therapy is instituted.

- Emami, Morrison, Rammage, and Bosch (1999) report that a combination of voice therapy and treatment of gastric reflux is effective in treatment of vocal fold contact ulcers and granulomas. They reserve surgical and injection treatment for those who are not helped by voice therapy and LPR treatment.

### Tonsillectomy

Some singers, particularly younger ones, may have tonsils that are chronically infected and swollen. Swollen tonsils compromise sound quality because the puffy tissues reduce space in the oral pharynx and absorb high frequency sound waves.

While tonsillitis that is caused by bacteria is often well treated by antibiotics, singers who experience multiple episodes of tonsil infection each year may wish to consult with an otolaryngologist (ENT physician) about the desirability of a tonsillectomy. This is typically a same-day-surgery procedure. After recovery, singers will need to stretch stiffened pharyngeal tissues gradually and regain control over raising the soft palate (Dayme, 2009). They will also need to adjust to their improved pharyngeal space, but that should be a happy experience.

## Choral conductor's role in maintaining vocal health

Choral conductors can support their singers' vocal health in a number of ways in the rehearsal setting. No one wins when singers emerge from rehearsal so hoarse that they can barely speak!

### The conductor's appearance and gestures

The way a conductor physically looks has a direct influence on the vocal health of the singers in the choir. Nonverbal communication has a strong and often unconscious effect upon singers. Conductors should always think about and practice gestures that encourage good vocal technique. Some of the myriad ways that conductors can facilitate vocal health through their gestures include:

- **Posture**—Practice what you preach. Avoid unnecessary physical motions and tension, especially in the neck and shoulders. Try not to lean in toward the ensemble, tipping the torso forward, in an effort to engage the singers—instead, have the singers produce the energy in their sound to bridge the gap to you.
- **Conducting pattern**—Conducting with a very large pattern all of the time will make everyone feel tense and tired, especially you. Also, make sure that your conducting pattern does not sway your body out of good postural alignment. Remember, the way you look when you conduct has a direct impact on both you and your singers. For example, conducting with the hands close to the body may lead to shallow breaths and unsupported singing.
- **Cues**—Prepare the singers' breaths and infuse your cues with a grounded inhalation whenever possible. Opening your mouth for the choir's inhalations is helpful. Breathing in through the shape of the vowel to follow is useful, as previously noted, so try showing the vowel shape yourself as you inhale with the choir.
- **Cutoffs**—Cutoffs should be clear and prepared. Whenever possible, avoid a rapid clamping shut of the fingers. Singers may respond to this gesture by closing their glottises or their mouths—an unhealthy and poor-sounding means of release as we have already established. Instead, prepare the cutoff a beat ahead with a gesture and simply show the place for the singers to sound the final consonant or inhale to stop the sound, if it is a vowel.
- **Hand shape**—When conducting without a baton, choral conductors should look carefully at the shape of their hands. This shape may well change depending on the tone quality desired. For example, fully extended tense fingers may result in a more intense, strident sound. Try to remind singers of pharyngeal space with your hand and mouth shapes. Generally you want to create a shape that looks relaxed yet engaged.
- **Facial expressions**—Attempt to stay relaxed in your face as you conduct. Show your intensity, connect with your singers, but avoid demonstrating tension, especially in the articulators. When difficult sections of music approach, show confidence in the ensemble on your face!
- **Difficult passages**—Often conductors do exactly the opposite of what their singers need in technically difficult sections of the repertoire. For example, for higher pitches, keep gestures low and grounded near the support muscles (abdominals) to encourage your singers to stay on their support. If the repertoire is fast and rhythmic, keep gestures more precise with little extraneous motion; be careful not to overconduct to

help your singers avoid unnecessary tension. Be a model of physical engagement without tension whenever possible.

While not part of a conductor's repertoire of gesture, remember to use a healthy, supported sound for your own speaking and singing. You don't need to have the tonal quality of a top-notch soloist, but you should use your voice in a healthy manner. A short personal warm-up for you (before rehearsal) will go a long way toward helping you stay vocally healthy too!

## Sight-singing

Sight-singing (sight-reading) is a vocally fatiguing activity for singers. When sight-singing, singers are fully occupied with achieving pitch and rhythmic accuracy and have few thoughts about vocal technique. Pitches and rhythms are frequently achieved "at all costs" including singing without consistent support. Often the articulators (teeth, lips, tongue) are overly involved and breath pressure as well as space for resonance is incorrect. Moreover, singers may experience substantial tension.

The result is that extended periods of sight-singing can leave singers vocally fatigued. It is difficult to avoid this sometimes—the first rehearsal of a concert of new repertoire will necessarily involve a great deal of reading. The goal then is to assist singers in progressing through the "reading" of music as quickly as possible, moving toward "recognizing" music instead. Some methods of achieving this include:

- Reading and learning music accurately, using a neutral syllable (e.g., "ba") to eliminate the difficulty of reading words and music at the same time. Solfège can be used if it is familiar to the singers. It is frustrating and time-consuming to "unlearn" a passage. Better to learn it well the first time.
- Encouraging the development of muscle memory by singing difficult intervals and passages slowly and concentrating on vocal technique while learning pitches.
- Looking for patterns or repetitions in the music and pointing these out to the singers so that there can be more immediate recognition.
- Rehearsing together sections of the choir that sing similar or complimentary lines. During this time other sections can mentally rehearse or rest.

## Standing, sitting, and taking breaks

Encouraging good posture is important. Make sure you remind your singers to sit and stand as discussed in Chapter 1 on posture. Although it may seem obvious, varying whether the group sits or stands throughout the rehearsal is desirable if at all possible.

Taking breaks for vocal rest is crucial to maintaining good vocal health. That said, vocal breaks do not need to be mental breaks—keeping singers engaged and invested in the rehearsal is important. Vocal breaks can still involve singing, but singing in a different way. Conductors can make some of the following choices in rehearsal to preserve their singers' vocal health:

- Instruct a voice part to "mentally rehearse" their line while another section sings.
- Have the accompanist play through a chord progression for the singers to hear.
- Ask the singers to speak a line in a sing-song, well-supported sound.
- Allow sections to change the range of a passage, for example by having the sopranos sing down an octave while learning a high section of music.
- Encourage the group to sing at a comfortable dynamic, especially when learning new music or with sections at the extremes of the range.

Mental breaks are also necessary—take time to talk with the choir briefly about the music, tell a story, share a laugh—these moments, rather than distracting the choir from your goal, will allow the singers to connect with you and relax for a minute within rehearsal.

Full breaks are important as well. Encouraging singers to get up, stretch, and talk with each other will build community as well as give their minds and voices a change of pace.

### Never skip the warm-up!

A thoughtful, well-planned warm-up, even as short as five to ten minutes, can make a huge difference to the vocal health of the ensemble. For many amateur singers, the choral rehearsal is the only singing that they do each week. Conductors should spend some time with them to establish the basics of the foundations of singing and then continue to remind them of these principles at every rehearsal. Their technique and stamina will improve and so will the sound of the ensemble.

### Include or encourage a cooldown

A cooldown is the chance to allow the voice to return to the normal mode of functioning for speech. Singers experience increased blood flow to the vocal folds and laryngeal muscles just as athletes do to the muscles they use when exercising. Taking a few minutes to sing some simple warm-up exercises *in reverse* will help prevent problems in muscle recovery. One possible way of implementing a cooldown process for a choral group would be to choose a group song or anthem with a moderate tessitura to close each rehearsal. Or singers could be encouraged to do some easy vocalizing on their own after rehearsal. Start exercises in the top or very bottom of the range and move toward the middle of the range. Move from faster, more complicated exercises to simple "stretches" like slides, including exercises using nasal consonants (e.g., humming exercises) and/or occluded vowels.

### Plan and pace rehearsals carefully

Choosing the order of rehearsal is crucial to an ensemble's success and their vocal health. A good rule of thumb is to start with repertoire that resembles an extension of the warm-up as a chance to apply the foundations of breath support and proper vowel formation. The first piece of repertoire should avoid extremes of range and be simple enough to allow singers to continue to think about their vocal production for a little while. Then, an alternation of pieces throughout rehearsal is desirable, whenever possible. As a rehearsal progresses, singers tire both physically and mentally. Finishing rehearsals with more familiar repertoire is often indicated.

Some specific elements to consider in planning a rehearsal sequence are:

- Tempo
- Key
- Accompanied vs. a cappella
- Tessitura
- Range
- Prevailing dynamic
- Language (familiar vs. unfamiliar)

Tessitura deserves special mention since a sustained high (or low) tessitura can result in tension and vocal fatigue. High tessitura is often a particular problem for the tenor and soprano sections. Remind singers to modify vowels when appropriate. Encourage good support and posture. Provide adequate time for rest and recovery by allowing the singers to sing a passage down the octave occasionally and by planning breaks in the singing.

### Support singers with voice health issues

Be patient with singers who are experiencing vocal health issues and are on vocal rest. While singers are ultimately responsible for their own vocal health, conductors play a crucial role in supporting them. Knowledge of the voice and careful planning will maximize what an ensemble can accomplish and minimize vocal health problems for individual singers.

# Chapter 16: A Productive Warm-Up

## Why are warm-ups important?

All voice teachers advocate a sequence of exercises to facilitate warm-up and development of technique during individual practice. Choral directors vary in their use of warm-ups, but we believe they are as important for the development of choral voices as they are for the development of solo voices. This chapter presents the elements of a good warm-up and provides comprehensive sequences of exercises to assist that process.

### Importance of choral warm-ups

If you are opposed to choral warm-ups you might say, "Why bother? Trained singers have probably warmed up already." Or, "Amateur singers are there to sing good music, not sing 'mm' or 'hang-ah,' or '[i], [e], [ɑ], [o], [u].' Besides, warm-ups waste valuable rehearsal time."

We argue, however, that warming up is a critical part of the choral rehearsal process. It is dangerous to assume that trained singers are already warmed up. Singers need a warm-up in the same way that warm-ups are desirable prior to a full engagement of muscles in physical exercise and athletics.

More importantly, a thoughtful warm-up process that addresses important aspects of vocal technique is essential for the vocal development of singers. In addition, rehearsal expectations (e.g., vowel colors) can be established during the warm-up.

As noted in the Introduction, singers benefit from multiple repetitions of warm-up exercises over time. This is essential for the development of muscle memory. Both massed practice (multiple repetitions within a given warm-up) and spaced practice (repetition over time) are necessary to learn and retain good vocal technique.

## Specific benefits of a thoughtful warm-up sequence

Warm-up time provides an opportunity for teaching vocal technique through a careful selection of exercises that will dramatically improve the sound of developing soloists and choral singers. Some of the possible benefits of a thoughtful, consistent warm-up are as follows:

- Warming up the vocal apparatus is essential for reducing tension and creating free production of higher pitches. Warm-ups help with production of higher pitches because the warm-up process makes muscles more extensible. This is extremely important for developing voices.
- Warm-ups increase blood flow, which improves oxygenation of muscle tissue. Oxygenation is critically important for proper muscle functioning.
- Warm-ups improve tonal quality. Amir, Amir, and Michaeli (2005) found that warm-ups reduced noise in the voice as well as disturbances in frequency and amplitude. The amplitude of the singer's formant was also increased.
- Warm-ups with the proper exercises improve resonance and vowel formation. In the choral setting vowel exercises will help to ensure that all singers produce their vowels in the same way, which enhances choral tuning and blending.
- Warm-ups can provide an opportunity to prepare for more difficult repertoire passages such as those requiring smooth onset of phrases beginning with vowels, staccato passages, and passages with melismas.

Most singers who have experienced singing without a warm-up can attest to being vocally fatigued a mere 20 minutes into rehearsal of repertoire. Individual practice sessions and choral rehearsals are more productive when prefaced by a good warm-up.

## Warm-up sequence

The sequence of exercises is almost as important as the exercises themselves. Think of preparing for a game of tennis—you would not start by hitting serves as hard as you can. Start with basic exercises and move to the more complicated.

1) Physical stretches to relieve tension
2) Breathing awareness
3) Connect breath with sound (onset can be addressed throughout or in detail here)
4) Vowels and resonance
5) Range reinforcement and extension
6) Linking of registers
7) Articulation, repertoire-specific exercises (address consonants here or throughout)

### Stretching/body awareness

Stretching and body awareness can involve very simple, small stretches or more rigorous activity. Children might need to work off some steam, while adults might need to release tension in the neck and shoulders.

### Breathing awareness

Breathing awareness can be as simple as taking a few deep, low breaths with reminders to expand the abdomen and ribs. More elaborate exercises without pitch can also be included.

### Connect breath with sound

Use simple exercises, lower register to mixed voice, such as humming/lip trills/tongue trills. The focus is on making sure sound is initiated in a healthy manner. And, as noted above, these exercises, which involve occlusion of the vocal tract, can protect vocal fold tissues as the laryngeal muscles and mucosal layers are being prepared for more strenuous singing to follow. In many respects they are similar to the stretching and flexing exercises that precede vigorous physical exercise (Titze, 2008a).

During these exercises, singers should think about a coordinated onset and work for a steady sound without too much breath escaping. Think about creating appoggio—the breath support governed by the abdominal and rib muscles that is essential for free vocal production.

### Vowels and resonance

Conductors and teachers should establish expectations for vowels—where they resonate (tongue, jaw, and lip position), the preferred tone color, etc. Work mainly with the five pure Italianate vowels [i], [e], [ɑ], [o], [u] in this order (the Vowel Spectrum) or, occasionally, the reverse. Sing in the middle range. One or two vowels needing special attention can also be isolated. For ensembles, listen for uniformity in pitch and vowel sound/color but do not fret about minor differences in external appearance of the singers.

Resonance will work hand in hand with vowels. If a singer lacks proper vowel formation, resonance will be affected. Work toward a basic tone quality that is vibrant and balanced. Add exercises that play with the tone color to encourage flexibility of sound. Vary the dynamic level to work toward a free, resonant sound regardless of dynamic.

### Range reinforcement/extension

Use simple exercises with a small to moderate range to stretch the voice up and down. Generally work in a rapid, sequential manner to avoid taxing the voice for prolonged periods. Begin with ascending exercises for upper range extension and descending exercises for the lower portions of the range. As singers become experienced and accomplished, try the reverse (begin on a higher pitch and descend). Use vowels that are comfortable—generally [ɑ] works for women and men, but with men modify to [ɔ] in the upper portion of their range.

### Linking of registers

Arpeggios, scales covering an octave or more, octave slides, etc. are all good exercises that will encourage singers to prepare to traverse registers. Singers should consider the variables (heavier versus lighter production, vowel modification, space, breath support, amount of glottal tension) as they ascend or descend.

### Special techniques

The sky is the limit! Choose exercises that address specific issues related to the repertoire to be sung or general skills that a singer or ensemble needs for further development. Some possibilities include: articulation, consonant pronunciation, coloratura, leaps, part independence in ensembles, intonation, dynamics, etc.

When creating and selecting exercises, our philosophy is that if the concept and/or technique is challenging, the exercise should be as simple as possible. Simple exercises permit singers to focus on the technical demands instead of being distracted by complicated composition.

## Concluding thoughts about exercise selection

Vocal exercises can be varied from rehearsal to rehearsal, but the underlying concepts (foundations and enhancements of vocal technique) should always govern the choice of exercises. The goal is to use exercises over time to develop singers' voices. Thoughtful repetition is the best way for singers to progress, so do not hesitate to keep certain exercises in warm-ups for longer periods of time.

## Sample warm-up sequences

The following sample sequences use brief descriptions of the exercises to be used. See the exercises at the end of this chapter or in the body of previous chapters for notation on staves, where relevant.

### Sample sequence one

1) Gently roll the shoulders both frontward and backward. Tip head forward, then upright, then back. Do the same side to side to stretch the neck.
2) Inhale slowly through the nose, then exhale through the mouth. Repeat. Listen to make sure both phases are silent.
3) Beginning on a D, hum (e.g., [m]) an ascending and descending major third; slide between pitches. Concentrate on staying connected to the breath. Repeat the exercise up a half step. Repeat again through the area of mixed voice, and then come back down to the starting pitch. You can switch from [m] to [n] to "ng."
4) Work through the Vowel Spectrum using pairs. Start with [i] to [e]. Sustain one pitch and move seamlessly from [i] to [e] and back to [i]. Concentrate on a fluid motion with no interruption of the resonance. Open the back of the jaw and allow it to lower a little when singing [e]. Move up and repeat. Then try [e] to [ɑ], [ɑ] to [o], and [o] to [u].
5) Sing an ascending and descending fifth on a cardinal (Italianate) vowel quite rapidly. Use a variety of vowels moving toward [ɑ] in the upper register. Work to maintain abdominal support throughout, sustaining the intensity of sound and resonance from top to bottom.
6) Starting around $C_4/C_5$ sing a stepwise descending fifth. Use [i] for the first four notes moving smoothly to [ɑ] for the final pitch. Continue descending by half steps well into the lower range.
7) Starting in C major, sing legato arpeggios on [o]. Ascend by half steps. Men should front the tongue as pitches get higher.
8) Sing "mamamia, mamamia, mamamia ma" using the following pitch sequence: do re mi do, re mi fa re, mi fa so mi do. Ascend and descend by half steps. Vary the tempo. Substitute different consonants. Concentrate on maintaining the correct vowel space and using quick, efficient articulation of the consonants.

### Sample sequence two

1) Stretch the arms over head. Bring the arms down and roll the shoulders slowly, both forward and back. Slowly bend forward allowing the arms to hang naturally. Slowly straighten the torso, rolling up to

a position with the sternum in a comfortably high position. Roll both shoulders slightly back into their sockets to assume excellent standing posture.

2) Inhale over 4 beats. Suspend for 4 beats *without closing the glottis* and without inhaling or exhaling. Exhale over 4 beats. Repeat over 5 beats, then 6. Singers should maintain rib and abdominal expansion during suspension and resist collapse during exhalation.
3) Using lip or tongue trills (or humming if not able to do trills), start in the lower register and move up and down in whole steps. Ascend and descend back to the starting pitch.
4) In the middle of the range, sing an ascending and descending major scale of a fifth. Sing on "ng" for the first 4 ascending pitches, then open to [ɑ] at the top and for the descent. Concentrate on making sure the palate lifts, opening space in the pharynx for a more resonant sound. Avoid "dropping" the jaw in the switch to [ɑ]—rather start with an open jaw while singing the ascending "ng." Men should start to modify to [ɔ] near the first passaggio. Ascend and descend by half steps. Vary the vowel to [e] and [o].
5) Sing a descending major or minor triad on "ja, ja, ja." Imagine the initial consonant to be an [i] vowel to increase focus and resonance. Work down by half steps.
6) Sing an ascending major scale plus a second, and then descend rapidly. Move up and down by half steps.
7) On a single pitch, sing a *messa di voce*—crescendo and diminuendo. Pace each phase over a number of counts—4, 6, 8, etc.

## Compendium of suggested exercises for warm-up

This section contains a variety of exercises for each part of the warm-up sequence. Many draw from exercises in earlier chapters, but some additional ones are featured as well. Exercises specifically geared toward younger singers can be found at the end of most chapters. Sources for adapted exercises which appear earlier are not contained in this chapter but rather are cited in the chapters in which they first appear.

Be creative with exercises as long as they are grounded in good technique. Any of these exercises can be modified by varying starting pitch, vowels, consonants, articulations, melodic patterns, etc. Choose/develop exercises to meet the needs of your singers.

## Physical stretches

McKinney (2005) and Henderson (1979) emphasize the importance of physical warm-ups prior to vocal warm-ups and have many suggestions for exercises. Here are a few that we have found most helpful:

- Roll the upper body in circles around the waist, first in one direction and then in the other
- Reach as high as you can; then bring the arms down slowly to your sides
- Lift and lower the shoulders three times in a relaxed fashion
- Pull the shoulder blades back slowly as though trying to make them touch
- Slowly roll the head around in circles, three times clockwise, three times counterclockwise
- Move the shoulders around in circles, first one direction and then the other
- Move the jaw up and down freely while saying "yah"
- Rag doll—let the body fall forward from the waist, keeping the knees flexed. Inhale and raise the trunk easily, exhaling slowly after returning to a standing position. Keep the sternum comfortably high.

During this period of the warm-up you can also use exercises for reducing tension from Chapter 14.

## Breathing awareness

- Try taking a noisy breath. Then contrast with a silent inhalation. Notice the sensations associated with each.
- Inhale through the nose then out through the mouth. Repeat. This exercise will slow down the inhalation phase and allow singers to more easily sense the passage of air into the lungs. (Breathe through the mouth when singing.)
- Place one hand over the center of the abdomen, with the lower portion just covering the navel. Inhale, then hiss and concentrate on not allowing the abdominal wall or the ribs to collapse until the very end. Having the hand in the above position helps to monitor the expansion of the abdominal area and the ribs and to provide feedback that will increase control over this process.
- Place both hands on the upper abdomen, thumbs touching lower ribs, little fingers near the waist, and middle fingers just touching. Then release the abdominal muscles and expand the ribs to fill the lungs from the bottom up. The middle fingers should part slightly. This is a good sign that abdominal muscles are allowing the diaphragm to descend

correctly. If some rib expansion is felt, this is a further good sign that the intercostal muscles are engaged.

- Hold this expanded position briefly and observe how it feels. Maintain this expanded position (within reason) while saying "s" and, ultimately, while singing. Make the "s" hissing sound with a minimum of breath pressure and a metered flow rate, while trying to keep the abdominal and rib area expanded (i.e., keeping fingers on the abdomen apart), allowing collapse only at the very end. For an extension of this exercise, try the voiced consonant [v]. This is more like singing and requires more engagement of the support muscles.
- Take a "snap-like breath," letting the abdomen spring out quickly (but naturally) for the intake of breath. Then meter the breath on exhalation. Breathe in silently when doing this exercise, as quick breaths are often associated with constriction in the vocal tract.

### Connect breath with sound

- Using intervals of a third, fifth, arpeggiated triads, etc., slide up and down engaging the support muscles throughout. Listen and feel for consistent breath pressure.
- Use tongue/lip trills (rrr/brrr) in short patterns. Listen for an "h" (small puffs of escaping air) between pitches and for consistent breath pressure/tone quality. If the trilling stops, so has the breath support!
- Focusing specifically on onset:

  Sing "Ha, Ha, Ha, Ha"—linger on the "h." This exercise gives singers the sense of a breathy onset.

  Sing "Uh, Uh, Uh, Uh"—close the glottis and then sing, lingering on the explosive initiation (almost like a grunt). This exercise gives singers the sense of the glottal onset.

  In between these two extremes is the coordinated onset:

  Sing [ɑ], [ɑ], [ɑ], [ɑ]—Images such as pulling a tissue gently from the box, or a scarf from out of a magician's hat are helpful. Performance of these physical actions while singing each "ah" can be very helpful. An extension of this exercise would be to imagine that the tissue box is located just above the navel and to perform the gesture as each "ah" is sung.

- Good onset, good phrase—sing a pitch three times, concentrating on onset. Immediately following the third attempt, sing a simple five-note ascending and descending scale. Once onset is consistently coordinated, sing the exercise without the "false starts." Use a variety of vowels, particularly [i], which is one of the most difficult with respect to achieving a coordinated onset.

- Inhale and exhale while attempting to keep the body relaxed without any unnecessary tension. Add a simple vocal exercise (i.e., a triad or scale), being conscious of the head and body during the breath cycle, onset, and release.
- Sing an ascending triad and then a descending triad on any vowel. On the top note of the ascending triad, stop the tone by closing the glottis to obtain a sense of a hard release. Then sing the ascending triad and stop the tone on the top note by breathing in. This is the coordinated release. An added bonus is that you have already inhaled to sing the descending triad. Be sure to initiate the top note of the descending triad with a coordinated onset.

## Vowels and resonance

- Start in the lower/middle portion of the range, slide up the octave and down again, allowing the jaw to open as necessary. Allow the vowel to shift/modify without predetermining its final jaw opening. Slide up and down on various vowels.
- Put your hand next to your ear and point your index finger up. Sing [ɑ] in the middle of the range. While sustaining the vowel, move your finger slowly around to a point in front of the nose, allowing the sound to brighten by increasing elevation of the hump of the tongue. Continue singing and bring the finger to the back of the head, shifting to a darker tone by depressing the hump. This exercise helps to illustrate physically the possibilities of vowel color. Generally the goal is to have a color that is neither too dark nor too light—"opposite the ear!"
- Sing "tele" (as in telephone) over and over on one pitch, concentrating on forming both the "t" and the "l" in the same place (tongue just behind the front top teeth). Return the tongue quickly back to its resting place for the vowel.

- Sing consonants that require tongue movement before a vowel such as [ɑ]—e.g., "la," "da," "ta," "na." Pronounce the consonant quickly and rapidly, returning the tongue to the resting place at the base of the lower incisors. Maintain vowel integrity throughout the exercise. Start on a single pitch, progress to more complicated melodic patterns. Vary the vowels. Try the spectrum in reverse.

- Sing [i], [e], [ɑ], [o], [u], sustaining one pitch. Progress through the Vowel Spectrum, listening to and feeling for consistency of tone and pitch.
- Move from one vowel to the next one on the Vowel Spectrum and then back to the first vowel, e.g., [iei], while optimizing jaw opening, tongue position, and lip position.
- Alternate [i] and [u] on one pitch, stretching the lips outward in a "Cheshire cat" smile for [i] and pulling them into slight pucker for [u]. Strive for consistency of resonance.
- Place a pencil just behind the lower canine teeth and let the top teeth contact the pencil naturally. Keep the tongue in contact with the base of the lower incisors. Vocalize in the middle of the range on all primary vowels.
- Sing "hang-gun-num-ee." On one pitch, move through the vowels quickly to sustain each nasal consonant ([ŋ], [n], [m]) finishing on the [i] vowel. The consonants to sustain are shown in blue. Maintain the open jaw space while singing the remainder of the exercise. Change the final vowel to [e], then to [a]. Next, try the exercise quickly. Then add an ascending and descending five-note major scale on the end.

- Ming, ming, ming—change vowels. Same on "kah, fah, vah."
- Ng-ah—start on the top note of a descending arpeggio. Sustain the "ng" nasal. Then slowly peel the tongue away from the roof of the mouth, close the soft palate, and feel the sound resonating in the pharynx. Descend through the rest of the arpeggio on [ɑ].
- Sing the German word "ja" on a descending triad (major or minor—ja, ja, ja). Imagine the initial consonant to be an [i] and move quickly into [ɑ].

## Range reinforcement and extension

- Slides of a fifth—start in the upper mixed voice and move through the second passaggio into the upper register. Do the same in reverse, descending into the lower register. Ascend/descend by half steps.
- Runs of a fifth ascending and descending, as above
- See-ah descending:

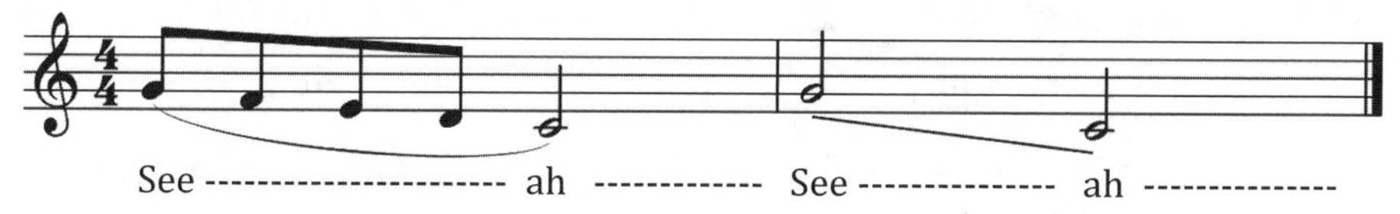


- Runs of a ninth ascending and descending:

## Linking of registers

- Arpeggios, ascending, descending or both
- Runs of a ninth, ascending and descending (see above)
- Arpeggios detaching each note, preparing the space and breath pressure in between pitches
- Arpeggio releasing after the top pitch, then descending
- Slides of an octave, ascending and descending
- For a more advanced exercise, try an ascending arpeggio followed by a descending arpeggio with a dominant seventh, covering the range of a twelfth. As with octave slides, start in the lower register. With choral groups, start singing a vowel that can be used in the upper register by both men and women, such as [ɔ], though women will have to modify this to [ɑ] at the highest pitches. Move the starting note up by half steps.

## Articulation, dynamic control, and repertoire-related exercises

- Vee-ah. Sing staccato descending as shown below.

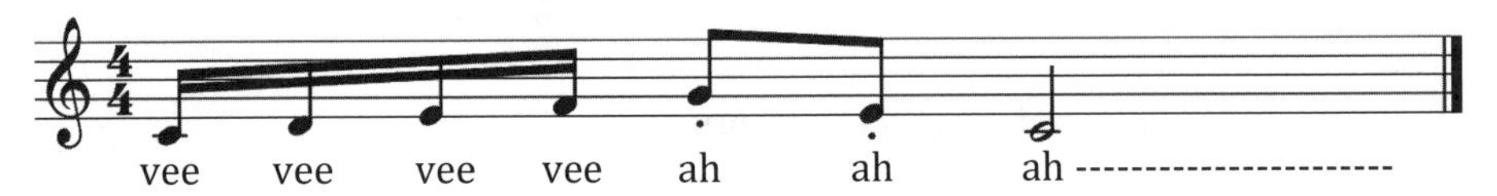


- Articulated runs—combine a run with onset and release. Release between each group. Quick tempo.

- Darts and Frisbees—on [i], ascending run of a fifth, two times in quick succession. Then sing legato on [ɑ].

- Rhythmic trill to gain a *sense* of vibrato—move slowly up a half step and back, repeat faster and faster. This is not an exercise to *achieve* vibrato.

- Ascending run of a fifth, staccato on the top pitch, repeat the top pitch staccato, then descending run of a fifth.
- Ascending run of a ninth with repetition of top two pitches.

- Mamamia, tatatia, zazazia, etc.

❖ Sing a *messa di voce*—gradually increase to forte and decrease. You can vary this exercise by taking away vibrato and adding vibrato.

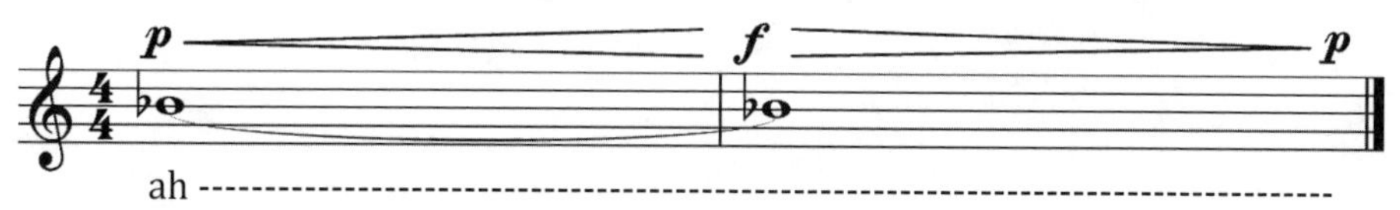


❖ Choose a voiced consonant and vary how long you sing it. For example, sing "mother" varying the length of [m]. Sing [m] quickly, then increase the duration to one or two beats. Try unvoiced consonants such as [s] as in "soft" and [k] in "cool" for a more challenging variation.

# Appendix A: IPA Symbols for Important Vowels and Consonants

| IPA Symbol | English Example | French Example | Italian Example | German Example |
|---|---|---|---|---|
| [i] | f*ee*t | b*i*stro | p*i*ccolo | B*ie*der |
| [ɪ] | h*i*p | — | — | dr*i*tte |
| [e] | b*a*se | *é*clair | r*e*pubblica | sp*ä*hen, s*e*hr |
| [ɛ] | p*e*t | n*e*ige | b*e*llo | *E*ngel |
| [ae] | f*a*ct, c*a*t | p*a*pillon | — | — |
| [ɑ] | f*a*ther | *Pa*ques | aff*a*re | V*a*ter |
| [ɒ] | *po*t (New England, U.S.) | — | — | — |
| [ɔ] | m*o*dern, r*o*d | pl*o*mb, b*o*nne | v*o*glia | Kn*o*pf |
| [o] | t*o*te | t*ô*t, f*au*x | cot*o*ne | T*o*d |
| [ʊ] | sh*oo*k | — | — | M*u*tter |
| [u] | p*oo*l | l*ou*p | fort*u*na | g*u*t |
| [ʌ] | m*o*ney, shr*u*g | — | — | — |
| [ə] | tak*e*n (schwa) | d*e*mandé | — | Ed*e*l |
| [y] | [i] space of [u] | f*u*mer, l*u*cide | — | f*ü*r |
| [ʏ] | [ɪ] space of [ʊ] | — | — | T*ü*chtig |
| [ø] | [e] space of [o] | Joy*eux* | — | Bl*ö*d |
| [œ] | [ɛ] space of [ɔ] | h*eu*re | — | G*ö*tze |

**Table A.1. IPA symbols for important vowels**

| IPA Symbol (Voiced) | Example | IPA Symbol (Unvoiced) | Example |
|---|---|---|---|
| **Pairs of Voiced and Unvoiced Consonants** | | | |
| [b] | *b*orn | [p] | *p*ower |
| [d] | *d*oor | [t] | *t*ape |
| [g] | *g*o | [k] | *c*all |
| [dʒ] | *j*ump | [tʃ] | *ch*ore |
| [ʒ] | le*s*ion | [ʃ] | *sh*ot, *s*ure |
| [ð] | *th*e | [θ] | *th*rough |
| [v] | *v*ery | [f] | *f*our |
| [z] | *z*ebra | [s] | *s*ea, *c*ease |
| [dz] | la*ds* | [ts] | *ts*ar |
| [w] | *w*eek | [hw] | *wh*ere |
| **Other Consonants** | | | |
| [m] | *m*en | [ç] | i*ch* (German) |
| [n] | *n*ote | [x] | a*ch* (German) |
| [ŋ] | si*ng* | [h] | *h*eart (aspirate) |
| [l] | fu*ll* | [j] | *y*ou |
| [r] (retro-flex) | *r*ed (pre-vocal) player (ending) | [ʁ] | *r*ester (French guttural) |
| [r] (rolled) | Pe*rr*o (Spanish) | [ɾ] (flipped) | Ca*r*o (Italian) |

Notes: Technically [ɹ] is the symbol for the "American" retroflex "r," but [r] is commonly used. The guttural [ʁ] is not used in cultured singing.

**Table A.2. IPA symbols for selected voiced and unvoiced consonants**

# Appendix B: Graphs of Formant Frequencies

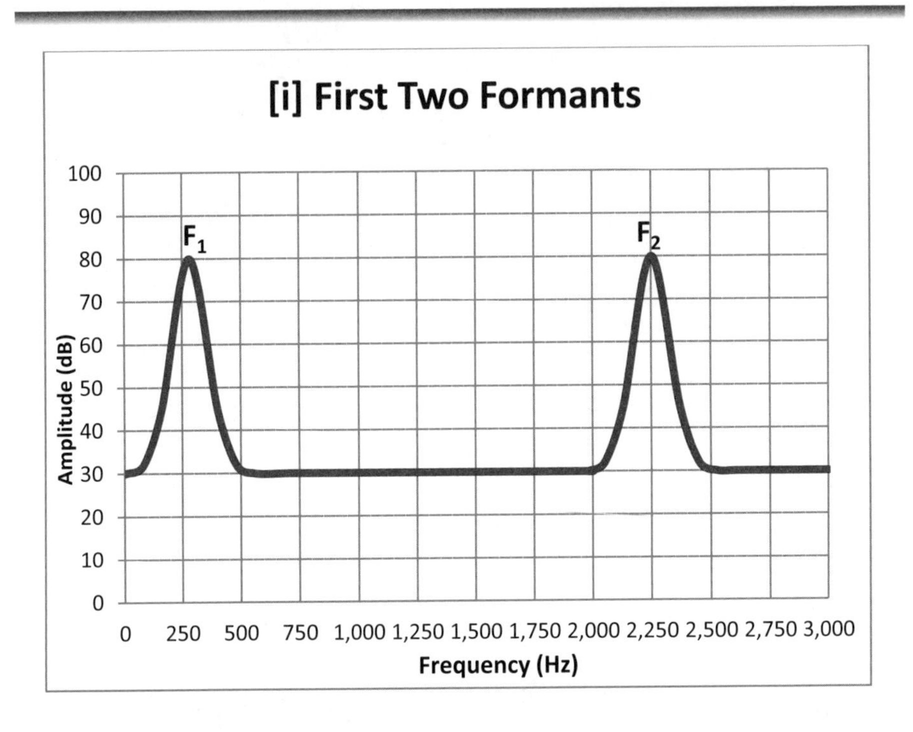
[i] First Two Formants
F1
F2
Amplitude (dB)
100
90
80
70
60
50
40
30
20
10
0
0 250 500 750 1,000 1,250 1,500 1,750 2,000 2,250 2,500 2,750 3,000
Frequency (Hz)

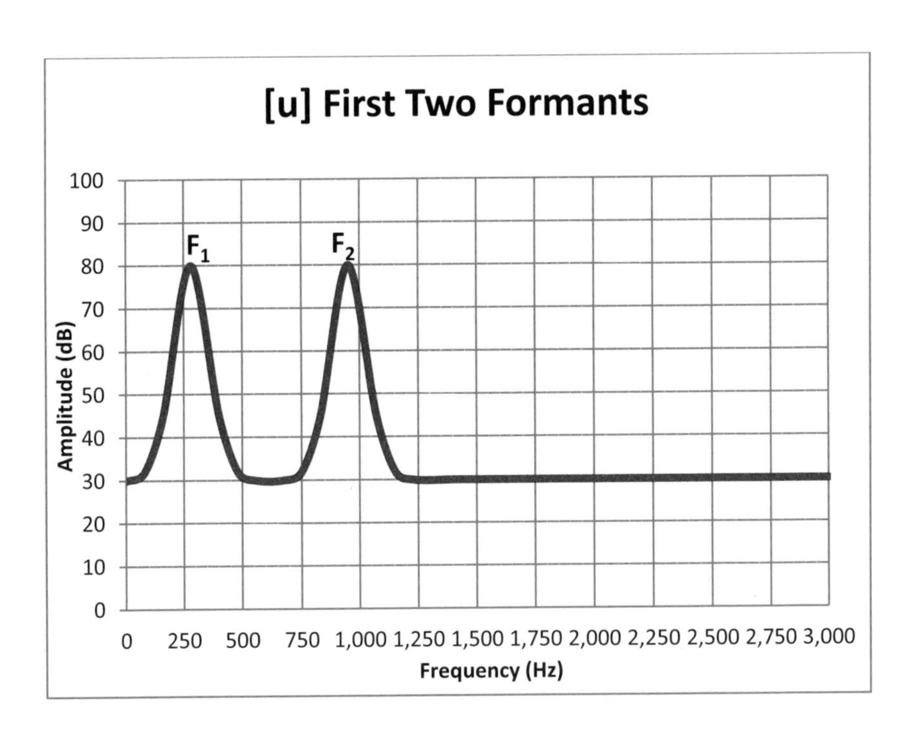
[u] First Two Formants
F1
F2
Amplitude (dB)
100
90
80
70
60
50
40
30
20
10
0
0 250 500 750 1,000 1,250 1,500 1,750 2,000 2,250 2,500 2,750 3,000
Frequency (Hz)

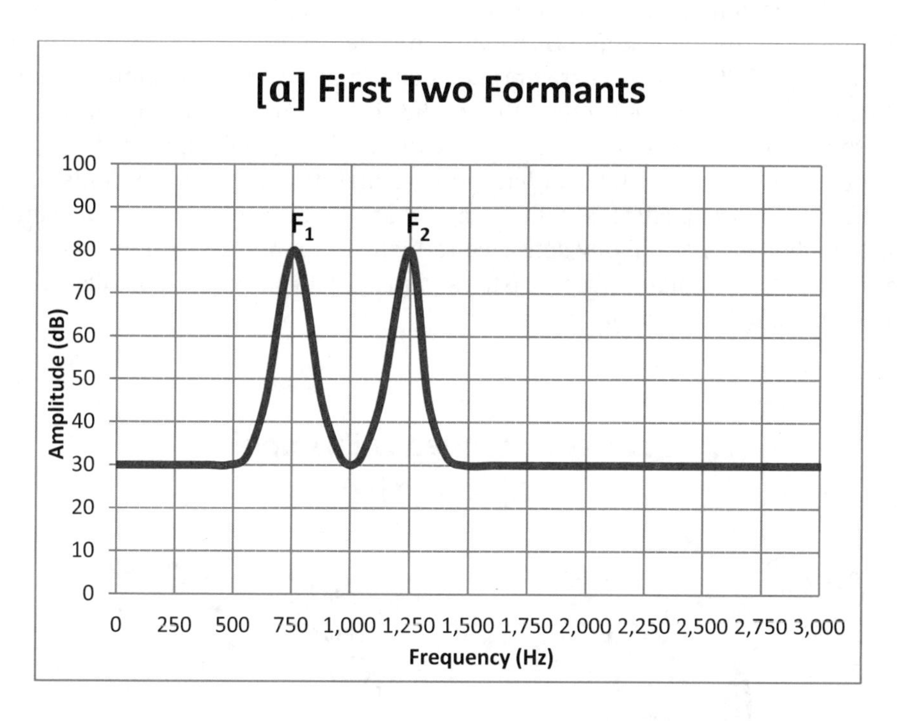


**Figure B.1 First and second formant frequencies for [i], [u], [ɑ]**

## $F_1$ and $F_2$ frequencies for [i], [ɑ], and [u]

Figure B.1 contains illustrations of $F_1$ and $F_2$ frequencies for [i], [ɑ], and [u]. In practice the harmonics amplified by $F_1$ and $F_2$ will not have exactly the same amplitude, and other harmonics will have some amplitude as well. The amplitudes in these graphs are similar to focus attention on the differences in the formant frequencies for these three vowels.

## Further illustration of formants

Figure B.2 illustrates formant frequencies and amplitudes for both a tenor and a soprano singing [ɑ] at $B_4$-flat. Though the fundamental frequency ($F_0$) is the same, the formant frequencies for the soprano are higher; this explains why a soprano sounds different from a tenor singing the same note.

The soprano shows the highest amplitude for the fundamental frequency, and the tenor shows the highest amplitude for the first formant, though the singer's formant for the tenor is quite high as well. (See the clustering of F3, F4, and F5 in the tenor graph that many consider to be the singer's formant.) Sundberg (1999) argues that sopranos depend more upon the amplitude of the fundamental frequency than that of the singer's formant. At higher pitches, the harmonic frequencies are more widely spaced, making it hard for the singer's formant to match the harmonics generated by the vocal folds. Sopranos are more likely to benefit from a strong fundamental or first formant, as listeners' ears are highly sensitive to high soprano pitches. However, sopranos singing in their lower register and in mixed voice typically will exhibit and benefit from a singer's formant.

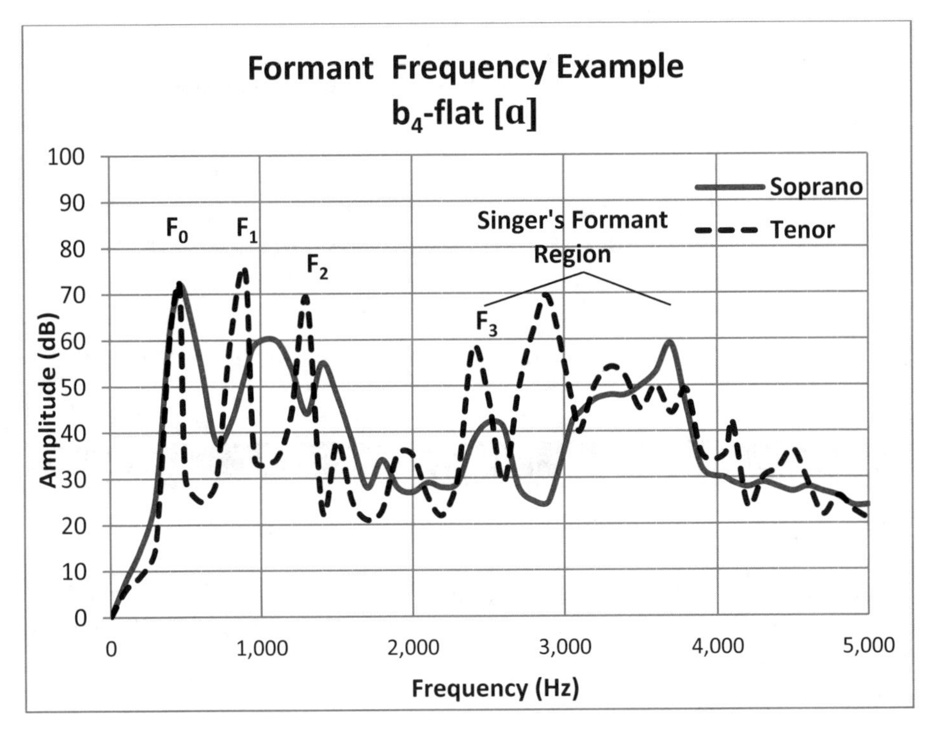


**Figure B.2 Further illustration of formants**

# References


Abitbol, J., Abitbol, P., & Abitbol, B. (1999). Sex hormones and the female voice. *Journal of Voice, 13*, 424–446.

Alderson, R. (1979). *Complete handbook of voice training*. West Nyack, NY: Parker Publishing Company.

American Academy of Teachers of Singing (1997). *Problems of tessitura in relation to choral music.* Retrieved Nov. 19, 2010 from http://Americanacademyofteachersofsinging.org/publications.html

Amir, O., Amir, N., & Michaeli, O. (2005). Evaluating the influence of warmup on singing voice quality using acoustic measures. *Journal of Voice, 19*, 252–260.

Amir, O., Biron-Shental, T., Muchnik, C., & Kishon-Rabin, L. (2003). Do oral contraceptives improve vocal quality? Limited trial on low-dose formulations. *Obstetrics & Gynecology, 101*, 773–777.

Appelman, D. R. (1986). *The science of vocal pedagogy: Theory and application*. Bloomington, IN: Indiana University Press.

Armstrong, L. E. (2002). Caffeine, body fluid-electrolyte balance, and exercise performance. *International Journal of Sport Nutrition and Exercise Metabolism, 12*, 189–206.

Armstrong, L. E., Pumerantz, A. C., Roti, M. W., Judelson, D. A., Watson, G., Dias, J. C., . . . Kellogg, M. (2005). Fluid, electrolyte, and renal indices of hydration during 11 days of controlled caffeine consumption. *International Journal of Sport Nutrition and Exercise Metabolism, 15*, 252–265.

Aspaas, C., McCrea, C. R., Morris, R. J., & Fowler, L. (2004). Select acoustic and perceptual measures of choral formation. *International Journal of Research in Choral Singing, 2*, 11–26.

Audsley, G. A. (1905). *The art of organ building (Volume I).* New York, NY: Dodd, Mead, and Company.

Augusto, L. G. (2006). Intranasal zinc in the management of the common cold. *Journal of Pharmacy Practice, 19*, 395–400.

Awan, S. N. (2006). The aging female voice: Acoustic and respiratory data. *Clinical Linguistics & Phonetics, 20*, 171–180.

Barbershop.org (2010). Retrieved May 31, 2010 from http://www.barbershop.org/youth-chorus-festival-judging-system.html

Bassinger, L. (2006). Acoustical analysis of choral voice matching and placement as it relates to group blend and tone. (Unpublished doctoral dissertation). Texas Tech University, Lubbock, TX.

Bernhard, C. (1973). (W. Hilse, Trans.). The treatises of Christoph Bernhard. In W. J. Mitchell, & F. Salzer (Eds.), *The Music Forum, Volume 3* (pp. 1–196). New York, NY: Columbia University Press.

Bicknell, S. (1996). *The history of the English organ*. Cambridge, UK: Cambridge University Press.

Biever, D. M., & Bless, D. M. (1989). Vibratory characteristics of the vocal folds in young adult and geriatric women. *Journal of Voice, 3*, 120–131.

Bloch C. S., Gould W. J., & Hirano M. (1981). Effect of voice therapy on contact granuloma of the vocal fold. *Annals of Otology, Rhinology & Laryngology, 90*, 48–52.

Blocker, R. (Ed.) (2004). *The Robert Shaw reader.* New Haven, CT: Yale University Press.

Bloomfield, S. F., Aiello, A. E., Cookson, B., O'Boyle, C. & Larson, E. L. (2007). The effectiveness of hand hygiene procedures in reducing the risks of infections in home and community settings including handwashing and alcohol-based hand sanitizers. *American Journal of Infection Control, 35*, S27–64.

Boeringer, J. (1989). *Organa Britannica: Organs in Great Britain: 1660-1860, Volume 3.* Lewisburg, PA: Bucknell University Press.

Boulet, M. J., & Oddens, B. J. (1996). Female voice changes around and after the menopause—an initial investigation. *Maturitas, 23*, 15–21.

Boydell, B. (1992). John Baptiste Cuvillie, Ferdinand Weber, and the organ of Trinity College Chapel, Dublin. *The Organ, 72*, 15–27.

Bunch, M. (1995). *Dynamics of the singing voice* (3rd ed.). Wien, Austria: Springer-Verlag.

Burney, C. (1775). *The present state of music in Germany, the Netherlands and United Provinces Volume 2* (2nd ed.). London, UK: T. Beckett, J. Robson, G. Robinson.

Bush, D. E., & Kassel, R. (Eds.) (2006). *The organ: An encyclopedia.* New York, NY: Routledge.

Carlsson, G., & Sundberg, J. (1992). Formant frequency tuning in singing. *Journal of Voice, 6*, 256–260.

Caruso, E., & Tetrazzini, L. (1975). *Caruso and Tetrazzini on the art of singing*. New York, NY: Dover Publications, Inc. (Original work published 1909, New York, NY: The Metropolitan Company)

Caruso, T. J., Prober, C. G., & Gwaltney, J. M. (2007). Treatment of naturally acquired common colds with zinc: A structured review. *Clinical Infectious Diseases, 45*, 569–574.

Cielo, C. A., Elias, V. S., Brum, D. M., & Ferreira, F. V. (2011). Thyroarytenoid muscle and vocal fry: A literature review. *Revista da Sociedade Brasileira de Fonoaudiologia, 16*, 362–369.

Coffin, B. (1980). *Coffin's overtones of bel canto*. Lanham, MD: Scarecrow Press, Inc.

Coleman, R. F. (1994). Dynamic intensity variations of individual choral singers. *Journal of Voice, 8*, 196–201.

Cooksey, J. M. (1977a). The development of a contemporary, eclectic theory for the training and cultivation of the junior high school male changing voice. Part II: Scientific and empirical findings; some tentative solutions. *Choral Journal, 18*(3), 5–16.

Cooksey, J. M. (1977b). The development of a contemporary, eclectic theory for the training and cultivation of the junior high school male changing voice. Part III: Developing an integrated approach to the care and training of the junior high school male changing voice. *Choral Journal, 18*(4), 5–15.

Cooksey J. M. (1993). Do adolescent voices 'break' or do they transform? *Voice, 2*, 15–39.

Cooksey, J. M. (1999). *Working with adolescent voices.* Saint Louis, MO: Concordia Publishing House.

Cottrell, D. (2010). Support or resistance? Examining breathing techniques in choral singing. *Choral Journal, 50*(9), 53–59.

Daugherty, J. K. (1999). Spacing, formation, and choral sound: Preferences and perceptions of auditors and choristers. *Journal of Research in Music Education, 47*, 224–238.

Dayme, M. B. (2009). *Dynamics of the singing voice* (5th ed.). New York, NY: SpringerWienNewYork.

Downes, O. (1927, February 9). The St. Olaf choir. *The New York Times*, p. 17.

Dromey, C., Carter, N., & Hopkin, A. (2003). Vibrato rate adjustment. *Journal of Voice, 17,* 168–178.

Echternach, M., Sundberg, J., Arndt, S., Markl, M., Schumacher, M., & Richter, B. (2010). Vocal tract in female registers—a dynamic real-time MRI study. *Journal of Voice, 24,* 133–139.

Ehmann, W., & Haasemann, F. (1982). *Voice building for choirs.* (B. Smith. Trans.). Chapel Hill, NC: Hinshaw Music, Inc.

Ekholm, E. (2000). The effect of singing mode and seating arrangement on choral blend and overall choral sound. *Journal of Research in Music Education, 48,* 123–135.

Emami, A. J., Morrison, M., Rammage, L., & Bosch, D. (1999). Treatment of laryngeal contact ulcers and granulomas: A 12-year retrospective analysis. *Journal of Voice, 13,* 612–617.

Emmons, S., & Chase, C. (2006). *Prescriptions for choral excellence: Tone, text, dynamic leadership.* New York, NY: Oxford University Press, Inc.

Eskelin, G. (2005). *Components of vocal blend: Plus: Expressive tuning.* Woodland Hills, CA: Stage Three Enterprises.

Fairbanks, G. (1940). Recent studies of fundamental vocal pitch in speech. *Journal of the Acoustical Society of America, 11,* 373–374.

Ferrand, C. T. (2002). Harmonics-to-noise ratio: An index of vocal aging. *Journal of Voice, 16,* 480–487.

Fishburn, H. (1964). *Fundamentals of music appreciation.* New York, NY: D. McKay Co.

Fisher, H. B. (1966). *Improving voice and articulation*. Boston, MA: Houghton Mifflin Co.

Fisher, R. A. (2010) Effect of ethnicity on the age of onset of the male voice change. *Journal of Research in Music Education, 58,* 116–130.

Fitch, W. T., & Giedd, J. (1999). Morphology and development of the human vocal tract: A study using magnetic resonance imaging. *Journal of the Acoustical Society of America, 106,* 1511–1522.

Fleming, R. (2005). *The inner voice: The making of a singer.* New York, NY: Penguin Books.

Fogle, R. H., Stanczyk, F. Z., Zhang, X., & Paulson, R. J. Ovarian androgen production in postmenopausal women. (2007). *The Journal of Clinical Endocrinology & Metabolism, 92*, 3040–3043.

Gackle, L. (1991). The adolescent female voice: Characteristics of change and stages of development. *Choral Journal, 31*(8), 17–25.

Gackle, L. (2006). Finding Ophelia's voice: The female voice during adolescence. *Choral Journal, 47*(5), 29–37.

Gackle, L. (2008, Oct.-Nov.). *Adolescent voice: A framework for understanding.* Presented at the 2008 Wisconsin State Music Conference, Madison, WI.

Galante, B. (2011). Vibrato and choral acoustics: Common voice science issues for the choral conductor. *Choral Journal, 51*(7), 67–78.

Ganassi, S. (1959). *Opera intitulata fontegara, Venice 1535.* H. Peter, (Ed.), (D. Swainson, Trans.). Berlin-Lichterfelde: Robert Lienau.

Gardiniere, D. C. (1991). Voice matching: A perceptual study of vocal matches, their effect on choral sound, and procedures of inquiry conducted by Weston Noble. (Unpublished doctoral dissertation). New York University, New York, NY.

Georg, K. (2005). Unifying the voice through registration: Reid's two-register concept of the voice versus Miller's vowel modification techniques. In A. Bybee & J. E. Ford (Eds.), *The modern singing master: Essays in honor of Cornelius L. Reid* (pp. 101–111). Lanham, MD: The Scarecrow Press, Inc.

Gilbert, H. R., & Weismer, G. G. (1974). The effects of smoking on the speaking fundamental frequency of adult women. *Journal of Psycholinguistic Research, 3*, 225–231.

Goodwin, A. W. (1980). An acoustical study of individual voices in choral blend. *Journal of Research in Music Education, 28*, 119–128.

Gregoir, E. G. J. (1865). *Historique de la facture et des facteurs d'orgue, avec la nomenclature des principales orgues placées dans les Pay-bas et dans les provinces Flamandes de la Belgique.* Anvers (Antwerp), Belgium: L. Dela Montagne.

Haasemann, F., & Jordan, J. (1991). *Group vocal technique.* Chapel Hill, NC: Hinshaw Music, Inc.

Heman-Ackah, Y. D., Sataloff, R. T., Hawkshaw, M. J., & Divi, V. (2008). How do I maintain longevity of my voice? *Journal of Singing, 64*, 467–472.

Henderson, L. B. (1979). *How to train singers: Featuring illustrated "natural" techniques and exercises.* West Nyack, NY: Parker Publishing Company, Inc.

Henrich, N. (2006). Mirroring the voice from Garcia to the present day: Some insights into singing voice registers. *Logopedics Phoniatrics Vocology, 31,* 3–14.

Henrich, N., Roubeau, B., & Castellengo, M. (2003, Aug.). *On the use of electroglottography for characterisation of the laryngeal mechanisms.* Paper presented at SMAC 03: Stockholm Music Acoustics Conference. Stockholm, Sweden.

Herman-Giddens, M. E., Kaplowitz, P. B., & Wasserman, R. (2004). Navigating the recent articles on girls' puberty in *Pediatrics*: What do we know and where do we go from here? *Pediatrics, 113,* 911–917.

Herman-Giddens, M. E., Slora, E. J., Wasserman, R. C., Bourdony, C. J., Bhapkar, M. V., Koch, G. G., & Hasemeier, C. M. (1997). Secondary sexual characteristics and menses in young girls seen in office practice: A study from the Pediatric Research in Office Settings network. *Pediatrics, 99,* 505–512.

Heustis, H. L. (2010) *The Osiris organ archive.* Retrieved Sep. 1, 2010 from http://www.wu.ac.at/earlym-l/organs/local.html

Hirano, M., Vennard, W., & Ohala, J. (1970). Regulation of register, pitch and intensity of voice: An electromyographic investigation of intrinsic laryngeal muscles. *Folia Phoniatrica et Logopaedica, 22,* 1–20.

Hirt, M., Nobel, S., & Barron, E. (2000). Zinc nasal gel for the treatment of common cold symptoms: A double-blind, placebo-controlled trial. *Ear, Nose & Throat Journal, 79,* 778–782.

Hixon, T. J., & Hoffman C. (1978). Chest wall shape during singing. In V. Lawrence (Ed.), *Transcripts of the Seventh Annual Symposium, Care of the Professional Voice* (pp. 9-10). New York: The Voice Foundation.

House, A. S. & Stevens, K. N. (1956). Analog studies of the nasalization of vowels. *Journal of Speech and Hearing Disorders, 21,* 218–232.

Howard, D. M. (1995). Variation of electrolaryngographically derived closed quotient for trained and untrained adult female singers. *Journal of Voice, 9,* 163–172.

Huff-Gackle, L. (1985). The adolescent female voice (ages 11-15): Classification, placement and development of tone. *Choral Journal, 25*(8), 15–18.

Hunter, E., & Titze, I. R. (2005). Overlap of hearing and voicing ranges in singing. *Journal of Singing, 61,* 387–392.

Iwarsson, J., & Sundberg, J. (1998). Effects of lung volume on vertical larynx position during phonation. *Journal of Voice, 12*, 159–165.

Jackson, C. (2007). An examination of vibrato: Use options for late Renaissance vocal music. *Choral Journal, 48*(1), 25–35.

Jackson, J. L., Lesho, E., & Peterson, C. (2000). Zinc and the common cold: A meta-analysis revisited. *Journal of Nutrition, 130*, 1512S–1515S.

Jers, H., & Ternström, S. (2004, Jun.) *Intonation analysis of a multi-channel choir recording*. Paper presented at the Joint Baltic-Nordic Acoustics Meeting 2004, Mariehamn, Finland.

Joliveau, E., Smith, J., & Wolfe, J. (2004). Vocal tract resonances in singing: The soprano voice. *Journal of the Acoustical Society of America, 116*, 2434–2439.

Jordan, J. (2007). *Evoking sound: The choral rehearsal. Volume One: Techniques and Procedures.* Chicago: GIA Publications Inc.

Juul, A., Teilmann, G., Scheike, T., Hertel, N. T., Holm, K., Laursen, E. M., . . . Skakkebæk, N. E. (2006). Pubertal development in Danish children: comparison of recent European and US data. *International Journal of Andrology, 29*, 247–255.

Kayes, G. (2004). *Singing and the actor* (2nd edition). New York, NY: Routledge.

Kemp, M. (2009). *The choral challenge: Practical paths to solving problems.* Chicago, IL: GIA Publications, Inc.

Killian, J. (1999). A description of vocal maturation among fifth- and sixth-grade boys. *Journal of Research in Music Education, 47*, 357–369.

Killian, J. N., & Basinger, L. (2007). Perception of choral blend among choral, instrumental and nonmusic majors using the continuous response digital interface. *Journal of Research in Music Education, 55*, 313–325.

Killian, J. N., & Wayman, J. B. (2010). A descriptive study of vocal maturation among male adolescent vocalists and instrumentalists. *Journal of Research in Music Education, 58*, 5–19.

Klein, A. M., & Johns, M. M. (2007). Vocal emergencies. *Otolaryngologic Clinics of North America. 40*, 1063–1080.

Knutson, B. J. (1987). Interviews with selected choral conductors concerning rationale and practices regarding choral blend. *Dissertation Abstracts International, 48*(12), 3067A.

Kochis-Jennings, K. A., Finnegan, E. M., Hoffman, H. T., & Jaiswal, S. (2011). Laryngeal muscle activity and vocal fold adduction during chest, chestmix, headmix, and head registers in females. *Journal of Voice*, in press.

Korkes, F., Costa-Matos, A., Gasperini, R., Reginato, P. V., & Perez, M. D. (2008). Recreational use of PDE5 inhibitors by young healthy men: recognizing this issue among medical students. *The Journal of Sexual Medicine, 5,* 2414–2418.

Koufman, J. A. (1991). The otolaryngologic manifestations of gastroesophageal reflux disease (GERD): a clinical investigation of 225 patients using ambulatory 24-hour pH monitoring and an experimental investigation of the role of acid and pepsin in the development of laryngeal injury. *Laryngoscope, 101,* 1–78.

Lamb, G. H. (1988). *Choral techniques* (3rd ed.). Dubuque, IA: William C. Brown, publishers.

Lamesch, S., Expert, R., Castellengo, M., Henrich, N., & Chuberre, B. (2007). Investigating voix mixte: a scientific challenge towards a renewed vocal pedagogy. In K. Maimets-Volt, R. Parncutt, M. Marin & J. Ross (Eds.), *Proceedings of the third conference on interdisciplinary musicology (CIM07),* Tallinn, Estonia, August 15–19, 2007.

Lamperti, F. (1877). *A treatise on the art of singing.* (J. C. Griffith, Trans.). London, UK: Ricordi.

Large, J. W. (1973). *Vocal registers in singing.* The Hague, Netherlands: Mouton.

Large, J. W. (1984). Male high voice mechanisms in singing. *Journal of Research in Singing, 8,* 1–10.

Large, J., & Iwata, S. (1976). The significance of air flow modulations in vocal vibrato. *The NATS Bulletin, 32,* 42-46.

Latimer, M. E., & Daugherty, J. F. (2006). F. Melius Christiansen: "Attitude of the director toward the composer: Personal opinion," an annotated edition with discourse analysis of an unpublished manuscript. *Choral Journal, 47*(1), 7–36.

Laukkanen, A-M., Horáček, J., Krupa, P., & Švec, J. G. (2011). The effect of phonation into a straw on the vocal tract adjustments and formant frequencies. A preliminary MRI study on a single subject completed with acoustic results. *Biomedical Signal Processing and Control,* in press.

Lee, S., Potamianos, A., & Narayanan, S. (1999). Acoustics of children's speech: Developmental changes of temporal and spectral parameters. *Journal of the Acoustical Society of America, 105,* 1455–1468.

Lehmann, A. C., Sloboda, J. A., & Woody, R. H. (2007). *Psychology for musicians: Understanding and acquiring the skills.* New York, NY: Oxford University Press, Inc.

Luchsinger, R., & Arnold, G. E. (1965). *Voice-Speech-Language.* Belmont, CA: Wadsworth.

MacClintock, C. (1976). Caccini's trillo: A re-examination. *Bulletin of the National Association of Teachers of Singing,* 33, 38–44.

Marafioti, P. M. (1922). *Caruso's method of voice production: The scientific culture of the voice.* New York, NY: D. Appleton and Company.

Marchesi, B. (1932). *The singer's catechism and creed.* London, UK: J.M. Dent & Sons.

Mason, R. M., & Zemlin, W. (1966). The phenomenon of vocal vibrato. *The NATS Bulletin, 22,* 12-17, 37.

Mayo Clinic (2010). Common Cold. Retrieved 2/7/2010 from www.mayoclinic.com/health/common-cold/DS00056.

McCoy, S. (2011). The choir issue, part I. *Journal of Singing, 67,* 297–301.

McKinney, J. C. (2005). *The diagnosis & correction of vocal faults: A manual for teachers of singing and for choir directors.* Long Grove, IL: Waveland Press Inc. (Original work published in 1994)

Mersenne, M. (1957). *Harmonie universelle: The books on instruments.* (R. E. Chapman, Trans.). The Hague, Netherlands: M. Mijhoff.

Miller, D. G. (2008). *Resonance in singing: voice building through acoustic feedback.* Princeton, NJ: Inside View Press.

Miller, D. G., & Schutte, H. K. (2005). 'Mixing' the registers: Glottal source or vocal tract? *Folia Phoniatrica et Logopaedica, 57,* 278–291.

Miller, R. (1993). *Training tenor voices.* Belmont, CA: Schirmer Books.

Miller, R. (1996). *The structure of singing: System and art in vocal technique.* Belmont, CA: Schirmer Wadsworth Group.

Miller, R. (2004). *Solutions for singers: Tools for every performer and teacher.* New York, NY: Oxford University Press, Inc.

Miller, R. (2006). Historical overview of vocal pedagogy. In B. Smith & R. T. Sataloff, (Eds.), *Choral Pedagogy* (2nd ed.) (pp. 91–115). San Diego, CA: Plural Publishing.

Mitchell, H. F., & Kenny, D. T. (2004). The impact of 'open throat' technique on vibrato rate, extent and onset in classical singing. *Logopedics Phoniatrics Vocology, 29,* 171–182.

Moens-Haenen, G. (1988). *Das vibrato in der musik des barock.* Graz, Austria: Akademische Druck-u. Verlagsanstalt.

Mürbe, D., Pabst, F., Hofmann, G., & Sundberg, J. (2002). Significance of auditory and kinesthetic feedback to singers' pitch control. *Journal of Voice, 16,* 44–51.

Mürbe, D., Zahnert, T., Kuhlisch, E., & Sundberg, J. (2007). Effects of professional singing education on vocal vibrato—a longitudinal study. *Journal of Voice, 21,* 683–688.

Murry, T., McRoy, D. M., & Parhizkar, N. (2007). Common medications and their effects on the voice. *Journal of Singing, 63,* 293–297.

Nakao, M., Yano, E., Nomura, S., & Kuboki, T. (2003). Blood pressure-lowering effects of biofeedback treatment in hypertension: A meta-analysis of randomized controlled trials. *Hypertension Research, 26,* 37–46.

National Digestive Diseases Information Clearinghouse (2010). Heartburn, gastroesophageal reflux (GER), and gastroesophageal reflux disease (GERD). Retrieved November 23, 2010 from http://digestive.niddk.nih.gov/ddiseases/pubs/gerd.

Neely J. L., & Rosen C. (2000). Vocal fold hemorrhage associated with coumadin therapy in an opera singer. *Journal of Voice, 14,* 272–277.

Neumann, F. (1993). *Performance practices of the seventeenth and eighteenth centuries.* New York, NY: Schirmer Books.

Neumann, K., Schunda, P., Hoth, S., & Euler, H. A. (2005). The interplay between glottis and vocal tract during the male passaggio. *Folia Phoniatrica et Logopaedica, 57,* 308–327.

Noble, W. H. (2005). *Creating the special world: A collection of lectures.* S. M. Demorest (Ed.). Chicago: GIA Publications, Inc.

Owen, B. (1999). *The registration of Baroque organ music.* Bloomington, IN: Indiana University Press.

Phillips, K. H. (1996). *Teaching kids to sing.* New York, NY: Schirmer Books.

Playe, S. J. (2010). You came to the ED for a cold? *Emergency Medicine News, 32*, 21.

Powell, S. (1991). Choral intonation: More than meets the ear. *Choral Journal, 77*(9), 40-43.

Praetorius, M. (2004) *Syntagma musicum III.* J. T. Kite-Powell (Ed. and Trans.). New York, NY: Oxford University Press. Original work published 1619.

Pratter, M. R. (2006). Cough and the common cold: ACCP evidence-based clinical practice guidelines. *Chest, 129*, 72S–74S.

Ramig, L. A., and Ringel, R. L. (1983). Effects of physiological aging on selected acoustic characteristics of voice. *Journal of Speech and Hearing Research, 26*, 22–30.

Ramig, L. O., Gray, S., Baker, K., Corbin-Lewis, K., Buder, E., Luschei, E., . . . Smith, M. (2001). The aging voice: A review, treatment data and familial and genetic perspectives. *Folia Phoniatrica et Logopaedica, 53*, 252–265.

Reid, C. L. (1950). *Bel canto: Principles and practices.* New York, NY: Joseph Patelson Music House.

Reid, C. L. (1983) *A dictionary of vocal terminology: An analysis.* New York, NY: Joseph Patelson Music House.

Robison, C. W., Bounous, B., & Bailey, R. (1994). Vocal beauty: A study proposing its acoustical definition and relevant causes in classical baritones and female belt singers. *The NATS Journal, 51*, 19–30.

Roers, F., Mürbe, D., & Sundberg, J. (2009). Predicted singers' vocal fold lengths and voice classification—a study of x-ray morphological measures. *Journal of Voice, 23*, 408–413.

Rossing, T. D., Sundberg, J., & Ternström, S. (1986a). Acoustic comparison of voice use in solo and choir singing. *Journal of the Acoustical Society of America, 79*, 1975–1981.

Rossing, T. D., Sundberg, J., & Ternström, S. (1986b). Acoustic comparison of soprano solo and choir singing. *Journal of the Acoustical Society of America, 79*, S93.

Rothenberg, M. (1981). Acoustic interaction between the glottal source and the vocal tract. In K. N. Stevens & M. Hirano (Eds.), *Vocal Fold Physiology* (pp. 305-328). Tokyo, Japan: University of Tokyo Press.

Rousseau, J. (1687). *Traité de la viole.* Paris, France: Ballard.

Rubin, H. J., LeCover, M., & Vennard, W. (1967). Vocal intensity, subglottic pressure and air flow relationships in singers. *Folia Phoniatrica (Basel), 19,* 393–413.

Sanford, S. (1979). Seventeenth and eighteenth century vocal style and technique. (Unpublished doctoral dissertation). Stanford University, Palo Alto, CA.

Sataloff, R. T., & Hawkshaw, M. (2006). Medical care of voice disorders. In B. Smith & R. T. Sataloff, (Eds.), *Choral Pedagogy* (2nd ed.) (pp. 29-59). San Diego, CA: Plural Publishing.

Schutte, H. K., Miller, D. G., & Duijnstee, M. (2005). Resonance strategies revealed in recorded tenor high notes. *Folia Phoniatrica et Logopaedica, 57,* 292–307.

Sears, T. A. (1977). Some neural and mechanical aspects of singing. In M. Critchley & R. A. Henson (Eds.), *Music and the brain* (pp. 78–94). London, UK: Heinemann Medical Books.

Seashore, C. E. (1938). *Psychology of music.* New York, NY: The McGraw-Hill Book Company, Inc.

Selby, J. C., Gilbert, H. R., & Lerman, J. W. (2003). Perceptual and acoustic evaluation of individuals with laryngopharyngeal reflux pre- and post-treatment. *Journal of Voice, 17,* 557–570.

Sell, K. (2005). *The disciplines of vocal pedagogy: Towards an holistic approach.* London, UK: Ashgate.

Shehab, N., Sperling, L. S., Kegler, S. R., & Budnitz, D. S. (2010). National estimates of emergency department visits for hemorrhage-related adverse events from clopidogrel plus aspirin and from warfarin. *Archives of Internal Medicine, 170,* 1926–1933.

Sherman, J., & Brown, L. R. (1995). Singing *passaggi*: Modern application of a centuries-old technique. *Choral Journal, 36*(1), 27–36.

Shipp, T., Doherty, E. T., & Haglund, S. (1990). Physiologic factors in vocal vibrato production. *Journal of Voice, 4,* 300–304.

Singh, M., & Das, R. R. (2011). Zinc for the common cold. *Cochrane Database of Systematic Reviews 2011,* Issue 2.

Singh, V., Cohen, S. M., Rousseau, B., Noordzij, J. P., Garrett, C. G., & Ossoff, R. H. (2010). Acute dysphonia secondary to vocal fold hemorrhage after vardenafil use. *Ear Nose Throat Journal, 89,* E21–22.

Skinner, P. H., & Antinoro, F. (1970). Critical-band theory and the auditory-evoked slow-wave V potential. *Journal of the Acoustical Society of America, 48,* 557–560.

Smith, B., & Sataloff, R. T. (2006). Choral singing: The singing voice and choral tone. In B. Smith & R. T. Sataloff (Eds.), *Choral Pedagogy* (2nd ed.) (pp. 171-187). San Diego, CA: Plural Publishing.

Sonninen, A. (1968). The external frame function in the control of pitch in the human voice. *Annals of the New York Academy of Sciences, 155,* 68–90.

Spaethling, R. (Ed.) (2000). *Mozart's letters, Mozart's life: Selected letters.* New York, NY: W. W. Norton & Company, Inc.

Spencer, M. L. & Titze, I. R. (2001). An investigation of a modal-falsetto register transition using helox gas. *Journal of Voice, 15,* 15–24.

Stark, J. (2003). *Bel canto: A history of vocal pedagogy.* Toronto, Canada: University of Toronto Press.

Stauffer, G. B., & May, E. (Eds.). (2000). *J. S. Bach as organist: His instruments, music and performance.* Bloomington, IN: Indiana University Press.

Sundberg, J. (1974). Articulatory interpretation of the "singing formant". *Journal of the Acoustical Society of America, 55,* 838–844.

Sundberg, J. (1977). The acoustics of the singing voice. *Scientific American, 236,* 82–91.

Sundberg, J. (1987). *The science of the singing voice.* DeKalb, IL: Northern Illinois University Press.

Sundberg, J. (1993). Breathing behavior during singing. *The NATS Journal, 49,* 49–51.

Sundberg, J. (1994). Perceptual aspects of singing. *Journal of Voice, 8,* 106–122.

Sundberg, J. (1995). Acoustic and psychoacoustic aspects of vocal vibrato. In *Vibrato* (P. H. Dejonckere, M. Hirano, & J. Sundberg, Eds.) (pp. 35–62). San Diego, CA: Singular Publishing Group, Inc.

Sundberg, J. (1999). The perception of singing. In D. Deutsch (Ed.), The *psychology of music* (pp. 171–214). San Diego, CA: Academic Press.

Sundberg, J., & Bauer-Huppmann, J. (2007). When does a sung tone start? *Journal of Voice, 21,* 285–293.

Sundberg, J., Thalén, M., & Popeil, L. (2011). Substyles of belting: Phonatory and resonatory characteristics. *Journal of Voice,* in press.

Tarneaud, J., & Borel-Maisonny, S. (1961). *Traité pratique de phonologie et de phoniatrie: La voix, la parole, le chant.* Paris, France: Moloine.

Ternström, S., & Sundberg, J. (1988). Intonation precision of choir singers. *Journal of the Acoustical Society of America, 84,* 59–69.

Thompson, A. R. (1995). Pharmacological agents with effects on voice. *American Journal of Otolaryngology, 16,* 12–18.

Titze, I., Riede, T., & Popolo, P. (2008). Nonlinear source-filter coupling in phonation: Vocal exercises. *Journal of the Acoustical Society of America, 123,* 1902–1915.

Titze, I. R. (1989). On the relation between subglottal pressure and fundamental frequency in phonation. *Journal of the Acoustical Society of America, 85,* 901–906.

Titze, I. R. (1992). Acoustic interpretation of the voice range profile (phonetogram). *Journal of Speech & Hearing Research, 35,* 21–34.

Titze, I. R. (1999). The use of low first formant vowels and nasals to train the lighter mechanism. *The Journal of Singing, 55,* 41–43.

Titze, I. R. (2000). *Principles of voice production* (Second printing). Iowa City, IA: National Center for Voice and Speech.

Titze, I. R. (2004). A theoretical study of $F_0$-$F_1$ interaction with application to resonant speaking and singing voice. *Journal of Voice, 18,* 292–298.

Titze, I. R. (2006). Voice training and therapy with a semi-occluded vocal tract: rationale and scientific underpinnings. *Journal of Speech, Language, and Hearing Research, 49,* 448–459.

Titze, I. R. (2008a). Getting the most from the vocal instrument in a choral setting. *Choral Journal, 49*(4), 34–41.

Titze, I. R. (2008b). Nonlinear source-filter coupling in phonation: Theory. *Journal of the Acoustical Society of America, 123,* 2733–2749.

Titze, I. R., Finnegan, E. M., Laukkanen, A., & Jaiswal, S. (2002a). Raising lung pressure and pitch in vocal warm-ups: the use of flow-resistant straws. *The Journal of Singing, 58,* 329–338.

Titze, I. R., Story, B., Smith, M., & Long, R. (2002b). A reflex resonance model of vocal vibrato. *Journal of the Acoustical Society of America, 111,* 2272–2282.

Titze, I. R., & Worley, A. S. (2009). Modeling source-filter interaction in belting and high-pitched operatic male singing. *Journal of the Acoustical Society of America, 126,* 1530–1540.

van den Berg, J. W. (1958). Myoelastic-aerodynamic theory of voice production. *Journal of Speech and Hearing Research, 1,* 227–244.

Vennard, W. (1967). *Singing: The mechanism and the technic* (Revised ed.). New York. NY: Carl Fischer.

Verdolini, K., Min, Y., Titze, I. R., Lemke, J., Brown, K., van Mersbergen, M., . . . Fisher K. (2002). Biological mechanisms underlying voice changes due to dehydration. *Journal of Speech, Language, and Hearing Research, 45,* 268–281.

Verdolini, K., Titze, I. R., & Fennell, A. (1994). Dependence of phonatory effort on hydration level. *Journal of Speech and Hearing Research, 37,* 1001–1007.

Verdolini-Marston, K., Sandage, M., & Titze, I. R. (1994), Effect of hydration treatments on laryngeal nodules and polyps and related voice measures. *Journal of Voice, 8,* 30–47.

Verdolini-Marston, K., Titze I. R., & Druker, D. G. (1990). Changes in phonation threshold pressure with induced conditions of hydration. *Journal of Voice, 4,* 142–151.

Vurma, A., & Ross, J. (2002). Where is a singer's voice if it is placed "forward"? *Journal of Voice, 16,* 383–391.

Vurma, A., & Ross, J. (2003). The perception of 'forward' and 'backward placement' of the singing voice. *Logopedics Phoniatrics Vocology, 28,* 19–28.

Walker, G. (2006). Good vibrations: Vibrato, science, and the choral singer. *Choral Journal, 47*(6), 37–48.

Ware, C. (1998). *Basics of vocal pedagogy: The foundations and process of singing.* Boston, MA: McGraw-Hill.

Warren, R. M. (1970). Elimination of biases in loudness judgments for tones. *Journal of the Acoustical Society of America, 48,* 1397-1403.

Wells, B. (2006). Belt technique: Research, acoustics, and possible world music applications. *Choral Journal, 46*(9), 65–76.

Williams, S. B. (2006). Turn the world around at the middle level. *Choral Journal, 47*(5), 123–124.

Willis, E. C., & Kenny, D. T. (2008). Effect of voice change on singing pitch accuracy in young male singers. *Journal of Interdisciplinary Music Studies, 2*, 111–119.

Winckel, F. (1967). *Music, sound and sensation: A modern exposition.* (T. Binkley, Trans.). New York, NY: Dover Publications.

Wooldridge, W. B. (1954). The nasal resonance factor in the sustained vowel tone in the singing voice. (Unpublished doctoral dissertation). Indiana University, Bloomington, IN.

Yearsly, D. (1998). The organ music of J. S. Bach. In N. Thistlethwaite, & G. Webber (Eds.), *The Cambridge companion to the organ* (pp. 236–239). Cambridge, UK: Press Syndicate of the University of Cambridge.

Ylitalo R., & Lindestad, P-A. (1999). A retrospective study of contact granuloma. *Laryngoscope, 109*, 433–436.

Zemlin, W. R. (1988). *Speech and hearing science: Anatomy and physiology* (3rd ed.). Englewood Cliffs, NJ: Prentice Hall.

# Index

## C

**G**



**H**



**I**

**N**



**O**



**P**

**R**

**S**

**Julia Davids, D.M.** enjoys a thriving career as a singer, conductor, and music educator. Dr. Davids is the Artistic Director of the Canadian Chamber Choir, Music Director for the North Shore Choral Society, and Director of Music Ministries at Trinity United Methodist Church. With over 20 years of experience teaching voice, she is sought after as a clinician and guest conductor. Julia has degrees from the University of Western Ontario, the University of Michigan, and Northwestern University, and is the Stephen J. Hendrickson Endowed Chair in Music at North Park University Chicago.

**Stephen LaTour, Ph.D.** is a psychologist, choral singer, and church soloist. Dr. LaTour's research has appeared in numerous psychological, management, and healthcare journals. He was a professor at Northwestern University for 17 years and is currently president of an international research and consulting firm. Memberships include the Acoustical Society of America, the research scientist honor society, Sigma Xi, and the American Psychological Association.